WELSH WOME
AN A

WELSH WOMEN'S POETRY 1460-2001: AN ANTHOLOGY

Selected and edited by
KATIE GRAMICH
and
CATHERINE BRENNAN

Translations by
KATIE GRAMICH
and others

THE ASSOCIATION FOR
WELSH WRITING IN ENGLISH
CYMDEITHAS LLÊN SAESNEG CYMRU

WELSH WOMEN'S CLASSICS

*First published by Honno in 2003, with the financial
support of the Arts Council of Wales.
Second edition published in 2017, with the financial
support of the Welsh Books Council.*
'Ailsa Craig', Heol y Cawl, Dinas Powys, Wales CF64 4AH.

1 2 3 4 5 6 7 8 9 10

Introduction © Katie Gramich and Catherine Brennan © The poets

All rights reserved. No part of this book may be reproduced,
stored in a retrieval system, or transmitted, in any form or by any means,
including electronic, mechanical, photocopying, recording or otherwise, without
clearance from the publishers.

Print ISBN: 978-1-909983-64-9
Ebook ISBN: 978-1-909983-65-6

Cover: Gabrielle, 1939 by Gladys Vasey
© Gladys Vasey Estate. Reproduced with kind permission of
Madeline Chappel-Gill and Robert Meyrick

Of the artist
Gladys Vasey: Blackpool 1889 – Aberystwyth 1981.
A self-taught painter of portraits, landscape and still-life, Gladys Johnstone grew up in rural Cheshire. She married Roland Vasey, an insurance surveyor, and began painting in the 1920s when both her children were away from home. She moved to Wales in 1943, first to Llanyblodwel, then Llanrwst and latterly Aberaeron, and painted many pictures of the Welsh landscape and portraits of friends and family. She exhibited widely for the Society of Women Artists, the Royal Society of Portrait Painters, the Royal Cambrian Academy and the Manchester Academy of Fine Arts, exhibiting 142 paintings between 1930 and 1968.

This portrait of Gabrielle Agnes Vasey (1915-1985), her eldest daughter, was exhibited in 1939. Against her parents' wishes, Gabrielle left the University of Manchester after a year to take a place at Studley Agricultural College for Ladies. This portrait was painted towards the end of that course, shortly before the outbreak of war.

Typeset and cover by: Graham Preston

Printed by Gomer Press

Contents

Introduction xvii

A Note on the Translations xliii

Gwenllïan ferch Rhirid Flaidd (*fl.* c.1460)
Nid er da bara'n y byd
(*Not for bread alone*) (englyn) 1

Gwerful Mechain (1462-1500)
I'r cedor *(On the vagina)* 2/3
I wragedd eiddigus *(To jealous wives)* 6/7
Rho Duw gal, rhaid yw gwyliaw
(If God gives a penis, it needs watching) 10/11
I'w gŵr am ei churo
(To her husband for beating her) (englyn) 12/13
Y gwahaniaeth *(The Difference)* (englyn) 12/13
I ateb Ieuan Dyfi am Gywydd Anni Goch
(In reply to Ieuan Dyfi for his cywydd on Red Annie) .. 14/15
Gweles eich lodes lwydwen (I'w thad)
(To her father) (englyn) 18/19
I ofyn telyn rawn i Ifan ap Dafydd
(To ask for a harp from Ifan ap Dafydd) 20/21
Dioddefaint Crist *(Christ's Suffering)* 22/23
Gwynflawd, daeargnawd, oergnu
(White flour, earthflesh, cold fleece) (englyn) 26/27
Eira gwyn ar fryn fry
(White snow on a high peak) (englyn) 26/27
I'w morwyn wrth gachu
(To her maid as she took a shit) 26/27
Fy mhais a wlychais yn wlych
(I got my petticoat wet and manky) 26/27

v

Rhown fil o ferched, rhown fwyn
(A thousand girls I'd give) 28/29
Y bedd *(The grave)* 28/29

Alis ferch Gruffydd ab Ieuan (ap Llywelyn Fychan) (C16)
Englyn ateb *(An englyn in response)* 30/31

Catrin ferch Gruffydd ap Hywel o Landdeiniolen (C16)
Ar haf oer 1555 *(On the cold summer of 1555)* 32/33

Katherine Philips [The Matchless Orinda](1631-64)
A marry[d] state 34
A Countrey Life 35
Friendship in Emblem, or the Seale,
to my dearest Lucasia 37
To my excellent Lucasia, on our friendship.
17th July 1651 41
A retir'd friendship, to Ardelia. 23rd Aug. 1651 42
On the Welch Language 44

Angharad James (1677-1749)
Ymddiddan rhyngddi a'i chwaer – detholiad
(A dialogue between herself and her sister) – extract 46/47
Nid ydi ein hoes ond cafod fer
(Our life is but the briefest shower) 50/51
Pan oedd bygythion y gyfraith ar ei gŵr
(When the law threatened her husband) 50/51

Catrin Gruffydd (*fl.* 1730)
Marwnad gwraig am ei merch
(A woman's elegy for her daughter) 52/53

Margaret Davies (*fl.* 1738)
Er bod gwŷr hynod eu henwau
(Though there are many men of renown) 54

Jane Brereton [Melissa] (1685-1740)
To Mrs Roberts on her Spinning.
Written on her Birth-day Jan. 6, 1731 55
On Reading some Dissertations,
in the Reverend Dr Foulkes's modern Antiquities 56

Contents

Elisabeth ferch William Williams ym Marog ymhlwy' Llanfair Talhaiarn (*fl.* 1714)

Cyngor hen wraig i fachgen – detholiad
(An old woman's counsel to a lad) – extract 58/59

Anna Williams (1706-83)

A sonnet to a Lady of Indiscreet Virtue.
In imitation of Spencer [sic] 60
The Nunnery 61

Anne Penny (*fl.* 1729-80)

Poem X 64
Poem XXXIII 65

Elisabeth Griffith (*fl.* 1712)

Ti ddyn 'styfnig melltigedig – detholiad)
(You stubbern accursèd man) – extract 66/67

Mary Robinson [Perdita] (1756-1800)

The Vision (extract) 70

Ann Julia Hatton [Ann of Swansea] (1764-1838)

Man as He is. Prose made into Poetry 71
Swansea Bay 73
A Man without Deceit 74
Roses Have Thorns 75
Resignation 76
The Mirror 77

Jane Cave (*fl.* 1770-96)

A Poem Occasioned by a Lady's doubting
whether the Author Composed an Elegy, to
which her Name is Affix'd 78
Thoughts, which occurred to the Author,
at Llanwrtid, in Breconshire, in walking
from Dol-y-Coed House to the Well 79
An Elegy on a Maiden Name 82
On Marriage 83

Ann Griffiths (1776-1805)

Dyma babell y cyfarfod
(Here we find the tent of meeting) 84/85

Mae bod yn fyw yn fawr ryfeddod
(What a wonder! To be living) 86/87
Am fy mod i mor llygredig
(Since I still remain corrupted) 88/89
Rhyfedda fyth, briodas ferch
(In endless wonder, bride, declare) 88/89
Wele'n sefyll rhwng y myrtwydd
(See him stand among the myrtles) 90/91
Gwna fi fel pren planedig, O fy Nuw
(Make me, my God, just like a tree that grows) 92/93

Felicia Hemans (1793-1835)
   The Cambrian in America 94
   The Rock of Cader Idris 94

Maria James (1795-1868)
   Wales 96
   The Meadow Lark 99
   To a Singing Bird 100
   The Broom 100

Jane Williams [Ysgafell] (1806-85)
   A Celtic Tradition from Cornwall, of a Funeral
   Among the Small People 103

Elin Evans [Elen Egryn] (1807-76)
   Dyhuddiant Chwaer Mewn Trallod ac
   Iselder Meddwl *(Consolation for a Sister
   suffering from depression and tribulation)* 106/107
   I Gydnabod y Bardd G. Cawrdaf am
   Hyfforddiad *(To thank the poet
   G. Cawrdaf for his instruction)* 108/109

Anne Beale (1816-1900)
   The Dog Violet 110
   To Mrs. Hemans 111

Emily Jane Pfeiffer (1827-90)
   Peace to the Odalisque 113
   Glân-Alarch, his Silence and Song (extract) 113
   Any Husband to Many a Wife 115
   Red or White? 115

Contents

Sarah Williams [Sadie] (1838-1868)
- Snowdon to Vesuvius — 117
- O Fy Hen Gymraeg! — 119

Sarah Jane Rees [Cranogwen] (1839-1916)
- Y Cyflwyniad *(Dedication – to her mother)* — 122/123
- Myfyrdod Nosawl *(Evening Meditation)* — 124/125
- Fy Ffrind *(My Friend)* — 128/129
- Diwedd y flwyddyn *(The end of the year)* — 134/135
- Fy Ngwlad – detholiad *(My Country)* – extract — 138/139

Catherine Prichard [Buddug] (1842-1909)
- Blodyn yr Eira *(Snowdrop)* — 142/143
- Cranogwen *(Cranogwen)* — 142/143
- Brwydr Dirwest a Bacchus
  (The battle of Temperance and Bacchus) — 144/145
- Mefus a Hufen *(Strawberries and Cream)* — 146/147
- Yr 'Hen' Ann Griffiths *('Old' Ann Griffiths)* — 148/149

Alice Gray Jones [Ceridwen Peris] (1852-1943)
- Manion am y Merched – detholiad
  (One or two details about women) – extract — 150/151
- Cyfarchiad dechrau blwyddyn – 1929
  (A New Year Greeting – 1929) — 150/151
- Cân Gwraig y Gweithiwr
  (Song of the Worker's Wife) — 154/155
- Manion – Aelwydydd Dedwydd – detholiad
  (More details – Happy Hearths) – extract — 156/157

Ellen Hughes (1862-1927)
- Tydi, aderyn bychan, mwyn
  (Oh bird, so tiny and so sweet) — 158/159

Elizabeth Mary Jones [Moelona] (1878-1953)
- Y Delyn ar yr Helyg *(The harp on the willow)* — 160/161
- Eto *(Again)* — 162/163

Eiluned Lewis (1900-1979)
- Departure — 164
- The Birthright — 164
- December Apples — 165

Dilys Cadwaladr (1902-1979)
    Bara – detholiad *(Bread)* – extract ... 166/167
Jean Earle (1909-2002)
    Old Tips ... 170
    Piccalilli ... 171
    Quaker's Yard Junction, 1950 ... 172
    Solva Harbour ... 173
Lynette Roberts (1909-1995)
    Poem from Llanybri ... 175
    Low Tide ... 176
    The Shadow Remains ... 177
    Fifth of the Strata ... 178
    Curlew ... 179
Margiad Evans (1909-1958)
    The Nightingale ... 180
    Nature and the Naturalist ... 180
    To my sister Sian ... 182
Brenda Chamberlain (1912-1971)
    I dream too much, over and over ... 184
    Now, on a shimmering sweet siren day ... 184
    Seal cave ... 185
    Women on the strand ... 187
    Talysarn ... 187
    Shipwrecked Demeter ... 188
    Dead ponies ... 188
Eluned Phillips (b. 1915?)
    Y Perthi Coll *(The Lost Hedges)* ... 190/191
Joyce Herbert (b. 1922)
    Death of an Old Country Woman ... 192
    The Childless Woman ... 192
    Poppies ... 193
    At the house of Ann Frank ... 194
    When I stood there among bullets ... 195
Alison Bielski (b. 1925)
    wild leek, Flatholm Island ... 197
    hunting the wren ... 197

sacramental sonnets (a selection):
    snowbound in Dyfed ... 202
    regeneration ... 203
    love's illusion ... 203
    the undefined ... 204
    walking with angels ... 204

Christine Furnival (b. 1931)
    Englyn: Spring ... 205
    Needles ... 205
    The Welsh Love-Spoon ... 206
    Rhiannon ... 207
    A Visit to Caldey Island Abbey (To my daughters) ... 209

Nest Lloyd (b. 1934)
    Iâr *(Hen)* ... 210/211
    Merched Llanio *(The Women of Llanio)* ... 216/217

Sally Roberts Jones (b. 1935)
    Narcissus ... 220
    To the Island ... 220
    Community ... 221

Gillian Clarke (b.1937)
    Catrin ... 223
    Shearing ... 224
    Lunchtime Lecture ... 225
    Letter from a Far Country (extract) ... 226
    Llŷr ... 231
    Clywedog ... 232
    Anorexic ... 233
    The King of Britain's Daughter – extract ... 235

Jane Edwards (b. 1938)
    Gwreiddiau *(Roots)* ... 236/237

Christine Evans (b. 1943)
    Second Language ... 238
    Tide ... 239
    Myxomatosis ... 239
    Llŷn ... 240

Nesta Wyn Jones (b. 1946)

Dawns y Sêr *(The Dance of the Stars)*
trans. Joseph P. Clancy 242/243
Ffarwèl y twrch daear *(Goodbye to the mole)*
trans. Tony Conran 244/245
Mêl Taid Cyplau *(Taid's honey)* trans. Joseph P. Clancy 246/247
Blodeuwedd *(Blodeuwedd)* trans. Joseph P. Clancy 250/251
Ymwrthod â geiriau *(Renouncing words)* 252/253
Hen Baentiad *(An old painting)* 254/255
Capel Celyn *(Capel Celyn)* trans. Joseph P. Clancy 256/257
Cwch *(Boat)* 258/259

Glenda Beagan (b. 1948)

Blodeuwedd 260
Vixen 261
Shaman 261

Marged Dafydd [Meg Elis] (b. 1950)

Y Milwr *(The Soldier)* 263

Einir Jones (b. 1950)

Gwraig I *(Woman I)* 264/265
Gwraig II *(Woman II)* 266/267
Angau *(Death)* 270/271
Byji *(Budgie)* 272/273
Sgwennais i 'rioed *(I never wrote)* 274/275
Y Goeden Geirios Gynnar *(The Early Cherry Tree)* 278/279
Lili *(Lily)* 280/281
Lladd-dŷ *(Slaughterhouse)* 282/283

Menna Elfyn (b. 1951)

Cân y di-lais i British Telecom
(Song of the voiceless to British Telecom)
trans. R. S. Thomas 284/285
Y gneuen wag *(The empty shell)* trans. Tony Conran 288/289
Eucalyptus *(Eucalyptus)* trans. Tony Conran 288/289
Siapau o Gymru *(The shapes she makes)*
trans. Elin ap Hywel 292/293
Pomgranadau *(Pomegranates)* trans. Gillian Clarke 294/295

Contents

Diwinyddiaeth Gwallt *(The Theology of Hair)*
trans. Elin ap Hywel 296/297
Coron Merch *(Crowning Glory)* trans. Elin ap Hywel 298/299
Enwi Duw *(The Many Names of God)*
trans. Elin ap Hywel 302/303
Dim ond Camedd *(Nothing but Curves)*
trans. Elin ap Hywel 304/305
Glanhau'r Capel *(Cleaning the Chapel)*
trans. Elin ap Hywel 308/309
Cusan Hances
(Handkerchief Kiss) trans. Gillian Clarke 312/313

Hilary Llewellyn-Williams (b. 1951)
The Woman Poet 314
Bagful 315
Breadmaking 316

Catherine Fisher (b. 1957)
Great-grandmother 318
Immrama 318
In a Chained Library 320
St Tewdric's Well 320
Blodeuwedd 321

Delyth George
Gwylnos *(Vigil)* 322/323
Treiffl a Threfn *(Trifle and Order)* 322/323

Gwyneth Lewis (b. 1959)
The Booming Bittern 326
Two Rivers 327
Wholeness (extract) 329
Welsh Espionage (extract) 331
Parables and Faxes (extract) 331
The Mind Museum (extract) 333

Merryn Williams
Michael 334
Black Mountain Cairns 334

Elin ap Hywel
    Cyn oeri'r gwaed *(Before the blood cools)* 336/337
    Cennin Pedr *(Daffodils)* 338/339
    Gwynt y Dwyrain *(The East Wind)* 340/341
    Gauloise yw'r gerdd *(The poem's a Gauloise)* 342/343
    Llithro Heibio *(Slipping By)* 342/343

Elin Llwyd Morgan (b. 1966)
    Rapunzel *(Rapunzel)* 346/347
    Madfall symudliw *(Iridescent lizard)* 348/349
    Machlud asid *(Acid sunset)* 350/351

Sarah Corbett
    The Red Wardrobe 352
    Ghost Mother 353

Elin Wyn Williams
    Moliannwn oll yn llon! *(Let us all give joyful praise!)* 354/355

Rose Flint
    In Waking 358

Kate Johnson
    Family Grave 359
    Blackberries 359

Kate Bingham
    Things I learned at University 361
    Nits 362
    In Passing 363

Esyllt Maelor
    Mam a gwraig tŷ *(Mother and housewife)* 364/365
    Nain *(Grandmother)* 366/367

Deryn Rees-Jones
    First 368
    I know Exactly the Sort of Woman
    I'd Like to Fall in Love With 368
    The Ladies 369

Frances Sackett
    Vanity 370
    Prinsengracht 263 – Amsterdam 371

Ann Griffiths
    Bechgyn Aberystwyth *(The lads of Aberystwyth)* 372/373
Kathy Miles
    Wash Day 376
    Polishing 377
    Ophelia 378
Samantha Wynne Rhydderch
    The X-Ray Room 379
    Part of the Furniture 379
Mererid Hopwood
    Dadeni – detholiad *(Rebirth – extract)* 380/381

Brief Biographies of poets 391

Acknowledgements 413

Introduction

BITEXTUALITY IN THE WELSH POETIC TRADITION

> Lord of the Running Rivers,
> I was given two languages
> to speak or, rather, they have spoken me
> through different landscapes from a common spring.
> *(Gwyneth Lewis)*

The Welsh bardic tradition is a venerable and venerated one. Nevertheless, it is a tradition which, until quite recently, has been assumed to have been an exclusive male preserve. It is one of the main objectives of this anthology to prove that the tradition is not, and never has been, exclusively male. Our contention is that women poets have been active in Wales from the earliest times and that it is only an unfortunate consequence of male dominance in the public culture of our country that relatively few works by women from the earliest periods of the tradition have been preserved. Nevertheless, the survival of a substantial body of work by the fifteenth-century poet, Gwerful Mechain, is a testimony not only of the existence of women poets at this time but of their full participation in the dominant poetic culture and the poetic discourse of the time. In other words, Gwerful Mechain's poetry belongs centrally to the Welsh bardic tradition: it is clearly not part of a feminine sub-culture nor of a separate female tradition; on the contrary, Mechain engages in poetic dialogues with her male contemporaries, using the same forms, metre, tropes, and vocabulary as they. Certainly, she often adopts a female point of view, and takes them to task for the arrogance and exclusiveness of their male stances, but she attacks them not from the position of marginality or outsiderness but rather as a full participant in the tradition, confident of her own craft and relishing what she depicts as the privilege of her female Otherness.

One of the most immediately striking characteristics of the poetry of Gwerful Mechain and the female poets of the sixteenth century is the easy coexistence in their oeuvre (depleted as it often is) of devotional and erotic works. Although in the twenty-first century many Welsh people have distanced themselves from organized religion, it is nevertheless true to say that the influence of Nonconformity still looms large in Welsh culture. Even those who have no direct connection with any of the Welsh Nonconformist sects are aware of the way in which Welsh history and culture has been shaped by that extraordinary efflorescence which was the Methodist Revival of the eighteenth century. After the scleroticism of the nineteenth century had put paid to the impassioned ecstasy so vividly portrayed in the poems of Ann Griffiths, Nonconformist religion came to be equated for many Welsh people of the later twentieth century with a barren asceticism, narrow-mindedness and sexual prudery. Perhaps this is why the unbridled relish of Gwerful Mechain and her female disciples for sexuality comes as such a surprise, particularly when it becomes clear that this relish is not considered by the poets concerned to be incompatible with religious devotion. Above all, perhaps, it is the humour and *joie-de-vivre* of these early poets which impress us the most: they are celebratory poets in the widest sense of that word. It might indeed be argued that the female poets of this period had more freedom than many of their male counterparts in that they were not obliged to sing empty praises of their patrons in order to earn their daily bread. On the contrary, their praise is reserved for those things which in their view was truly worthy of praise, whether they be the female genitals or Jesus Christ.

The fifteenth and sixteenth century Welsh poets were therefore not afflicted with the self-destructive dilemma of the 'poetess'. This was a creature of a later age, namely, the early nineteenth century. As Germaine Greer has eloquently described:

> 'The poetess accepts that she must display characteristics associated with femininity, such as delicacy, modesty, charm, domesticity, hypersensitivity and piety, as well as the filial, sororal, and maternal affections. What the poetess does not aspire to is the revelation of gut truths of womanhood, or any negative feelings of rage, contempt, protest, despair, or disbelief . . . The poetess typically presents a sanitized version of herself; she and her poetry are deodorized, depilated and submissive . . . The poetess's stride is encumbered by a train of esses.'[1]

There is nothing 'deodorized, depilated or submissive' about the early Welsh women poets. Indeed, it would be possible to argue that it is their very lack of inhibition and their head-on engagement with the 'gut truths of womanhood' that has prevented most of their work from seeing the light of day until now. Gwerful Mechain's poetry, along with that of three of her male peers, was the subject of a University of Wales MA thesis by Leslie Harries as far back as 1933 but when he came to publish his research as a book twenty years later, he decided not to include her work along with the others. The reason for this strange decision can be found in the attitudes displayed in the thesis itself:

---

1. *Germaine Greer, Slip-shod Sibyls: Recognition, Rejection and the Woman Poet* (London: Viking Penguin, 1995), pp. xv-xvi; p. 37.

Y peth pwysicaf i'w gofio wrth feirniadu barddoniaeth Gwerful Mechain, yn enwedig ei chaneuon aflendid, yw na dylid ei barnu yng ngoleuni egwyddorion moesol y ganrif hon. Tueddiadau ac egwyddorion ei hoes hi ei hunan a benderfyna safon ei gwaith. Yng ngoleuni yr ugeinfed ganrif nid yw Gwerful Mechain namyn putain, ond yn ei chanrif ei hun yr oedd canu caneuon aflan yn beth cyffredin bron, yn enwedig ar y Cyfandir.[2]

(The most important thing to remember in evaluating the poetry of Gwerful Mechain, especially her pornographic songs, is that she should not be judged in the light of the moral principles of this century. The tendencies and principles of her own age are those which determine the standard of her work. In the light of the twentieth century, Gwerful Mechain is nothing more than a whore, but in her own century singing dirty songs was more or less a common thing to do, especially on the Continent.)

That the male student doth protest too much is, in retrospect, amusingly apparent. The allegedly 'enlightened' morals of early twentieth-century Wales, when, for example, unmarried girls who fell pregnant were ignominiously expelled from chapels, and when women who were foolhardy enough to marry were debarred from the professions, might today be considered somewhat doubtful. Also interesting is the attempt to pass erotic poetry off as a foreign, perhaps essentially French, habit, thus conserving Wales's image as 'the land of the white gloves' (*gwlad y menig gwynion*).

---

2. Leslie Harries, *Barddoniaeth Huw Cae Llwyd, Ieuan ap Huw Caes Llwyd, Ieuan Dyfi, a Gwerful Mechain* (MA thesis, University College of Wales, Swansea, 1933) p. 26. My English translation follows.

Despite his own prejudices, Leslie Harries carried out extremely valuable work in preparing scholarly editions of a range of Gwerful Mechain's poetry. The task is tricky because her poems – there are forty extant – appear in many different manuscript versions. This, in itself, as Ceridwen Lloyd-Morgan has pointed out[3] is testimony to the popularity of Gwerful Mechain's work: her 'cywydd' to Jesus Christ, for instance, is found in no fewer than 49 different manuscripts. Also notable is the fact that her poetry seems to have been known and admired by later Welsh women poets, as indicated by its appearance in manuscript copies such as the 'Red Book' of Angharad James. In this context, it is important to acknowledge that there existed in Wales alongside the relatively erudite strict-metre poetic tradition an oral, popular tradition of song, consisting of 'hen benillion' (old verses) of anonymous authorship. Many critics believe that the anonymous authors of these lyrical verses, often very simple and proverbial in style, and dealing with elemental human passions and experiences, were predominantly women. Certainly, the oral tradition has proved influential on the work of a number of later female poets, from Ann Griffiths to Nesta Wyn Jones. It may even be that the alleged laxness which Leslie Harries and other male critics have censured in the work of Gwerful Mechain can be seen to derive from the influence of the folk verse traditions upon her. She is taken to task by Harries for 'not keeping to the rules very carefully'. He shakes his head in despair over Gwerful's ineptitude: *'Deuthum ar draws nifer o wallau cynganeddol a beiau gwaharddedig'*[4] (I came across a number of mistakes in the cynghanedd and prohibited faults). It may be, of course, that she was not concerned to keep carefully to the rules and

---

3. Ceridwen Lloyd-Morgan, "'Gwerful Ferch Ragorol Fain': Golwg Newydd ar Gwerful Mechain" *Ysgrifau Beirniadol XVI* (1990) pp.-84-96.
4. Leslie Harries, op. cit. p. 25.

that she adopted an attitude to composition more analogous with the composers of the anonymous verses which were passed on orally from generation to generation. That Gwerful Mechain's own poetry was often preserved in this way is suggested by Leslie Harries, who concludes from his struggle to produce scholarly editions of her poems from the manuscript sources that 'the copies were frequently written down from memory and that they had been corrupted by those who copied them, or those who recited them' (*bod y copïau'n fynych wedi eu codi oddi ar gof a'u llygru gan y rhai a'i copïai, neu a'u hadroddai*). Fortunately, the lack of a scholarly edition of the work of Gwerful Mechain has finally been amended, with the publication in 2001, of Nerys Ann Howells' *Gwaith Gwerful Mechain ac Eraill*[5] (The Work of Gwerful Mechain And Others). Howells' valuable work is testimony to the fact that feminist intellectual approaches are finally making inroads upon Welsh academia. The title of her work is a neat riposte to Leslie Harries's *Gwaith Huw Cae Llwyd Ac Eraill (The Work of Huw Cae Llwyd **And Others**)*; Gwerful Mechain was, in 1933, among the Others, the 'also rans' but in 2001 she takes pride of place.

If, as we contend, there did not exist a separate female tradition of strict metre poetry in fifteenth-century Wales, it is possible to argue that such a tradition did begin to develop subsequently, as more women became literate and aware of the existence of other female poets. The situation in Wales is also complicated by the fact that another language, namely English, crept into the equation from the early modern period onwards. Thus, with the advent of 'Anglo-Welsh' poets such as Katherine Philips, the 'Matchless Orinda', in the seventeenth

---

5. Nerys Ann Howells, *Gwaith Gwerful Mechain ac Eraill* (Cardiff: University of Wales Press, 2001). Howells disputes the authorship of some of the poems listed in this book as by Gwerfil Mechain. In these cases, we have marked the poems (?).

Introduction xxiii

century, it is necessary to pose an additional question: not only, was there a distinct female poetic tradition in Wales? but also, was there a single female poetic tradition in two languages, or two separate traditions developing side by side?

By the time of her death in 1664 Katherine Philips (The Matchless Orinda) had achieved public recognition as an important literary figure in the male-dominated Restoration court culture under Charles Stuart. Philips was English Presbyterian by birth and upbringing, and Welsh Parliamentarian by marriage and geographic location. Despite these allegiances her loyalties inclined towards a High Anglican and royalist sensibility. Much of Philips' poetry takes the form of panegyric addressed to members of the English Royal Family and aristocracy. A number of her poems are elegies to dead neighbours in the West Wales gentry. By far the most interesting and successful of her works, however, is the body of poems addressed to her circle of female friends, in particular to Anne Owen of Orielton (Lucasia). In these pieces Philips demonstrates a self-consciously female aesthetic, proposing friendship between women as a viable alternative, in life and in terms of poetic inspiration, to heterosexual romance, to secular power and to religious faith. As a royalist under the recently restored monarchy Philips was anxious to promote the maintenance of the new *status quo*, and to secure the position of her former Cromwellian husband in the new dispensation. Thus many of her public poems lionize the virtues of the dominant patriarchal and patrilineal order. The female economy which the Lucasia poems describe, however, present a challenge to prevalent notions of love, power and spirituality, and in these works Philips attempts to redefine public values through examination of private relationships.

Like Gwerful Mechain in the Welsh language context before her, Philips is a confident and accomplished participant in the male-dominated English poetic tradition of her time. Philips certainly values the otherness of the female subject position, investing it with profound potential for social renewal. Unlike Mechain, however, Philips does not revel in the 'privilege' of woman's position; rather she chafes against the constraints of its marginality, not primarily in terms of her personal frustrations but with reference to society's moral depletion by it. Thus, despite the assured tenor of, and public acclaim afforded to her poetic voice, it is also possible to see Philips as a pioneer contributor in the tradition of women's poetry, specifically Welsh women's poetry in English.

Philips is the most prominent of the early Anglo-Welsh women poets, but there are others who followed. Later in the seventeenth century Jane Brereton [Melissa] built on the nascent 'tradition' established by Philips by pursuing a considerably less high profile writing career. Philips was a courtly writer whose poetic voice tends to be somewhat public in tone, even in poems dealing with intimate emotions between close friends. Brereton, as wife to the wastrel son of an army major, lived in genteel and somewhat threadbare obscurity. Brereton did not write for the court, nor even for public consumption at all; having resisted all pressure to publish during her lifetime, her volume of verse appeared posthumously in 1744. Here, there is a parallel with the Welsh-language tradition of female verse: women's writing tended to circulate in manuscript copies and orally. It was not until 1850 that the first fully-fledged volume of Welsh poetry by a woman, namely *Telyn Egryn*,[6] was published. The National Library of Wales contains a wealth of hand written books of poems – personal anthologies, really – dating from the eighteenth century and containing the work of a wide

---

6. *Telyn Egryn*, new edition by Ceridwen Lloyd-Morgan and Kathryn Hughes (Honno, 1998).

range of female and male poets. Women poets themselves, such as Angharad James and Margaret Davies, kept such books; this anthology, unfortunately, can include only a fraction of this neglected manuscript material.

Like Philips, Brereton relishes her friendships with other women, using them as starting points for a number of poems. Although Brereton's poems to her female friends do not make the same bold claims for platonic female love as do Philips' provocative explorations, she is clearly comfortable to work within the genre promoted by her famous predecessor. Moreover, Brereton is explicit about her debt to Philips, in her 'Epistle to Mrs Anne Griffiths' she acknowledges the connection: 'First our Orinda, spotless in her Fame,/As chaste in Wit, rescu'd our Sex from Shame'.[7]

Clearly Brereton takes Philips as her model in so far as her apparent purity and chastity are concerned, and does not focus on the potentially subversive qualities of much of Philips' verse. In a departure from Philips' poetic style, some of Brereton's work uses the domestic as a site for poetic excursion. In her poem 'To Mrs Roberts on her Spinning', Brereton focuses on the distinctly female occupation of spinning, drawing links between woman's work at the spinning wheel and the spider's web. The poem has some interesting points to make about the constant movement and growth of that which the spinner produces, and the tedium and toil required to give it substance. It celebrates the skill of the spinner and the beauty and inspirational qualities of her 'web'. At the same time it calls into question the value system which 'despises' this explicitly female (and implicitly 'lower class') mode of creativity.

Brereton's work is interesting in terms of tracing a tradition of Anglo-Welsh women's poetry because

---

7. Jane Brereton, *Poems on several Occasions*, London, 1744, p. 34.

in her poems Brereton's Welshness manifests itself more explicitly than does Philips', who limits her Welsh identification to dedicating some poems to dead neighbours among the West Wales gentry and a poetic disquisition on the 'Welch' language. In her 'On Reading some Dissertations . . .' Brereton demonstrates an interest in Welsh history and identity. The poet is no Welsh nationalist heroine: the piece praises the restored monarchical order, and describes Wales' integration into unity with England as 'savage Liberty restrain'd'. She does, however, identify herself in the poem as a 'Cambro-Briton' and draws upon the resources of Welsh history, landscape and culture as vehicles for her creative impulse. To this extent it is possible to locate Brereton as part of the tradition of Anglo-Welsh women's poetry: the poems demonstrate an awareness of the marginality of women's creativity, albeit without the assertive charge which Philips' work carries; at the same time Brereton avers herself a Welsh woman writer and thus complicates the issue of national identity as a component of the woman poet's subject position.

The late eighteenth-century interest in primitivism led to an increased enthusiasm in literature for Celtic culture; consequently, the tendency to deploy Welsh themes and motifs in poetry became increasingly prevalent in the period. Anglo-Welsh women poets, spurred on not only by literary fashion, perhaps, but also by the connections they felt with Wales, were among the practitioners in this trend. Anne Penny, Jane Cave and Ann Julia Hatton certainly use Wales and Welsh topics in their work. Penny's *oeuvre* includes 'Taliesin's Poem to Prince Elphin' which celebrates the Welsh bardic tradition.

By the mid eighteenth century women's poetry has clearly shifted from the celebration of otherness visible in Katherine Philips' work to an acute awareness of, and frustration with, women's marginality. Cave and Hatton both write as aspiring members of what Leonore Davidoff and Catherine Hall refer to as the 'middling ranks' of British society.[8] Davidoff and Hall have detailed the complex function of women's role in consolidating middle-class dominance in the period, and it is possible to discern in the textual fabric of their writing Cave and Hatton's unease with women's position. Both Cave and Hatton's poetry engages with areas of women's experience: both, for example, are interested in marriage, and both demonstrate a desire to subvert romanticized understandings of gender relations to ironic and often humorous effect. In Cave's work a concern with women's health and education is apparent, and the importance of care and support among women is foregrounded. Many of Hatton's poems demonstrate a concern with sexuality and carnal appetite: the poet is often self-consciously provocative in her treatment of sexual conduct, challenging prevalent ideas about women as sexual beings and about women as writers of poetry.

Interestingly, both poets also draw on their respective relationships with Wales to explore a range of issues relating to gender, class and nationality. Both poets identify themselves with Wales, Hatton even taking the pen-name 'Ann of Swansea' after her adopted home. For Cave, it is Welsh landscape and religion which attract her as channels through which to engage with ideas about women and society; for Hatton ancient Welsh history offers a site for dramatizing many of the same concerns. For all their extreme differences – Cave's work is sharply observed and witty but devoutly pious and in terms of prevalent sexual morality, without reproach, whilst much of Hatton's poetry, by

---

8. Leonore Davidoff and Catherine Hall, *Family Fortunes: Men and Women of the English Middle Class, 1780-1850* (London: Hutchinson, 1987), passim.

contrast, is highly suggestive of the colourful adventures undertaken by the poet herself, and includes some decidedly racy pieces – both Cave and Hatton's poetic depictions of Wales and Welshness are used as the basis for explorations which challenge dominant patriarchal notions about women as writers and members of particular class groupings.

Cave's attachment to the enthusiastic approaches to religious observance favoured by the Calvinist Methodist community at Trefecca where she was brought up, allows her poetic space from which to resist not only the comparatively uninspiring practice of High Anglicanism, and by implication English attitudes generally, but also to chafe against the inequalities of the class system of her time when compared with the more democratic structures of Calvinist ideology. Hatton demonstrates an interest in the position of the dis-located exile, and her use of ancient Welsh history provides the apparatus with which to challenge social codes which disenfranchise those who fail to conform to the expectations of the dominant order.

The broadly chronological arrangement of the poems in this anthology offers scope for comparison of Welsh-language and English-language poets of similar periods. Initially, one is struck by difference, such as the startling disparity between the poems of Anglophone writers such as Mary Robinson and their Welsh-language peers, such as Ann Griffiths. As Moira Dearnley has shown in her book, *Distant Fields*,[9] an analysis of the depiction of Wales and the Welsh in eighteenth-century fiction, the notorious Mrs. Robinson, though Bristol-born, had strong Welsh connections and set some of her works in Wales. Her poetry, however, is suffused with the conventions of the age in English poesy. Her pastorals are inhabited by languid Damons, Phillises, Colins

---

9. Moira Dearnley, *Distant Fields: Eighteenth-Century Fictions of Wales* (Cardiff: University of Wales Press, 2001).

and Delias; unlike her somewhat feisty novels, her poems are the insipid products of a true poetess, in Germaine Greer's definition of the term. Most of her poems are about or are addressed to women, such as Stella, Emma, and Matilda. Clearly, this mode of female-focused poetry is a convention of English verse of the age and, in the hands of a poet like Katherine Philips, can be the medium for some vigorous and even subversive, female-centred poetry. However, in the case of Mary Robinson, it seems obvious that the poet is constrained by the convention: as a woman who (unsuccessfully) is attempting to uphold her public respectability ('Hymn to Virtue' and 'An Ode to Wisdom' are two of her methinks-she-doth-protest-too-much effusions in her *Poems*)[10] it is out of the question for her to write love poems addressed to male objects of desire. Conversely, Ann Griffiths' hymns are, of course, love poems addressed to Christ. He is the object of her speaker's most intense desire. Thus, under the auspices of a Methodism which Mary Robinson lampooned in her memoirs, Ann Griffiths found release from the poetic conventions of her day. Nevertheless, that Ann Griffiths and Mary Robinson belong to the same age, even if they do not share the same language, is clear from their poetic discourse: birds, boughs, groves, streams, and the myrtle, abound in both their poetic landscapes. Moreover, it is clear that the piety of a poet such as Jane Cave and the religious fervour of Ann Griffiths spring from the same early Methodist enthusiasm. It is also evident that women writing in either language during the eighteenth century are broadly aligning themselves with a lyrical tradition: we find women poets writing songs or hymns, rather than epics, strict metre forms, or blank verse narratives. In a period when male poets in English and Welsh tended to be strongly influenced by

---

10. Mary Robinson, *Poems* (London: T. Silsbury & Son, 1795).

Classical models and to aspire toward the erudite and grand utterance[11] women poets eschewed such models and forms. This is not to suggest an excessive timidity on the part of the female poets: Ann Griffiths' work is remarkable for its boldness and quasi-masculine forcefulness.[12] One might argue, then, that the female poets of Wales in the seventeenth and eighteenth centuries shared certain characteristics and concerns which may be a consequence of their shared gender but there is very little evidence of a mutual cross-fertilization between the two language traditions during this period. The Anglophone poets tend to look resolutely outwards towards an English audience, even when they are dealing with Welsh themes or subject-matter. Katharine Philips' poem 'On the Welch Language' is a case in point: while romanticizing the ancient tongue and extolling the Celts' august past, there is no indication of the poet's awareness that this language is spoken around her every day and that sister poets not many miles distant were composing verses in it.

As the nineteenth century progressed and literacy among women increased, a number of Welsh and Anglo-Welsh women writers emerged; throughout the period women poets from all parts of Britain and America were increasingly concerned to explore the so-called 'woman question'. The practical, emotional and psychological demands of living, as a woman and a poet, under the prevalent ideology of separate spheres for men and women is explored in the work of all the nineteenth century poets in this anthology. In the context of

---

11. Examples of such poets and works are numerous but one might think of Alexander Pope and Goronwy Owen as representative of their age.
12. Saunders Lewis famously asserted that of the two great eighteenth-century Welsh hymnists, William Williams Pantycelyn and Ann Griffiths Dolwar-fach, it was Ann who was the more 'masculine' poet.

nineteenth century Wales it is difficult to overestimate the impact on cultural life effected by the 1847 'Blue Books' *Report of the Commission of Enquiry into the State of Education in Wales*. Ostensibly a government enquiry into education in Wales, the report also discussed the sexual morality of the Welsh, with Welsh women coming in for particular criticism in this area. Inevitably the act of writing as a woman and a poet during this period, already encumbered by constraints imposed by Victorian patriarchal codes of femininity, was further problematized for the Welsh woman poet. Poets such as 'Cranogwen', 'Ceridwen Peris', 'Buddug', and 'Moelona' all espouse feminist agendas in their work, though their particular brand of feminism might be difficult for a contemporary woman to identify as such. All are impassioned devotees of Temperance and it emerges from their writings that the ideology of Temperance is, for them, a feminist ideology. As Ceridwen Lloyd-Morgan has pointed out[13] in nineteenth-century Wales feminism had a particular religious inflection, so that for many radical women, temperance was a campaign they were willing to espouse even when they perceived suffrage as something alien or dangerous. However, as Moelona's work reveals, a number of Welsh women poets were active suffragists, as well as advocates of Temperance and cultural nationalism.

While women writing in Welsh were engaged with defending their sex against the allegations of the Blue Books and the depredations of the demon drink, their sisters writing in English were, understandably, not so concerned with such issues. Anglicised Welsh women were often Anglican (i.e. inclined to be sympathetic to the Blue Books' attack on

---

13. Ceridwen Lloyd-Morgan, 'From Temperance to Suffrage?' in *Our Mother's Land: Chapters in Welsh Women's History 1830-1939* ed. Angela John (Cardiff University of Wales Press, 1991), pp.-135-158.

Nonconformity) and felt no need to defend the morality of the Welsh. The most prominent of the nineteenth century Anglo-Welsh women poets is Felicia Hemans, author of such enduring anthology staples as 'Casabianca' and 'The Stately Homes of England'. Though Hemans may be regarded as the example par excellence of Germaine Greer's 'poetess', she is the only nineteenth-century Welsh woman poet to have generated significant critical attention from the English literary establishment. A minor industry of textual analysis and theoretical application has grown up around her work since the 1980s. Many feminist critics have attempted to interrogate the poet's reputation as arch gender-political conservative of the Victorian age. In a good deal of her poetry Hemans lives up to her name for safe and saccharine depictions of women and domesticity, with much of her work celebrating and promoting the Victorian ideology of separate spheres in gender relations. Nevertheless, in some poems the poet dramatizes to poignant effect the costs involved for the women who are subject to the dominant cult of the domestic, for women are depicted as paying a high price in terms of their creativity and their full humanity.

Hemans also follows in the tradition of earlier Anglo-Welsh women poets in that she uses Wales as poetic resource. Hemans' correspondence shows that the poet felt a strong connection with her adopted home in Wales, going as far as to learn the language in order to empathize more fully with her neighbours. Hemans' volume *Welsh Melodies*, published in 1832, is predominantly a collection of the poet's versions of ancient Welsh historical scenes and bardic lyrics. The poems in *Welsh Melodies* romanticize ancient Welsh culture and celebrate Cambria's 'proud' history (very much in the same vein as Katherine Philips' poem on the Welsh language). It is difficult, however, to reconcile these sentiments with the English imperialist and jingoistic tenor of much of Hemans' *oeuvre*. Hemans is chronologically a Romantic poet and, in her case, a taste for Welsh bardic culture may well have been influenced more strongly by the Romantic enthusiasm for the Celtic sublime, than her desire to subvert the English imperial project, to which she self-evidently wholeheartedly subscribes. Interestingly, however, Hemans' use of Welsh resources is also connected to her preoccupation with the idea of home. The poet's interest in the domestic as site of fulfillment and frustration for the female subject recurs throughout her work. In the Welsh poems these complexities are rehearsed to similar effect. The Cambrian speaker in America (in the only *Welsh Melodies* piece not set in ancient times) experiences a dream of home which conflicts with his economically motivated desire to succeed in the New World, just as the successful and economically motivated woman poet is perplexed by her compulsion to meet the demands of the Victorian domestic ideal.

It is interesting to compare Hemans' work with that of Emily Pfeiffer. Hemans' profound influence on Victorian culture occurred despite the fact that she died in 1835, two years before Victoria's accession to the throne; Emily Pfeiffer's writing career spanned the 'high' Victorian era. By contrast with Hemans, Pfeiffer was a declared feminist, and many of her poems explore ideas about social justice, particularly in relation to women's position in the dominant patriarchal and imperialist ideology of Victorian Britain. Like Hemans, Pfeiffer uses Welsh themes and settings in her poetry, but in Pfeiffer's hands the resource is used to more radical effect. In her long poem, 'Glân-Alarch, his Silence and his Song', the poet explores complex issues of national identity, arguing against the imperialist urge and for a more inclusive sense of Britishness which will accommodate and draw strength from diversity in nationhood.

Felicia Hemans and Emily Pfeiffer are representative of most Anglo-Welsh women poets writing throughout the nineteenth century in that both emerge from the middle class. From the early part of the nineteenth century middle-class influence had burgeoned and by the 1850s middle-class sensibility had become the unassailable ideology of Britain. Indeed, one might argue that the attack represented by the Blue Books was as much one motivated by class antagonism as by religious intolerance and racial tensions, for Wales was and long remained a predominantly working-class society. Nevertheless, throughout the century the majority of women who had the education and leisure necessary to write poetry tended to be members of the middle class; since in Wales an indigenous middle class was slow to develop, it is not surprising that all but one of the nineteenth-century Anglo-Welsh women poets in this collection are middle-class.

The exception to this rule is Maria James, a working-class poet whose family emigrated from Wales to America in the 1800s, where, at the age of ten, James was found a position as a domestic servant in the home of a wealthy family. Originally a monoglot Welsh speaker, the young James was forced to learn English on board the ship to America in order to survive. James enjoyed the patronage of her employers in whose home she lived, and it was the advantages of education and encouragement that this relationship afforded which allowed her to produce and publish her one volume of verse. In common with many of her fellow Anglo-Welsh poets, James' work engages with ideas about gender, class and national identity. James' poems are particularly interesting in that her treatment of these issues suggests a subject position which is more intensely problematic than that of any of the other poets in this collection. When James explores ideas about home and the domestic, the sense of confinement is particularly acute as she dramatizes conflicting senses of imprisonment and insecurity in the domestic environment. Issues of class in the American context are similarly fraught in James' work; the poems indicate tensions between the promise of fulfillment apparently offered in the 'land of opportunity' and the reality of life there as a woman and a servant. James' poetic ruminations on her original home in Wales dwell significantly on the issue of language. The poet is preoccupied with the loss of her mother tongue, and her poem 'Wales' explores a sense of inadequacy in English as a medium of poetic expression. The added perspective of linguistic dis-location distinguishes James from the other nineteenth century poets in this anthology. This distinction, along with the poet's working-class identity, complicate the notion of a tradition of Anglo-Welsh women's poetry.

Interestingly in one of her poems, 'The Album', James dismisses, among others, the work of Felicia Hemans as in any way influential on her own creativity, claiming that nature is her inspiration, rather than the work of other women poets.[14] Given her fraught position in relation to the class structures, gender constraints and linguistic hegemony of the time, it is perhaps not surprising that James is less than willing to acknowledge a debt to her native English-speaking, distinctly middle-class and therefore relatively privileged contemporaries. Despite her rejection of poetic tradition in the formation of her own creative voice, James' work nevertheless contributes to the body of poetry by nineteenth century Welsh women writing in English in ways which accentuate and problematize the unchallenged middle-class domination of literary culture in the period.

---

14. See Maria James, 'The Album', *Wales and Other Poems* (New York: John S. Taylor, 1839), p. 74.

Moving on to the twentieth century in 1987, *Poetry Wales* published a Symposium among five contemporary English-language Welsh women poets,[15] entitled 'Is there a Women's Poetry?'.[16] Of the five contributors only Gloria Evans Davies is unequivocally positive about the existence of a women's poetry and about her desire to be seen as contributing to it:

> The question . . . coincides with my current collection, which I hope is Women's Poetry.[17]

Sheenagh Pugh, conversely, is vehemently opposed to the concept, focusing on what she sees as the universality of truly illuminating poetry:

> In short, if there is such a thing as a poetry which is limited to part of humanity, I think there is a simpler name for it than women's poetry, black poetry or whatever. I think the word in question is mediocre.[18]

(Unsurprisingly, Pugh refused permission for us to include her work in this anthology.)

Christine Evans, in a piece which is resonant of Virginia Woolf's criticism of *Jane Eyre* in *A Room Of One's Own*,[19] is uncomfortable with the anger which she sees as inherent in much contemporary women's poetry. While she acknowledges that women's lived experience inevitably affects the rhythms and the poetic sensibilities of their

---

15. The poets concerned were: Sheenagh Pugh, Gloria Evans Davies, Christine Evans, Sally Roberts Jones and Val Warner.
16. *Poetry Wales*, 23, 1987.
17. Ibid, p. 37.
18. Ibid, p. 31.
19. Virgina Woolf *A Room of One's Own*, 1928, in *A Room of One's Own and Three Guineas*, Michele Barrett ed., (Harmondsworth: Penguin, 1993).

writing, Evans is reluctant to accept that 'imagination is subject to the limitations of gender'.[20] Welsh-language poets of the same generation often share similar anxieties about the potentially limiting label of 'woman poet': both Einir Jones and Nesta Wyn Jones are prominent poets who have expressed such anxieties publicly. Nevertheless, both allowed their work to be included in the pioneering anthology of Welsh women's poetry, *Hel Dail Gwyrdd* (*Collecting Green Leaves*, Gomer Press, 1985). Menna Elfyn was the editor and inspirational force behind that anthology and a succeeding one, *O'r Iawn Ryw (Of the Right Sex*, Honno Press, 1991). Elfyn's own feminist commitment is clear, both in her poems, and in the introductions to the two anthologies. Her 1985 celebration of women's achievements sounds very forthright and bold in comparison with the lukewarmness of the five poets interviewed by *Poetry Wales* just two years later:

> Cyfrol sy'n ceisio gwneud iawn am ddiffygion y gorffennol, ynghyd â nawsio dyheadau ac awyddfrydau merched heddiw, yw ffrwyth y Flodeugerdd hon, ac un sydd yn rhan o'r profiad mawr cyffrous o fod yn ferched, yn Gymry Cymraeg, ac yn feirdd. Cip yn unig fydd y gyfrol ar y byd ymryddhaol a chaethiwus honno. (Nodyn: benywaidd yw byd, am y tro)[21] [The harvest of this anthology is a volume which attempts to make amends for the failures of the past, as well as to give a flavour of the desires and aspirations of women today, and it is also a part of that big, exciting experience of being women, Welsh-speakers, and poets. This book gives just a glimpse of that liberating and constricting world. (Note:

---

20. Ibid, p. 45.
21. Menna Elfyn, Rhagymadrodd (Introduction) *Hel Dail Gwyrdd* (Collecting Green Leaves) Llandysul: Gomer, 1985, p. xvi.

> Menna takes liberties with the gender of the noun for world, *byd*, making it, as she says, female for the present.)]

This range of attitudes among a relatively small group of Welsh women poets is an indication of the complexity of the task facing the editors of a volume of Welsh Women's Poetry. It may be that some women poets' reluctance to embrace a specifically female public identity is connected with the fact that Welsh literary culture generally has suffered from the effects of a crisis in confidence particularly since the middle of the nineteenth century, perhaps connected with the Blue Books Report discussed above. As Gillian Clarke has noted, Anglo-Welsh literature has been regarded 'as not good enough or too local' for inclusion on exam board syllabuses.[22] It is not surprising then that contemporary women writers in the Anglo-Welsh tradition are reluctant to embrace the prospect of the further psychological incumbrances upon their creativity represented by the assertion of a women's poetry to which their work may belong.

It is Sally Roberts Jones who attempts, in the *Poetry Wales* symposium, to locate the women's poetry debate in a specifically Welsh context. Jones sees class as a far more urgent limiting factor in the emergence of a poet than gender, noting that neglected women artists recovered by feminist scholars tend to be middle class when 'potential working class artists in whatever medium rarely, if ever, had . . . [the] benefit of developing their artistic ability'.[23] Jones then goes on to make strong claims for the Welsh literary environment as unconstrained by the issue of class and thus inclusive of women in ways not possible for mainstream English culture:

---

22. Gillian Clarke, 'Ffiw: Referendum Reactions', *The New Welsh Review 38* (Autumn 1997), p. 11.
23. Ibid. p. 52.

> In Wales things are different; social class has little or nothing to do with being a published poet . . . and, relative to their numbers, women are equally well represented in anthologies and publishers' lists, and equally well discussed by critics.[24]

Jones' contentions on behalf of the Welsh literary establishment are tempered by her parenthetical qualification, 'relative to their numbers': she skims over the obvious question of why, given the intensely democratic nature of Welsh cultural structures which she asserts, there are relatively few women poets compared to men.

In this anthology we consider the issues of historic specificity with which the contributors to the *Poetry Wales* symposium struggle. By addressing the work of women writers from the medieval period to the present day we trace the emergence of a tradition of Welsh women's poetry in both languages. The anthology includes examples of writing by Welsh women from the genesis of their poetic tradition as part of the bardic culture in pre-modern works, through English language poetry produced out of seventeenth century gentry culture, eighteenth-century works in English by aspirant middle-class poets, a spectrum of poets writing in Welsh and English against a range of material and psychological prohibitions throughout the nineteenth and twentieth centuries, to work by women who inherit, inhabit and reconfigure that tradition in the new millennium.

Mindful of the need not to be perceived as too 'hysterical' in our championing of female poets of the past, our editorial procedure was to select work by as wide a range of poets as possible but never to include poems simply for their 'representative' qualities, i.e. we did not feel constrained to include poems we did not like simply because the poet in

---

24. Ibid, p. 52.

question happened to be neglected and female. Our problem, which might come as a surprise to some readers, was not a dearth of suitable material but far too much material to include in a single volume.

As we have seen, a number of contemporary Welsh women poets express varying degrees of resistance to the idea that their work should be seen, not as part of mainstream literary culture, but as part of a separate women's tradition. What is clear, however, from the work of pre-twentieth-century writers in this anthology, is that each poet engages with literary and social history; each interrogates her place in the literary and social culture of the day. The intersections of class, gender and national identity explored in the poems are always complex and historically specific. Notwithstanding the reluctance of some, contemporary Welsh women poets inherit the literary history forged by, among other artists, their foremothers in Welsh and Anglo-Welsh women's poetry. By the same token the work of contemporary Welsh women poets contributes to that tradition. It is to be hoped that in the new millennium the optimism invested by these writers in the inclusiveness of the contemporary literary establishment is justified, and that the women's poetry which this volume attempts to illustrate will be read as a crucial component of Welsh literature and literary culture generally.

Despite the apparently separate growth of the two language traditions in poetry, it is also true to say that the borders around poetic territories have never been hermetically sealed. In the Middle Ages, for example, the Welsh poetic tradition was profoundly affected by influences from elsewhere, notably France. Gradually, the influence of English and English poetry becomes evident in Welsh-language poetry, at least from the nineteenth century onwards; what is even more striking, perhaps, is the reciprocal influence of Welsh on Anglophone writing, particularly in the twentieth century. Homi Bhaba has said that 'All forms of culture are continually in a process of hybridity' and this is as true of the culture of Welsh as of a promiscuous, imperial language such as English. Elaine Showalter has stated, with reference to American literature, that:

> 'The languages of various groups are perpetually intersecting, translating each other; minority or post-colonial cultures appropriate and subvert the language of the dominant through the strategies of neologisms, syntactic fusion, interlanguages, substitutions, and allusion. Indeed, 'interlinguistic play' and bilinguality is one of the most striking features of minority literatures. Such writing is always double-voiced, what Henry Louis Gates, speaking of Afro-American Literature calls 'two-toned' . . . or Naomi Schor, speaking of women's literature, calls 'bitextual.'[25]

The influence from England had been growing from the early modern period onwards but there was a decisive shift in the relationship between Welsh and English in the early twentieth century, when English became the mother tongue of the majority of the Welsh people. English was no longer a dominant neighbour to be emulated or despised but a presence within the most intimate realms of the Welsh psyche. Thus, in the twentieth century particularly, the 'seepage'[26] between English and Welsh poetry (in both directions) has been profound. A cursory glance at the Welsh poetry of this century, written in both Welsh and English, confirms that there is a distinctive poetic tradition, united

25. Elaine Showalter, *Sister's Choice: Tradition and Change in American Women's Writing* (Oxford: Oxford University Press, 1994), p. 7.
26. Tony Conran, 'Introduction', *Welsh Verse* (Bridgend: Poetry Wales Press, 1986).

by a shared experience of migration, industrialisation, war, language loss, and a post-colonial identity crisis. Clearly, the attitude towards the Welsh language is likely to be different in a poet who writes in Welsh and one who writes in English; nevertheless, both are writing in the same context of encroachment upon and erosion of that native tongue. Often, and perhaps unexpectedly, poets in both languages express a similar sense of commitment. It might be argued that, just as a self-identification in terms of race is often seen to override gender issues, in Wales the language issue has occluded gender as a site of meaning and identification for modern poets.

Yet it is not as clear-cut an issue as it may at first appear. Indeed, the whole notion of 'identity' is by no means a simple, single statement. Psychoanalytically-inflected literary theory has taught us the value of discussing the notion of 'subjectivity' and 'subject-positions', which are more fluid and shifting than the rather monolithic and fixed notion of a stable identity. When we begin to explore modern Welsh women's poetry as we do in this anthology, we can see that language politics, notions of nationality and belonging, and the complexities of gender and sexuality all tend to intersect in the poets' exploration of Welsh women's subjectivity. Thus, Menna Elfyn's poetry is never simply about The Language; it is about the language, and women's experiences, sexual relationships, motherhood, poetry, religious faith, war, issues of justice and freedom across the world, and the possibility of expressing all these things in the words available at the time given in the gender assigned.

Katie Gramich and Catherine Brennan

A Note on the Translations

Every translator must be afflicted with a fascination with what is difficult. Translating Welsh poetry certainly has its peculiar and endlessly fascinating problems. Verse in the traditional bardic strict metres is particularly tricky, owing to the complexity of its structure, which is bound by strict rules. Any translator of Welsh to English has to bend and often flout these rules because of the differing textures and sounds of the two languages. Welsh is richly endowed with consonants, which means that complex patterns of internal rhyme and alliteration are possible, indeed, *de rigeur* for any strict metre poet. English is less consonantally rich, so that the translator has to use some ingenuity to give a hint of the flavour of the original without lapsing into semantic nonsense. My approach throughout has been to try to be true to the tone and mode of the original, while sticking as closely as possible to literal meanings. Some readers will undoubtedly think that I have been 'too free' in my versions but I would rather be accused of this than be congratulated on literal accuracy in prose. Prose translations of poetry are undoubtedly useful for scholars but they are useless for readers who enjoy the music and verbal excitement of poetry. They are like the ingredients for a cake, rather than the cake itself and, after all, trying to ingest spoonfuls of flour, raw egg, butter, and sugar leads to nothing but nausea.

The main strict metre forms represented in this anthology are the **cywydd** and the **englyn**. The cywydd is a poem of seven-syllable rhyming couplets, each line of which includes complex patterns of **cynghanedd** (internal sound patterns, rhymes and alliteration). In addition, alternate lines end on a stressed and an unstressed syllable. The cywydd can be anything from twenty to about fifty lines long. It is a flexible, sinuous form, which lends itself both to racy narrative and to epigrammatic precision. Another feature of the cywydd is a practice known as **dyfalu** (invention) which means that the poet piles up line upon line of increasingly ingenious similes and metaphors to describe something often quite ordinary. It is as if the poet is self-consciously displaying her skill to an appreciative audience and having a jolly good time in so doing. The englyn, in contrast, is a brief, four-line form, whose challenge is succinctness. There are many different types of englyn, which is still a very popular form in Welsh verse, and it can be used for the most heart-rending of epitaphs or the most frivolous of comic squibs. Again, the englyn contains complex cynghanedd and usually one main end-rhyme, though the first instance of this is, rather strangely for a non-Welsh reader, three-quarters of the way through the first line.[27]

Despite the difficulty, I have had enormous fun shaping these translations. In writing some versions of Gwerful Mechain's rude and energetic narratives, I have found myself chuckling aloud at her sheer audacity. I have also relished translating some of the Victorian poems, which are much more conventional and lack the challenge of strict metre, but have a period charm and a superbly slick facility for rhyme. In each case I have tried to render the tone of the original, though I confess that some seriously-intended poems, such as 'The Battle of Temperance and Bacchus' today perforce read rather tongue-in-cheek.

---

27. For those interested in knowing more about Welsh metrics, I warmly recommend Tony Conran's 'Appendix on Metres' in his aforementioned anthology of translations, *Welsh Verse* (Bridgend: Poetry Wales Press, 1986).

A Note on the Translations   xlv

In some cases I have been very fortunate in finding translators who have done the job far better than I could ever hope to do. Ann Griffiths' hymns are notoriously difficult to translate successfully and I was relieved and delighted to find the superb translations by Alan Gaunt included here. He has managed to render the freshness and vigour of Ann Griffiths' work in a way which demonstrates at last for the non-Welsh reader what a unique voice hers was. Similarly, I have been very grateful for the excellent translations of Menna Elfyn's poems by a range of contemporary poets, who have had the benefit of discussing their work with Menna herself. This has led to some wonderfully subtle versions which are undoubtedly poems in their own right. But whose are they – Menna's or the translators'? Fortunately, they are yours – enjoy!

Katie Gramich

My translations are dedicated to
Tony Conran
and
Joseph Clancy
inspirational translators and
champions of Welsh women's writing.

Gwenllïan ferch Rhirid Flaidd
(fl. c. 1460)

Nid er da Bara'n y byd[1]

Nid er da bara'n y byd – o'r diwedd
    Y deuai ferch Ririd
    At y gwas bras o Brysaeddfed;
Adnebydd dywydd dafad.

Not for any kind of bread

Not for any kind of bread to break her fast
    Did Rhirid's daughter come at last,
    But that rogue of Prysaeddfed court to damn;
Because she knows too well when a ewe will lamb.

---

1. This is a poem in answer to one by a male poet called Gruffudd ap Dafydd ap Grono, namely:

    Gwenllian druan drwyn ysgrafell – bren,
        A ŵyr brynu bara gradell;
    Doeth i Fôn a'i hun fantell
    Rhag newyn o Benllyn bell.

    Poor Gwenllian, whose nose is sharp as a comb,
        She needs some bread because she's got none at home;
    She came to Anglesey in her only cloak
    Fleeing the famine of Llanuwchlyn's yokel folk.

The englyn is a typical poetic insult, such as was often traded by poets of the period. Gwenllian's riposte is a little more unusual. She refutes his taunts and as a final challenge suggests she's coming to confront him with her pregnancy – presumably she claims that he is the father.

Gwerful Mechain (1462-1500)

I'r cedor

Pob rhyw brydydd, dydd dioed,
Mul rwysg wladaidd rwysg erioed,
Noethi moliant, nis gwarantwyf,
Anfeidrol reiol, yr wyf
Am gerdd merched y gwledydd
A wnaethant heb ffyniant ffydd
Yn anghwbl iawn, ddawn ddiwad,
Ar hyd y dydd, rho Duw Dad.
Moli gwallt, cwnsallt ceinserch,
A phob cyfryw fyw o ferch,
Ac obry moli heb wg
Yr aeliau uwch yr olwg.
Moli hefyd, hyfryd tew,
Foelder dwyfron feddaldew,
A moli gwen, len loywlun,
Dylai barch, a dwylaw bun.
Yno, o brif ddewiniaeth,
Cyn y nos canu a wnaeth,
Duw yn ei rodd a'i oddef,
Diffrwyth wawd o'i dafawd ef.
Gado'r canol heb foliant
A'r plas lle'r enillir plant,
A'r cedor clyd, hyder claer,
Tynerdeg, cylch twn eurdaer,
Lle carwn i, cywrain iach,
Y cedor dan y cadach.
Corff wyd diball ei allu,
Cwrt difreg o'r bloneg blu.

To the vagina

Every poet, drunken fool
Thinks he's just the king of cool,
(Every one is such a boor,
He makes me sick, I'm so demure),
He always declaims fruitless praise
Of all the girls in his male gaze
He's at it all day long, by God,
Omitting the best bit, silly sod:
He praises the hair, gown of fine love,
And all the girl's bits up above,
Even lower down he praises merrily
The eyes which glance so sexily;
Daring more, he extols the lovely shape
Of the soft breasts which leave him all agape,
And the beauty's arms, bright drape,
Even her perfect hands do not escape.
Then with his finest magic
Before night falls, it's tragic,
He pays homage to God's might,
An empty eulogy: it's not quite right:
For he's left the girl's middle unpraised,
That place where children are conceived,
The warm bright quim he does not sing,
That tender, plump, pulsating broken ring,
That's the place I love, the place I bless,
The hidden quim below the dress.
You female body, you're strong and fair,
A faultless, fleshy court plumed with hair.

Llyma 'nghred, gwlad y cedawr,
Cylch gweflau ymylau mawr,
Cont ddwbl yw, syw seingoch,
Dabl y gerdd â'i dwbl o goch,
Ac nid arbed, freuged frig,
Y gloywsaint wŷr eglwysig
Mewn cyfle iawn, ddawn ddifreg,
Myn Beuno, ei deimlo'n deg.
Am hyn o chwaen, gaen gerydd,
Y prydyddion sythion sydd,
Gadewch yn hael, gafael ged,
Gerddau cedor i gerdded.
Sawden awdl, sidan ydiw,
Sêm fach len ar gont wen wiw,
Lleiniau mewn man ymannerch,
Y llwyn sur, llawn yw o serch,
Fforest falch iawn, ddawn ddifreg,
Ffris ffraill, ffwrwr dwygaill deg.
Pant yw hwy no llwy yn llaw,
Clawdd i ddal cal ddwy ddwylaw.
Trwsglwyn merch, drud annerch dro,
Berth addwyn, Duw'n borth iddo.

Gwerful Mechain (1462-1500)

I proclaim that the quim is fine,
Circle of broad-edged lips divine,
It's a valley, longer than a spoon or hand,
A cwm to hold a penis strong and grand;
A vagina there by the swelling bum,
Two lines of red to song must come.
And the churchmen all, the radiant saints,
When they get the chance, have no restraints,
They never fail their chance to steal,
By Saint Beuno, to give it a good feel.
So I hope you feel well and truly told off,
All you proud male poets, you dare not scoff,
Let songs to the quim grow and thrive
Find their due reward and survive.
For it is silky soft, the sultan of an ode,
A little seam, a curtain on a niche bestowed,
Neat flaps in a place of meeting,
The sour grove, circle of greeting,
Superb forest, faultless gift to squeeze,
Fur for a fine pair of balls, tender frieze,
A girl's thick glade, it is full of love,
Lovely bush, blessed be it by God above.

I wragedd eiddigus

Bath ryw fodd, beth rhyfedda',
I ddyn, ni ennill fawr dda,
Rhyfedda' dim, rhyw fodd dig,
Annawn wŷd yn enwedig,
Bod gwragedd, rhyw agwedd rhus,
Rhwydd wg, yn rhy eiddigus?
Pa ryw natur, lafur lun,
Pur addysg, a'i pair uddun?
Meddai i mi Wenllïan,
Bu anllad gynt benllwyd gân,
Nid cariad, anllad curiaw,
Yr awr a dry ar aur draw.
Cariad gwragedd bonheddig
Ar galiau da, argoel dig.
Pe'm credid, edlid adlais,
Pob serchog caliog a'm cais,
Ni rydd un wraig rinweddawl,
Fursen, ei phiden a'i phawl.
O dilid gont ar dalwrn,
Nid âi un fodfedd o'i dwrn:
Nac yn rhad nis caniadai,
Nac yn serth er gwerth a gâi.
Yn ordain anniweirdeb
Ni wnâi'i ymwared â neb.
Tost yw na bydd, celfydd cain,
Rhyw gwilydd ar y rhiain
Bod yn fwy y biden fawr
Na'i dynion yn oed unawr,
Ac wyth o'i thylwyth a'i thad,
A'i thrysor hardd a'i thrwsiad,
A'i mam, nid wyf yn amau,
A'i brodyr, glod eglur glau,

Gwerful Mechain (1462-1500)

To jealous wives

Jealousy is the strangest attitude
It's no good thinking that everyone's lewd;
When you think of it, it's really not nice
You might even say it's a terrible vice,
But wives take on this inconvenient stance
They're so suspicious, they look at me askance!
What is it in their nature, tell me please
Makes them act like that, never at their ease?
My friend Gwenllïan told me one time
That she'd heard sung a dirty old rhyme
Which said it wasn't love on which women are sold
That yearning which thrives on unreachable gold,
But what really gets wives going, bless their little cotton socks,
Is, pardon me for saying it, the love of good, big cocks.
OK, don't get het up, just believe me when I say
All these well-hung blokes are after me, desperate for a lay,
But these blinking wives, so respectable,
Just won't give up their pricks delectable,
Though they want to follow a pussy in the field
Not an inch from their hand will these wives yield
They're not having any, come what may,
Not for any price, no way José.
This jealous wife won't share the fun,
She won't do a deal with anyone.
Oh damn, it really is a pain,
This woman simply knows no shame
What she likes best is a big prick and a good lay
It means more to her than her family, any day,
Her own father and eight of her relations,
All her jewels and her fashionable creations,

A'i chefndyr, ffyrf frodyr ffydd,
A'i cheraint a'i chwiorydd:
Byd caled yw bod celyn
Yn llwyr yn dwyn synnwyr dyn.
Peth anniddan fydd anair,
Pwnc genfigen a'i pair.
Y mae i'm gwlad ryw adwyth
Ac eiddigedd, lawnedd lwyth,
Ym mhob marchnad, trefniad drwg,
Tros ei chal, trais a chilwg.
Er rhoi o wartheg y rhên
Drichwech a'r aradr ychen,
A rhoi er maint fai y rhaid,
Rhull ddyfyn, yr holl ddefaid,
Gwell fydd gan riain feinir,
Meddai rai, roi'r tai a'r tir,
A chynt ddull, rhoi ei chont dda
Ochelyd, na rhoi'i chala,
Rhoi'i phadell o'i chell a'i chost
A'i thrybedd na'i noeth rybost,
Gwaisg ei ffull, rhoi gwisg ei phen
A'i bydoedd na rhoi'r biden.
Ni chenais 'y nychanon,
Gwir Dduw hynt, ddim o'r gerdd hon,
I neb a ffurfeidd-deb y ffydd
A fyn gala fwy no'i gilydd.

Gwerful Mechain (1462-1500)

Even her mother, I'm sad to say,
And her brothers, cousins, sisters, all away,
It's a tough old world when a common-or-garden dick
Strips a woman of her senses – don't it make you sick?
I know libel is distinctly unsavoury,
But it's envy that causes it, don't you agree?
For there's a blight on this, my country
And that heavy weight is jealousy,
It's just bad news in every marketplace,
Fighting over her penis in your face.
Some say a pretty girl would sooner
Than give up her very own peter,
Sacrifice eighteen of the landlord's cows
Or even the oxen that pull the ploughs,
Or the entire flock of sheep, so rash,
Or the estate, the buildings, and the cash,
Or even her own pussy, would you believe,
All the pans in her kitchen, you can't conceive,
The trivet they stand on but not her naked post,
Rather her headdress and finery be forever lost
Along with all her worldly goods, whatever the cost.
And let me tell you now at the end of my song
This satire's not for one who just wants a huge dong.

Rho Duw gal, rhaid yw gwyliaw (?)

Rho Duw gal, rhaid yw gwyliaw
Arnad a llygad a llaw.
Am hyn o hawl, pawl pensyth,
Yn amgenach bellach byth.
Casa hoelbren wyd gennyf,
Corn cod na chyfod na chwyf.
Ystyr gof, ystryw gofiant,
Gostwng pen planbren y plant.
Rhwy d'adain cont rhaid ydiw
Rhag cwyn rhoi ffrwyn yn dy ffriw.
I'th atal mal na'th llitier,
Eilwaith clyw anobaith clêr.
Traws hoel myrdd, trosol morddwyd,
Troi'n ael y blew, trwyn wlyb wyd.
Ystum llindag ceiliagwydd,
Yn cysgu yn ei blu blwydd.
Pleidflwng ei wddw paladflith,
Pendarn himp paid ar chwimp chwith.
Corgi ymlaen hollti hon,
A glasu'n ôl ei gloesion.
Un â tholo yn ei thalcen
A wŷl pob gwreignyth yn wen,
Pestel crwn, gwn ar gynnydd,
Purdan ar gont fechan fydd,
Tebren arffed merchedau,
Tafod cloch yw'r tyfiad clau.
Llodred wyd o anlladrwydd,
Llwn dro gwrn, asgwrn gwddw gŵydd.
Hoel drytholl, hawl drythyllwg,
Hoel drws a pair hawl a drwg.
Crair, calennig gwragedd da Cred,
Clorffon ceufol, coel arffed,
Y fonllist winau finllwyd
Ynghafn nos anghyfion wyd.
Cefn trosol, cyfion traserch,
Cloigyn clawr moeldin merch.

Gwerful Mechain (1462-1500) 11

If God gives a penis, it needs watching

If God gives a penis, it needs careful watching;
Mark it well – who knows what it's hatching?
Proud-headed post, full of its own importance,
Always in search of more and better dalliance.
You peg, you horn with sacs,
You quiver that refuses to wax,
You smith's tool, you cunning hothead,
Lowering your tip like the shrub the kids planted.
Through two wings of the quim you must go and not falter
Rather than moan about having your head in a halter.
It's no good trying to stop you, it can't be done:
You're the clergy's despair when you want to have fun.
Strong as a myriad nails, you sceptre of thighs,
You're a dripping wet nose of . . . considerable size.
You gander's neck, asleep in its soft plumage,
Head like a shoot, you should be on the rampage.
Cur, you go on splitting this one open wide
As she swoons you take a ride on the flood tide,
On that wave you carry in your loaded brow
As every girl can see all too well now.
Curved pestle, cocked pistol,
You purgatory for a small hole,
Poker of girls' groins, you well-hung
Bell's tongue, you clay erection,
A trouserful of wantonness, fount of all that's loose,
An urn's curving handle, the neck bone of a goose.
You lustful screw, you wanton desire,
You doornail whose claims just never tire.
Reliquary, Christian goodwives' New Year relief,
Empty-bellied spear holder, a groin's belief.
You brown, grey-lipped phallus,
In the dead of night you can be callous.
Sceptre's shaft, righteous passion,
Great covering cloak for a girl's bare bottom.

I'w gŵr am ei churo

Dager drwy goler dy galon – ar osgo
　I asgwrn dy ddwyfron;
　Dy lin a dyr, dy law'n don,
　A'th gleddau i'th goluddion.

Y gwahaniaeth (?)

Dau beth odieth didol – siom gariad
　Sy'n gyrru'n gynhwynol;
　Gwen ireiddwen gain raddol
　Sy ffeind a minnau sy ffôl.

To her husband for beating her

A dagger through your heart's stone – on a slant
    To reach your breast bone;
  May your knees break, your hands shrivel
  And your foes take your weapons to make you snivel.

The Difference

Two things we must distinguish – for love's pains
    Send one mad with anguish;
  Fair Gwen who is tender, kind, and fresh,
  And me, for I'm quite, quite foolish.

I ateb Ieuan Dyfi am Gywydd Anni Goch

Gwae'r undyn heb gywreindeb,
Gwae'r un wen a garo neb;
Ni cheir gan hon ei charu
Yn dda, er ei bod yn ddu.
Lliw yr un nid gwell o rod
Y nos pan elo'n isod.
Gwen fonheddig a ddigia,
Naws dydd, oni bydd was da.
Nid felly y gwna'r ddu ddoeth:
Ei drinio a wna drannoeth.
O dyfod Ieuan Dyfi
Rhai drwg yn amlwg i ni,
Rhai o'r gwynion fydd gwenwyn,
A rhai da a urdda dyn.
Merch a helethe Eneas,
Ddu rudd, ac oedd dda o ras.
Gwenddolen a ddialodd
Ei bai am na wnaid ei bodd.
Gwraig Ddyfnwal yn gofalu
A wnâi les rhwng y ddau lu.
Marsia ffel, gwraig Guhelyn,
A ddaeth â'r gyfraith dda ynn;
A gwraig Werydd, ddedwydd dda,
Heddychodd, hyn oedd iacha',
Rhwng dau lu, mawr allu maeth,
Mor felys rhag marfolaeth.
Mam Suddas, oedd ddiraswr,
Cywir a gwych carai'i gŵr,
A gwraig Beiled, pei credid,
Y gwir a ddywad i gyd.
Elen merch Goel a welynt,
Gwraig Gonstans, a gafas gynt

Gwerful Mechain (1462-1500) 15

In Reply to Ieuan Dyfi for his cywydd on Red Annie

Woe betide the man without honesty,
And the girl who retains her chastity;
This man won't have a tête-à-tête
With her because she's a brunette.
But a pretty girl's colour's not worth a jot
Under cover of darkness, when she gets hot.
A well bred white girl will go all coy
By day, if at night she gets no joy;
But the wise dark girl will have her say:
She'll give him what for next day.
Oh Ieuan Dovey, do come along,
When you say all girls are bad, you're just plain wrong,
For some of the white ones really are poison
While some of us dark ones have virtue and reason.
It was a woman who made Aeneas rich
Dido was of high birth and dark as pitch.
Gwenddolen was one who got her own back
When her will wasn't done, she had the knack.
Tonwen, she who was Dyfnwal's wife,
When she reigned, kept the land free from strife.
Intelligent Marcia, Cuhelyn's consort,
Sorted our Laws and cleaned up the court.
Genuissa, she who was Gwerydd's wife,
She too brought peace and long life,
She stood between two raging battalions
Bringing sweetness, not death to the rapscallions.
Tiborea, the mother of Judas the traitor,
She was a proper, loving wife, don't hate her,
And Pontius Pilate's wife as well
Was the soul of truthfulness, so they tell.
Ellen, the daughter of Coel,

Yn gywir hardd, ai gwir hyn?
Ni allodd merch, gordderchwr,
Diras ei gwaith, dreisio gŵr,
Dig aflan, o dôi gyfle,
Ymdynnu a wnâi, nid am ne'.
Gad yn wib, godinebwr,
Galw dyn hardd gledren hŵr.
Efô fu'n pechu bob pen,
Ac o'i gallon pe gwelen'.
Y Groes lle y lladdwyd Iesu,
A'r gras, ac nis llas mo'i llu.
Wrth Gwlan, fu un waneg,
A ddoeth yr un fil ar ddeg
O'r gweryddon i'r gradde
Am odde a wnaeth, i Dduw Ne'.
Gwraig Edgar, bu ddihareb,
A wnaeth yr hyn ni wnaeth neb:
Cerdded yr haearn tanllyd
Yn droednoeth, goesnoeth i gyd,
A'r tân ni wnaeth eniwed
I'w chroen, mor dda oedd ei chred.
Eleias a ddanfonasyd
At wraig dda i gael bara a byd.
Gwraig a wnaeth pan oedd gaetha'
Newyn ar lawer dyn da,
O'r ddinas death at gasddyn
Dig i ddywedyd i'r dyn;
Troesai ei boen tros y byd,
Disymwth y dôi symud.
Susanna yn sôn synnwyr,
Syn a gwael oedd sôn y gwŷr.
Mwy no rhai o'r rhianedd,
Gwell no gwŷr eu gallu a'u gwedd.
Brenhines, daeres dwyrain,

Gwerful Mechain (1462-1500)

And wife of Constance, got by toil
The cross on which Jesus died,
And its grace, and her legions cried.
Gwlan was another wise woman
Who endured enormous pain
But she received her reward in Heaven.
Edgar's wife was proverbial among men
She did what no other soul
Dared: walked barefoot on hot coal,
And the fire did her no harm
Since her faith just kept her warm.
Elias the prophet sent out a message
To bake bread, the world's famine to assuage;
This good woman did as she was asked,
As many starved, she balked not at the task.
Meanwhile in the city a man in bad humour
Decided to give out false rumour;
He spread pain through the world
But he suddenly had to eat his words.
Susanna was good and full of good sense;
The men's rumours of her were to give offence.
Girls are the mildest of creatures,
They're better than men, in ability and features.
Queen and heiress of the Orient
Was the Sibyl, most excellent,
She was the very first to say
That 'fore God there'd be a judgement day;
For her wisdom all revered her
She was named truth-teller of the future.
Tell me, Ifan, I'm asking you,
Tell me now, isn't all this true?
And when all is said and done
No woman could rape a mother's son,
Whatever the traitor had gone and done.

Sy' abl fodd, Sibli fain,
Yn gynta' 'rioed a ddoede
Y down oll gerbron Duw Ne';
Hithau a farn ar yr anwir
Am eu gwaith, arddoedyd gwir.
Dywed Ifan, 'rwy'n d'ofyn,
Yn gywir hardd, ai gwir hyn?
Ni allodd merch, gordderchwr,
Diras ei gwaith, dreisio gŵr,
Dig aflan, o dôi gyfle,
Ymdynnu a wnâi, nid am ne'.
Gad yn wib, godinebwr,
Galw dyn hardd gledren hŵr.
Efô fu'n pechu bob pen,
Ac o'i galon pe gwelen'.
Dywed Ifan, ar dafawd,
Rhodiog ŵr, cyn rhydu gwawd,
Ai da i ferch golli'i pherchen,
A'i phrynt a'i helynt yn hen?
Yr un ffŵl a neidio wrth ffon
Neu neidio wrth lw anudon,
Aed ffeilsion ddynion yn ddig,
Duw a fyddo dy feddyg.

Gweles eich lodes lwydwen (i'w thad) (?)

Gweles eich lodes lwydwen – eiddilaidd,
   Hi ddylai gael amgen;
Hi yn ei gwres, gynheswen,
Chwithau 'nhad aethoch yn hen.

Stop your hypocrisy, you pervert,
You, who call a lovely girl a tart.
You who sin from morn to night
Even in your heart, if I could see aright.
Tell me, Ifan, do you think it's just
For a wife to be chucked when her husband's lust
Decides she's too old for his whim?
An old fool leaps a stick to keep in trim,
Or to the magistrate's call gives a leap and a hop,
For false men like you just get in a strop;
I can't mend your pretended pain:
Let God heal your precious bane.

To her father

I saw your grey-white lass – she's feeble
   But deserves a bit of class;
Her warm youth attracts your lust so bold,
But father, face it, you – you're just too old.

I ofyn telyn rawn i Ifan ap Dafydd

Gwerful wyf o gwr y lan,
O Fferi, lle hoff arian.
Cynnal arfer y Fferi
Tafarn ddi farn ydd wyf i;
Llanw yn hy, nid llawen hyn,
'Mysg tylwyth eisiau telyn.
Pan feddyliais, gwrtaisrodd,
Ble cawn delyn rawn o rodd,
Gyrrais gennad, rhoddiad rhydd,
I dŷ Ifan ab Dafydd;
Barwn yn rhoddi bara,
Barwniaid ei ddeudaid dda.
E'i dygwn o waed agos
Yn gâr i'r rhai gorau'r Rhos;
A'i geraint nis digarodd,
A'i gares wyf a gais rodd.
Rhodd hynod a'm gwnâi'n fodlawn,
Os da rhodd ag ystôr rhawn;
Ag ebillion ei llonaid
O'i cwr bwygilydd y'i caid;
A'r cweirgorn wrth ei chornel
A ddaw ple bynnag ydd êl,
A'i gwddw fal un o'r gwyddau,
A'r cefn yn ddigon cau.
Yma caf am y cywydd
Yn rhodd, ac Ifan a'i rhydd.
Minnau roddaf i Ifan
Rost a medd os daw i'r man,
A chroeso pan gano'r gog,
A'i ginio er dwy geiniog.
Cryswen lwys croesawa'n lan
Y gwŷr a ddaw ag arian,
Mynnwn fod, wrth gydfod gwŷr,
Fyd diwall i'm lletywyr,
A chanu yn lân gyfannedd
Yn eu mysg wrth lenwi medd.

Gwerful Mechain (1462-1500) 21

To ask for a harp from Ifan ap Dafydd

I'm Gwerful from the river bank,
The Ferry, where money's happy.
I uphold the Ferry's tradition,
It's a tavern open to everyone;
It fills up regular, but the only blot
Is its lack of a harp – the company's not
Amused. When I pondered where I'd get
A harp as a present, I thought I'll bet
That Ifan ab Dafydd, a free generous man,
Will come up trumps on this if anyone can,
So I sent a messenger to the baron's pad
He's baron of bread-giving, just like his dad.
Actually, his blood is close to mine,
He's beloved of all the Rhos – the cool and fine;
His relatives he surely would not refuse,
And I'm his kinswoman, so I just can't lose.
Such a rare gift would make all fair,
If it's packed in a nice case of horse hair;
And has holes made with a tidy awl
Wherever it comes from, it'll grace a good hall,
Elegant as a goose's throat
Its back curved like the keel of a boat.
I'm sure I'll get one for this verse
Our Ifan will soon open his purse.
Me, in return I'll give dear Ifan
A roast and mead if he comes to the tavern,
And a welcome when the cuckoo sings
And his dinner, though it costs two pennies.
Clean white linen will welcome
The men who bring the handsome
Cash. I'll make sure my guests get their fill
And the company's crack will fit the bill,
Jubilant song will soar from below
While the mead cups overflow.

Dioddefaint Crist

Goreudduw gwiw a rodded
Ar bren croes i brynu Cred,
I weled, gweithred nid gau,
O luoedd Ei welïau;
Gwaed ar dâl gwedi'r dolur,
A gwaed o'r corff wedi'r cur.
Drud oedd Ei galon drwydoll
A gïau Duw i gyd oll.
Oer oedd i Fair, arwydd fu,
Wrth aros Ei ferthyru,
Yr hwn a fu'n rhoi'i einioes
I brynu Cred ar bren croes.
Gŵr â'i friw dan gwr ei fron,
A'r un gŵr yw'r Oen gwirion.
Prynodd bob gradd o Adda
A'i fron yn don, frenin da.
Ni cheir fyth, oni cheir Fo,
Mab brenin mwy a'n pryno.
Anial oedd i un o'i lu
Fwrw dichell i'w fradychu:
Siwdas wenieithus hydwyll,
Fradwr Duw, a'i fryd ar dwyll,
Prisiwr fu, peris ar fwyd,
Ddolau praff, ddal y Proffwyd.
Duw Mercher wedi 'mwarchad
Ydd oedd ei bris a'i ddydd brad.
Trannoeth, heb fater uniawn,
Ei gablu'n dost gwbl nid iawn,
A dir furn cyn daear fedd
A'i 'sgyrsio ymysg gorsedd
Oni gad, enwog ydiw,
Glaw gwaed o'r gwelïau gwiw.
Duw Gwener cyn digoni
Rhoed ar y Groes, rhydaer gri,
A choron fawr, chwerw iawn fu,
A roesant ar yr Iesu,
A'r glaif drud i'w glwyfo draw

Christ's Suffering

Christ immaculate, due to our vanity,
Was nailed to the cross to redeem humanity.
Behold the legion of his lacerations
The dear blood after the humiliation
His body's blood after the passion!
The price his pierced heart paid was high
God's flesh itself was cut and men stood by,
There was a sign and Mary stayed in bitterness
Her only son's martyrdom to witness,
He who freely made the great sacrifice
On the cross to free mankind from vice.
With a wound beneath his breast this man,
This same man is the tender Lamb:
He bought every single Adam,
The good King, his breast a flood of blood.
Never again will we see one so good,
No King's son to buy us, unless he comes again.
It was harsh that one of his own men
Should have betrayed him at the last,
It was the scheming flatterer Judas,
Betrayer of God, bent on dishonesty, the cur
Took the pieces of silver and after supper,
With strong bonds, he snared the Prophet
It was on Wednesday after market;
Cheap was his price on that ashen day.
With no justification, on the next day
He was brutally beaten to the floor
And scourged alike by rich and poor,
Until, as we all know, there streamed
Out so much blood that like rain it seemed.
On Friday before they had their fill
They put him on the Cross, a cry rang shrill,
And they placed a bitter crown
On Jesus' head as he gazed down,
And as he did so Longinus the blind was healed
By the blood which dropped and his eyes unsealed.

O law'r dall i'w lwyr dwyllaw.
Trwm iawn o'r tir yn myned
Oedd lu Crist wrth ddileu Cred
A llawen feilch, fellýn fu,
Lu Sisar pan las Iesu.
Wrth hud a chyfraith oediog
Y bwrien' Grist mewn barn grog
Er gweled ar Ei galon
Gweli fraisg dan gil Ei fron.
Ni bu yn rhwym neb un rhi,
Ni bu aelod heb weli.
Marw a wnaeth y mawr wiw nêr
Yn ôl hyn yn ael hanner.
Ar ôl blin yr haul blaned
A dduodd, crynodd dir Cred.
Pan dynnwyd, penyd einioes,
Y gŵr grym o gyrrau'r groes,
Sioseb a erchis Iesu
I'w roi'n ei fedd, a'i ran fu.
Pan godes, poen gyhydedd,
Cwrs da i'r byd, Crist o'r bedd,
Yna'r aeth, helaeth helynt,
Lloer a'r haul o'u lliw ar hynt,
A phan ddug wedi'r ffin ddwys
Ei bridwerth i baradwys,
Troi a wnaeth Duw Tri yn ôl
I'r ffurf y bu'n gorfforol.
Duw Naf i'r diau nefoedd
Difiau'r aeth, diofer oedd,
Yn gun hael, yn gynheiliad,
Yn enw Duw, yn un â'i Dad.
Un Duw cadarn y'th farnaf,
Tri pherson cyfion a caf.
Cawn drugaredd a'th weddi,
Down i'th ras Duw Un a Thri.
Cael ennill fo'n calennig
Pardwn Duw rhag Purdan dig:
Profiad llawen yw gennym
Praffed gras y Proffwyd grym.

With heavy hearts did Christ's disciples, humbled,
Leave that place as their world crumbled,
But Caesar's mob were merry and elated
Like cackling birds as they killed the man they hated.
Old laws and ignorance of good
Meant they nailed Christ to the rood,
Though they saw above his heart
A huge wound cleaving his breast apart.
Never was such a king so abused,
No-one there failed to see, yet no-one accused.
And then the great lord God died
In the middle of the day, the turning of the tide.
After this torment the great sun took
A hue of darkness, and Christendom shook.
From the cross they took down his body dear
And there approached Joseph of Arimathea,
Who laid him in his own grave, and thus it was.
When Christ rose up from the tomb,
After so much pain, to save us from our doom,
Then suddenly both sun and moon
Were dark both at midnight and noon,
And when he crossed like everyone who dies,
Paying the price to enter Paradise,
God of the Trinity turned back once more
Returning to the form of man, the mortal shore.
The Lord God whose Heaven is certain
He was wholly good, and endured great pain,
Oh generous sublime, our mainstay,
At one with your Father, be with us every day.
Though I can see but one great Lord,
He is Three Persons in accord.
Grant our prayer that we have your mercy,
Grant that we gain the grace of the Trinity.
Let our New Year gift be to win
God's pardon from the Purgatory of sin:
Our most pure and precious asset
To gain grace of the powerful Prophet.

Gwynflawd, daeargnawd, oergnu (?)

Gwynflawd, daeargnawd, du oergnu – ym mynydd,
   Manod wybren oerddu;
Eira'n blât, oer iawn ei blu,
Mwthlan a roed i'm methlu.

Eira gwyn ar fryn fry (?)

Eira gwyn ar fryn fry – a'm dallodd,
   A'm dillad yn gwlychu;
O, Dduw gwyn, nid oedd genny'
Obaith y down byth i dŷ.

I'w morwyn wrth gachu

Crwciodd lle dihangodd ei dŵr –'n grychiast
   O grochan ei llawdwr;
Ei deudwll oedd yn dadwr',
Baw a ddaeth, a bwa o ddŵr.

Fy mhais a wlychais yn wlych

Fy mhais a wlychais yn wlych – a'm crys
   A'm cwrsi sidangrych;
Odid Gŵyl Ddeinioel foelfrych
Na hin Sain Silin yn sych.

Gwerful Mechain (1462-1500)

White flour, earthflesh, cold fleece

White flour, earthflesh, black mountain – with cold fleece,
    Cold black snow-laden horizon;
  A plate of snow, feathers frozen,
  A soft snare to trip me sudden.

White snow on a high peak

    White snow on a high peak blinded me,
        And my clothes were soaked;
    I really thought I'd never manage,
    Oh dear God, to reach the village.

To her maid as she took a shit

She crouched where her water cascaded quick, seething
    Like a cauldron out from her knicks;
Her twin holes created a great hubble bubble,
Then a liquid arc squirted and dirt at the double.

I got my petticoat wet and manky

  I got my petticoat wet and manky – and my shirt's
    Soaked and my wrinkly satin hanky;
  I'll still be spattered by St. Deiniol's, no lie,
  Nor by Saint Silin's will I be high and dry.

Rhown fil o ferched, rhown fwyn

Rhown fil o ferched, rhown fwyn – lances,
    Lle ceisiais i orllwyn,
  Rhown gŵyn mawr, rhown gan morwyn
  Am un llanc ym min y llwyn.

Y bedd (?)

Och! lety, gwely gwaeledd, – anniddan
    Anheddle i orwedd,
  Cloëdig, unig annedd,
  Cas gan bawb yw cwsg y bedd.

A thousand girls I'd give

A thousand girls I'd give, the sweetest lasses,
    A hundred virgins, the prettiest that live,
As under the hedge I try to lie in wait,
For that one fine lad who's always late.

The grave

Oh rude lodging, beggarly bed – uneasy
    Abode in which to lay one's head
    Locked, lonely enclave,
Scorned by all the sleep of the grave.

*Alis Ferch Gruffydd ab Ieuan
(ap Llywelyn Fychan) (C16)*

Englyn ateb

Nid wylo, ond cwyno i'm câr yr ydwy'
    Tra rodwy' y ddaear
    Na alle fod yn llai' i fâr
    Na dilyn Gwen o'r Dalar. (Alis ai cant)

Alis Ferch Gruffydd ab Ieuan (ap Llywelyn Fychan)

An englyn in response

I'm not weeping but moaning for what it's worth –
                                         to my lover,
   The one for whom I'd give the whole earth,
That he should be so untrue to me
As to follow Gwen from the headland for all to see.
(Alis sang this)

Catrin Ferch Gruffydd ab Hywel o-Landdeiniolen (C16)

Ar haf oer 1555

Gwynt chwiban cadarn ar torddydd ar drall
    Yn dryllio dail newydd
   Nid gwarêb o dôb yn dydd
   Ond troi gaeaf tragowydd.

Gwyn glaw a ddaw mow ddifaru a chynllysg
    A chynllwyn pob oerni
   Am waith Duw nid waith Towi
   Gayaf yn lle haf yw hi.

Gwyliwch ryfeddod mi a goiliaf beth
    Ni wn byth ai gwelaf
   Mai gwynt oer fel gwynt oiraf
   Mewn ram cefnfor Gannow Gaf.

Y ffordd gan Ferddin wr ffraeth a rgwili
    Mi choiliwn ni rbwrth
   Fo droad wr y Iardaniaeth
   Fo dwy to byd i gyd yn gaeth.

On the cold summer of 1555

Howling heavy wind at break of day
    Tearing new leaves to shreds
  No-one knows if the new day will come
  Or if perpetual winter has begun.

White rain and sleet come to make us sad
    And the cold has made a cunning plan
  Is this really God's handiwork? – I fear
  This winter that comes in the midst of the year.

Look at this wonder: I can hardly credit it
    I don't think I'll ever feel again
  Such a cold wind, like the coldest
  On the sea at midwinter that blows without rest.

It's like when that clever Merlin
    You'd never believe it, shameless fellow,
  Turned the Creation on its head
  Keeping the whole world enchanted.

Katherine Philips
['The Matchless Orinda'] (1631-64)

A marry[d] state

A marry[d] state affords but little ease:
The best of husbands are so hard to please.
This in wifes Carefull faces you may spell,
Tho they desemble their misfortunes well.
A virgin state is crown'd with much content,
It's always happy as it's inocent.
No Blustering husbands to create your fears,
No pangs of child birth to extort your tears,
No children's crys for to offend your ears,
Few worldly crosses to distract your prayers.
Thus are you freed from all the cares that do
Attend on matrimony and a husband too.
Therefore, madam, be advised by me:
Turn, turn apostate to love's Levity.
Supress wild nature if she dare rebel,
There's no such thing as leading Apes in hell.[2]

---

2. Proverbial: spinsters dying unmarried were supposed to 'lead apes in hell'. Orinda was only fifteen or sixteen years old when she wrote this poem. Ironically, she herself married soon after, in 1648.

A Countrey Life

How sacred and how innocent
  A countrey life appears,
How free from tumult, discontent,
  From flatterye and feares.
That was the first and happiest life,
  When man enjoy'd himselfe;
Till pride exchanged peace for strife,
  And happinesse for pelfe.
'Twas here the poets were inspired,
  And sang their mysteries,
And while the list'ning world admired,
  Men's minds did civilize.
That golden age did entertaine
  No passion but of love;
The thoughts of ruling or of gaine
  Did ne're their fancyes move.
None then did envy neighbour's wealth,
  Nor plot to wrong his bed:
Happy in friendship and in health,
  On rootes, not beasts, they fed.
They knew no law nor physique then,
  Nature was all their witt;
And if there yet remaine to men
  Content, sure this is it.
What blessing doth this world afford
  To tempt or bribe desire?
Her courtship is all fir and sword,
  Who would not then retire?
Then welcome dearest solitude,
  My great felicity;
Though some are pleas'd to call thee rude,
  Thou art not so, but we.
Such as do covet only rest,
  A cottage will suffice:
It is not brave to be possest

Of Earth, but to despise.
Opinion is the rate of things,
    From hence our peace doth flow;
I have a better fate then Kings,
    Because I think it so.
When all the stormy world doth roare,
    How unconcern'd am I?
I can not feare to tumble lower
    That never would be high.
Secure in these unenvied walls
    I think not on the state,
And pitty no man's acse that falls
    From his ambition's height.
Silence and Innocence are safe;
    A heart that's nobly true
At all these little arts can laugh
    That do the world subdue.
While others revel it in state,
    Here I'le contented sit,
And thinke I have as good a fate
    As wealth or pompe admit.
Let some in Courtship take delight,
    And to th'exchange resort;
There revel out a winter's night,
    Not making love, but sport.
These never knew a noble flame,
    'Tis lust, scorne, or designe:
While Vanity playes all their game,
    Let peace and honour mine.
When the inviting spring appears,
    To Hide park let them go,
And hasting thence be full of feares
    To loose Spring garden show.
Let others (nobler) seeks to gaine

   In knowledge happy fate,
And others busy them in vaine
   To study wayes of state.
But I, resolved from within,
   Confirmed from without,
In privacie intend to spin
   My future minuts out.
I from this hermitage of mine
   Do banish all wild toyes,
And nothing that is not divine
   Shall dare to tempt my joyes.
There are below but two things good,
   Friendship and honestie,
And only these of all I would
   Aske for felicitie.
In this retir'd integritie,
   Free from both warre and noise,
I live not by necessitie,
   But wholly by my choice.

Friendship in Emblem, or the Seale, to my dearest Lucasia

1

The hearts thus intermixed speak
A Love that no bold shock can break;
For Joyn'd and growing, both in one,
Neither can be disturb'd alone.

2

That meanes a mutuall knowledge too;
For what is't either heart can doe,
Which by its panting centinell
It does not to the other tell?

3

That friendship hearts so much refines,
It nothing but it self designs:
The hearts are free from lower ends,
For each point to the other tends.

4

They flame, 'tis true, and severall ways,
But still those flames doe so much raise,
That while to either they incline
They yet are noble and divine.

5

From smoak or hurt those flames are free,
From grosseness or mortality:
The hearts (like Moses bush presum'd)
Warm'd and enlighten'd, not consum'd.

6

The compasses that stand above
Express this great immortall Love;
For friends, like them, can prove this true,
They are, and yet they are not, two.

7

And in their posture is express'd
Friendship's exalted interest:
Each follows where the other Leanes,
And what each does, the other meanes.

— 8

And as when one foot does stand fast,
And t'other circles seeks to cast,
The steddy part does regulate
And make the wanderer's motion streight:

9

So friends are onely Two in this,
T'reclaime each other when they misse:
For whose're will grossely fall,
Can never be a friend at all.

10

And as that usefull instrument
For even lines was ever meant;
So friendship from good angells springs,
To teach the world heroique things.

11

As these are found out in design
To rule and measure every line;
So friendship governs actions best,
Prescribing Law to all the rest.

12

And as in nature nothing's set
So Just as lines and numbers mett;
So compasses for these being made,
Doe friendship's harmony perswade.

13

And like to them, so friends may own
Extension, not division:
Their points, like bodys, separate;
But head, like soules, knows no such fate.

14

And as each part so well is knit,
That their embraces ever fitt:
So friends are such by destiny,
And no Third can the place supply.

15

There needs no motto to the Seale:
But that we may the Mine reveale
To the dyll ey, it was thought fit
That friendship onely should be writt.

16

But as there is degrees of bliss,
So there's no friendship meant by this,
But such as will transmit to fame
Lucasia's and Orinda's name.

To my excellent Lucasia, on our friendship. 17th July 1651

I did not live until this time
   Crown'd my felicity,
When I could say without a crime,
   I am not Thine, but Thee.
This Carkasse breath'd, and walk'd, and slept,
   So that the world believ'd
There was a soule the motions kept;
   But they were all deceiv'd.
For as a watch by art is wound
   To motion, such was mine:
But never had Orinda found
   A Soule till she found thine;
Which now inspires, cures and supply's,
   And guides my darken'd brest:
For thou art all that I can prize,
   My Joy, my Life, my rest.
Nor Bridegroomes nor crown'd conqu'rour's mirth
   To mine compar'd can be:
They have but pieces of this Earth,
   I've all the world in thee.
Then let our flame still light and shine,
   (And no bold feare controule)
As inocent as our design,
   Immortall as our Soule.

A retir'd friendship, to Ardelia, 23rd Aug. 1651

1

Come, my Ardelia, in this bowre,
  Where kindly mingling Souls a while,
Let's innocently spend an houre,
  And at all serious follys smile.

2

Here is no quarrelling for Crowns,
  Nor fear of changes in our fate;
No trembling at the Great ones frowns,
  Nor any Slavery of State.

3

Here's no disguise, nor treachery,
  Nor any deep conceal'd design;
From blood and plots this place is free,
  And calme as are those looks of thine.

4

Here let us sit, and blesse our Starres
  Who did such happy quiet give,
As that remov'd from noise of warres
  In one another's hearts we live.

5

Why should we entertain a feare?
   Love cares not how the world is turn'd:
If crouds of dangers should appeare,
   Yet friendship can be unconcern'd.

6

We weare about us such a charme,
   No horrour can be our offence;
For mischief's self can doe no harme
   To friendship and to innocence.

7

Let's mark how soone Apollo's beams
   Command the flocks to quit their meat,
And not intreat the neighbour – streams
   To quench their thirst, but coole their heate.

8

In such a scorching Age as this,
   Whoever would not seek a shade
Deserve their happiness to misse,
   As having their own peace betray'd.

9

But we (of one another's mind
   Assur'd,) the boistrous world disdain;
With quiet souls, and unconfin'd,
   Enjoy what princes wish in vain.

On the Welch Language

If honour to an ancient name be due,
Or Riches challenge it for one that's new,
The Brittish Language claims in either Sence,
Both for its Age, and for its Opulence.
But all great things must be from us remov'd,
To be with higher Reverence belov'd:
So Lantskips which in prospects distant ly,
With greater wonder draw the pleased Ey.
Is not great Troy to one dark ruine hurl'd?
Once the fam'd Scene of all the fighting World.
Where's Athens now, to whom Rome learning ows,
And the safe Lawrells that Adorn'd her brows?
A strange reverse of Fate she did endure,
Never once greater, then she's now obscure.
Ev'n Rome her self can but some footstepps shew
Of Scipio's times, or those of Cicero:
And as the Roman and the Grecian State,
The Brittish fell, the spoyle of Time and Fate.
But though the Language hath her beauty Lost,
Yet she has still some great remains to boast;
For 'twas in that, the scared Bards of Old,
In deathless numbers did their thoughts unfold.
In Groves, by Rivers, and on fertil plaines,
They civilized and taught the Listening Swains;
Whilst with high Raptures, and as great success,
Virtue they cloath'd in musick's charming dress.
This Merlin spoke, who in his gloomy Cave,
Ev'n Destiny her self seem'd to enslave.
For to his sight the future time was known,
Much better than to others is their own:
And with such state, Predictions from him fell,

Katherine Philips ['The Matchless Orinda'] (1631-64)

As if he did Decree, and not foretell.
This spoke King Arthur; who, if fame be true,
Could have compell'd mankind to speak it too.
In this once Boadicia valour taught,
And spoke more nobly then her souldiers fought:
Tell me what Hero could do more than she,
Who fell at once for Fame and Liberty?
Nor could a greater sacrifice belong,
Or to her children's, or her Countrey's wrong.
This spoke Caraticus, who was so brave,
That to the Roman fortune check he gave;
And when their yoak he could decline no more,
He it so decently and nobly wore,
That Rome her self with blushes did beleive
A Brittain would the Law of Honour give;
And hastily his chains away she threw,
Least her own Captive else should her subdue.

Angharad James (1677-1749)

Ymddiddan rhyngddi a'i chwaer – detholiad
*Ymddiddan rhwng dwy chwaer un yn dewis gŵr oedrannus
a'r llall yn dewis ieuenctid, i'w canu ar Fedle Fawr
(Angharad James ai canodd ar ymddiddan a fu
rhyngddi ai chwaer, Margaret)*

MJ: Yn wir om rhan tra fyddwi fyw
    Yn enw Duw mi gara
    Yr hardda ei bryd yn wir heb wad
    Yw newis gariad gora
    Cael glaslanc mwyn ifanc mewn afiaeth ydyw mryd
    Yn ddedwydd ar gynnydd dda beunydd yn y byd.

AJ: Os wyt Began mor ben chwiban a mynd i garu
    Hogiau purlan anniddan fydd dy fyd
    Nid wrth 'madroddion ofer Ddynion y mae coelio
    Eitha ei calon ai moddion hoywon hyd
    Y gŵr ifanc tecca ei ddawn
    Bydd anodd iawn ei ddirnad
    Fe dry ei ffydd pan ddêl yn ffraeth
    Dan gwlwm caeth offeiriad
    Fe â'n gastiog afrowiog ŵr tonnog eirie tyn
    Heb wenu ni chwery ond hynny mwy am hyn.

MJ: Ow na choethoch ar hyfrydwch, ma'i gŵr ifanc
    Au diddanwch yn harddwch tegwch tir
    Perl aur gemau purion tlysau, dethol ran dawn
    Daeth o'r India Hawddgarau gorau gwir
    Ni choncwerir dim yn siŵr
    Mo londid gŵr a'i fodde
    Y fi ni chara hen Ddyn fyth
    Tra byddo chwyth i'm gene
    Dau mwynach na chliriach yn bwbach afiach yw
    Cael llencyn ireiddwyn pen felyn teg i fyw.

A dialogue between herself and her sister – extract
*A dialogue between two sisters, one choosing an elderly
husband and the other opting for youth, to be sung to the
tune of 'Y Fedle Fawr'. (Angharad James sang this song,
based on a debate she had with her sister, Margaret)*

MJ: Truly for my part while I live
In God's name I'll gladly love
The handsomest one every time:
He's the one I would were mine.
To have a young sweet naïve lad full of life – that's my desire,
To grow in happiness every day, driven by passion's fire.

AJ: Maggie, if you're such an airhead that you'll go for dapper,
Pretty, boring boys, you're sure to come a cropper
It's not the words of men you should believe
But their hearts and ways you should perceive,
For the best looking young man
You make him out if you can,
For he'll soon change once he hears the bann
Called solemnly by the clergyman:
He'll turn moody and nasty, all anal retentive
He won't smile and won't flirt for he has no incentive.

MJ: Oh don't get hard on handsomeness, a dreamboat
Is amusing in himself and makes you gloat;
Pearls, gold, lovely jewels, you name it, give me a gem
Of India, let's have him; granted, niceness is the best item
Though sure enough it won't sweep me off my feet
But a man's good nature and good temper sure are sweet.
But me, I'll never go for an old man
My stomach turns, I never can,
A man who mopes 'round like an ancient goblin,
No, a virile blonde hunk will, for me, always win.

AJ: Cymer gyngor meinir weddol, os yw dy fwriad
 Yn arferol bun raddol i ble yr eir
 Na fêd yn gynta cyn cynhaea, gwaetha y grifia
 Yr yd aeddfetta yw'r gore yn siŵr
 A felly gŵr mewn oedran
 Drwg ywd 'amcan am ŵr da
 Yn wir debyga'i Began.
 Cans ddewis yn ddilys un moddus gweddus gwâr
 Di falchedd go sobredd da rinwedd cyrredd câr.

MJ: Henaint go brydd aiff yn Goubren, rydwi'n tybied
 Hyn fy hunan mae gwaetha iw'ch amcan chwi
 Gwell cymdeithas llance peraiddlais, nid yw'ch cyngor
 Ond rhy ddiles im pwrpas addas i
 Yr impin iredd braf o bryd
 Yw'r goreu ei gyd i gara
 Ai feddwl mwyn au fodde
 Cyn mentro ymrwymo ar un pan grycho'r grudd
 Mi brofa mi ymgroesa yn wir mi arhosa yn rhydd

AJ: Gwiliwch funud gam gymeryd, mae'ch mawrfryd
 Yn eich gwynfyd i gael dedwydd fyd da
 Pam brioder chwi a rhyw swagor, yn gwit y derfydd
 Yr holl fwynder ar gwychder hoywder hâ
 Odid un pan bwyso'r byd
 Na newidia ei bryd ai fodde
 Ni welir Gwen fel yr ydoedd gynt
 Fe aeth gyda'r gwynt or eirie
 Yn sicr bun eglur in welir feinir fael
 Y sobre'r mwyneiddia a fuase gore ei gael.
 Duw gadwo i mi fel dyma'r gwir
 A garu yn hir o amser
 Ag i Farged lysti lance
 O swagrwyr ifanc ofer.

Angharad James (1677-1749)

AJ: Take my advice, good girl, if your intention
Is sensible, you won't mind if I mention:
If you harvest before the crop is ripe, you'll rue
The day, for the ripest corn is the best, you know
So go for a mature man, do,
Your lad will bring you only sorrow.
Maggie, believe me, I'm right.
Choose a decent man who's seen the light,
Your pride in him will grow and love will soon shine
    bright.

MJ: Old age will soon wither into death, that's my view,
Whatever you say I'd much rather have the new,
The company of a pure-voiced young lad, your counsel
Is no good at all for what I'm after:
A naughty scamp full of fun and a real looker,
Being in love with him I think I'd do quite well,
With his tender mind and his sweet manner,
I'd rather have him than a withered cheek –
I'd rather stay single and be seen as a freak.

AJ: Hang on a minute – before the step is done,
You fancy that you'll find some kind of paradise
When you marry some swaggerer, but it's unwise:
All the sweetness of summer will soon be gone.
But go for one who has the world's measure
Who won't be fickle but regard you as a treasure,
Who won't stop smiling as he used to do,
For the lad's smile flew off with his fine song,
Believe me, you're better off, a girl like you
With a sober one who's sensible, for he won't do you
    wrong.
May God find such a one for me
That I can love forever
And for Maggs a lusty lad:
Young swaggerer and deceiver.

Nid ydi ein hoes ond cafod fer

Nid ydy ein hoes ond cafod fer
A roed o flinder bydol:
Ymwnawn' ni gawn gan Un a Thri
Lawenydd di-derfynol
Mewn hapusrwydd yn y Ne'
Da diddan, le dedwyddol.

Pan oedd bygythion y gyfraith ar ei gŵr

Mae llawer o drafferth i'n hindro ni, ysywaeth,
A gofid am gyweth anhyweth yw hwn
Os cawn ein diddanu yn nheyrnas yr Iesu,
Er adfyd a chyni, na chrynnwn.
Er maint sy' fygythion, ni thorrai mo'm calon,
Rho' mhwys ar Dduw cyfiawn erfynion hyd fedd.
Os credwn yn ddilys a gwneuthur ei 'wyllys
Cawn barchus wir felys orfoledd.
(Angharad James ai cant)

Our life is but the briefest shower

Our life is but the briefest shower
Of worldly woe, a torrent:
But one day the Trinity
Will bring us endless ecstasy,
We'll share the bliss of Heaven
That place of sheer content.

When the law threatened her husband

Troubles beset us, sad to say
And cares, they do oppress,
But if in Christ's kingdom our trust we lay
We fear not, despite our distress.
These looming threats will not break our heart
If our faith in a just God goes not amiss,
For if in doing his will we play our part
We shall drink of the sweet wine of bliss.

Catrin Gruffydd (fl. 1730)

Marwnad gwraig am ei merch

Rwyf yn dymuned ar Dduw Cyfion
Roi i mi bur fodlondeb calon
Am fy annwyl eneth gynnes
Sydd y rŵan yn Dy fynwes.
Mae ei henaid hi'n cael canu peraidd fiwsig
Dda nodedig yn ddi-wadu
Crist ei hun a fo im cysuro, dda gynorthwy,
Fel y gallwy fyned yno.
Ar gyfer hynny o amser hynod
Bu Grist ddioddef am ein Cymod
Y daeth Duw o'i fawr drugaredd
I dynnu 'ngeneth i o'i chyfyngedd
Ai henaid aeth i'r Nefoedd uchod, at yr Iesu
I gael yno ganu mawr-glod
A'i chorphyn bach a roed i bydru, nes y delo
Duw i'w cheisio oddi yno i fyny
Fe dderfydd hyn o drymder calon
Mae fy ngobaith i ar Dduw cyfion
Y ca'i fynd i'r Nef i dario
Lle na ddaw dim drwg im blino
Er bod hiraeth arna'i beunydd, trwm a thramawr,
Hynny yn ddirfawr mi wn a ddrfydd
Duw a'm dyco i at fy Neli, f'annwyl eneth
Yn gu lanweth i'r goleuni.
Un Duw cyfion a'i drugaredd
A faddeuo i mi y'nghamwedd
Fel y gallwy' fod yn sicir
O fwynhau geiriau yr Ysgrythur
Ni ddown i'r mynydd dedwydd didwyll, pan ddêl
                                                    Barnwr
Yn ddi-gynnwr' euraidd gannwyll
I'r cyfarfod hynod hynny, penn' pennod
Yn y diwrnod y bo yn barnu.

A woman's elegy for her daughter

I pray to you, oh righteous Lord,
Grant me a heart of pure content,
For the sake of my dearest daughter
Who was to your bosom sent.
Her soul now sings sweet music
That no-one can deny,
Let Christ himself give me comfort,
That I may join her by and by.
Let me recall that strangest of times
When Christ suffered for our sins,
Just so, God came from his great mercy
To draw my daughter from her pains,
And her soul went up to Jesus
And to sing there his praise
While her little body was left to rot, 'til
God comes again her corpse to raise.
This song springs from a heavy heart
But my hope still rests with the righteous Lord
That I may go to my dear girl in Heaven,
Where no evil will come and all live in accord.
Though I long for her daily, heavy in heart,
The end will soon enough be in my sight,
For God will take me up to Nell, dear girl,
Clean and pure in the dazzling light.
One righteous God in all his mercy
Will forgive me every trespass,
So that I can be truly certain
To relish the words of the mass:
I will come to the mountain of truth,
In great calm, bearing a golden flame,
I shall come, all passion spent,
On that great Day of Judgement.

Margaret Davies (fl. 1738)

Er bod gwŷr hynod eu henwau

Er bod gwŷr hynod eu henwau, gwir oedd
A thiroedd a thyrau
Yn llaw Duw gŵyr llwyr wellau
Mwy dawn, mae mywyd innau.

Though there are many men of renown

Though there are many men of renown, it's true
Rich in rural lands and houses in town,
It's not in them but in God I place my trust
I place my life in his hands, 'fore I turn to dust.

Jane Brereton [Melissa] (1685-1740)

To Mrs Roberts on her Spinning.
Written on her Birth-day Jan. 6, 1731

Penelope did thus her Time employ,
Till her lov'd wand'ring Lord return'd from *Troy*;
While he was fated thro' strange Realms to roam,
The prudent Queen play'd the good Wife at Home;
While he the various Turns of Fortune knew,
She ply'd the Loom, and th'Ivory Shuttle threw.
So the dull Hours you at your Wheel deceive,
And draw a Web, fit for a Queen to weave.

Wise the Resolve, when to your Wheel you sate,
The Wheel, best Emblem of our worldly State;
Still changing, varying, always moving found,
Where high and low, alternate, take their round,
With skilful Hand you manage this Machine,
May like Success thro' all your Life be seen!
May each revolving Year with Joy be crown'd,
And this your Natal Day still happy found!

Let no proud Dame the Spinning Art despise,
Which from the wife *Minerva* took its Rise;
And which *Aliza* for Amusement chose
To lighten Absence, and to soften Woes.

On Reading some Dissertations, in the Reverend Dr Foulkes's modern Antiquities

Some will, perhaps, think they've a Right to blame,
When to these Lines they see a Woman's Name.
Why shou'd I then obnoxious Praise bestow,
And unavailing Honour strive to shew?
Well then, – lest I shou'd prejudice the Cause,
And draw a Censure, by my weak Applause;
I'll not attempt the panegyrick Strain,
Nor fond expatiate on this Work, in vain:
Be that the Province of judicious Friends:
To say – I'm pleased – is all my Muse pretends.

A *Cambro-Briton* must with Pleasure trace
The Means which Heav'n ordain'd to save our Race.
Tho', in the Fight, our warlike Fathers prov'd
Fierce as their Wolves, and as our Rocks unmov'd;
Yet Heav'n be prais'd that here, the Eagles flew,
And *Roman* Arts that Fierceness cou'd subdue;
That Laws prevail'd, which their just Rights maintain'd;
And but from savage Liberty restrain'd!

Still honour'd by our Sex, still dear to Fame,
Be the first *Edward*'s great, and glorious Name!
Who abrogated that unrighteous Power,
By which our Sex enjoy'd nor Land nor Dower.
No Wonder for this Prince the much-lov'd Wife
Should risqué her own to save his dearer Life!
(The Surgeon's Art, when ineffectual found,)
Shou'd brave e'en Death, and suck the poison'd Wound!

Let Fame to latest Times his Virtues tell;
And own his Laws, our *Howel Dda*'s excel!

Superior Blessings, still, to us allow'd,
See! pure religion breaking thro' a Cloud,
The Mist of SUPERSTITION clear'd away,
Diffusive shine in her own Heav'nly Ray!

May Rage, and Ignorance, attempt in vain
To rule our Temples, or our Courts again;
And may their horrid Offspring, here no more,
Glut *her* fierce Thirst, with Draughts of human Gore:
May *Britons* ne'er the hellish Fury feel,
Her Chains, her Whips, her Gibbets, Fire, or Wheel!
But bless'd with equal Laws, and Gospel Light,
May Peace, and Charity, their Hearts unite!

O Heav'n-descended Charity! 'tis thine
To rule our Spirits, and our Hearts refine.
Th'angelick Mission Thou! can'st best instill;
"To God give Glory, and to Men Goodwill."
Thy divine Spirit if we can't attain;
Our Hope's ill-grounded, and our Faith in vain.
The grand *Criterion*, Thou! celestial Grace!
Of the Disciples of the Prince of Peace.
For Thee! a new Commandment we receive!
(He, both the Precept, and th'Example gave;)
"Love one another," The blest Saviour said:
O *Britons*! let the Mandate be obey'd.

Elisabeth Ferch William Williams ym-Marrog ymhlwy Llanfair Talhaiarn (fl. 1714)

Cyngor hen wraig i fachgen – detholiad

Gwrando Machgen yn ddiymdro
Cymer gyngor gan dy garo
Gwilia ei ollwng chwaith yn ofer
Meddwl beth am hwn yn d'amser.

Dod dy galon yn wastadol
I roi moliant i Dduw nefol
Ac na ollwng fyned heibio
Heb it ddyfal gofio am dano

Ar dda byd na rown mo'n hyder
Rhown ein gobaith yn yr uchelder
Gan nas gwyddom wrth ei gasglu
Pwy fydd fory i'w feddiannu.

Ac os gofyn neb yn ddibaid
Pwy a linie hyn o ganiad
Un sy a'i gweddi nos a bore
Ar Dduw fadde iddi ei beie.

Elisabeth yw ei henw hi unwaith
A dwbwl W ai dyblu eilwaith
Sydd a'i gobaith ar Dduw nefol
O gael trugaredd yn tragwyddol.

An old woman's counsel to a lad – extract

Listen Lad, don't mess about,
From one who loves you, never doubt,
Take advice and let vain things go
Think hard and long or risk some woe.

Remember that we all must die.
Put your heart on an even keel
To worship God, get down and kneel
Don't let Time just pass you by.

I wouldn't trust in worldly good
Let's place our faith in God's own rood
When we gather wealth we harvest sorrow
For who may claim it on the morrow?

And if anyone asks the whole day long
Who can have shaped this little song
It's one who prays by night and day
That God will wash her sins away.

Her name is Elisabeth, just the once,
Then a double u, doubled twice,
Whose hope in mighty God has placed
That she might gain eternal grace.

Anna Williams (1706-83)

A sonnet to a Lady of Indiscreet Virtue. In imitation of Spencer (sic)

While you, fair Anna, innocently gay,
And free and open, all reserve disdain,
Wherever fancy leads securely stray,
And conscious of no ill, can fear no stain,
Let calm discretion guide with steady rein,
Let early caution twitch your gently ear;
She'll tell you censure lays her wily train
To blast those beauties which too bright appear.
Ah me! I feel the monster lurking near,
I know her haggard eye and pois'nous tongue,
She scans your actions with malicious leer,
Eager to wrest and represent them wrong:
Yet shall your conduct, circumspect and clear,
Nor baleful touch, nor fangs envenom'd fear.

The Nunnery

What wond'rous projects form'd the fickle fair?
How stately rose the castle built in airs
When maids their charms from lovers' eyes to screen
Made a rash vow no longer to be seen?
Whose pen shall dare to tell what secret cause,
Incited nymphs to spurn great Hymen's laws?
Or shew how soon the fatal cov'nant fail'd,
And mirth, and flattery, and shew prevail'd?
Of maids a beauteous bevy late disdain'd,
In matrimonial fetters to be chain'd;
All banish man with one consenting voice,
Some think by force, but more agree by choice.

But how this bold rebellion to maintain,
A thousand stratagems fill every brain;
Through diff'rent ways their resolutions tend,
But all unite in the same fatal end.

Round the tea table many a time they sate,
Th'important scheme at leisure to debate;
Till one prolifick Head above the rest,
With serious mien th'assembled Fair addrest.

How blest the nymphs in cloister'd walks immur'd
From all the follies of the world secur'd;
With what contempt its empty pomp they view,
And with its pleasures bid its cares adieu;
Whatever joys they see, they enjoy none,
Because no state is equal to their own.
Triumphant votaries! Whose hearts possess
Unshaken peace and genuine happiness.

This bliss shall no good Protestant obtain?
Shall only Papists break the nuptial chain?
Forbid it, Stars! Let English wit contrive,
At equal ease and liberty to live.
If you, my sisters, this advice approve,
My scheme our ills will cure, our fears remove.

Each fleeting will more durably to bind,
Let all our fortunes in one stock be join'd;
Then where some gloomy grove or lonely plain,
Hears the faint murmurs of the distant main,
Let modest art a pleasing mansion build,
With thirty willing vot'ries to be fill'd;
But volunteers alone let choice admit,
One cross'd in love is but a hypocrite.
One only male our vestal floor shall tread,
Of blameless manners and of learning tried,
To read good lessons, and good books provide.
Hereafter on the hours we will agree,
For pray'r, for work, for reading and for tea.

Thus spoke the Fair: The project all commend,
And all their wishes to the Nunnery bend
The Chaplain nam'd, and articles begun,
Full half the work appear'd already done:
Whene'er they met they spoke of future joys,
And the Nuns' Castle all their thoughts employs.
But when their various statutes were survey'd,
And nicely read by each judicious maid,
What sudden changes in their looks appear!
Some are too mild, and some are too severe.
Dorinda cry'd, are visits then a crime?
And shall we see no friends at any time?
Shall dancing be allow'd, Sempronia said,

And yet no partner never to be had?
Must no man enter here? Brisk Lucia cry'd:
Then burn the plan, fair Thestylis reply'd:
Let fellows rather stile me wife than Nun.
And thus the castle sunk ere yet begun.

Anne Penny (fl. 1729-80)

Poem X

Little trifling, silly, Heart,
Why art thou? so prone to smart;
Why art thou? so apt to Joy,
Why does Air, thy Thoughts employ?
What but Air, are Fancy's Dreams,
What but Air, are Earthly Scenes;
What but Air, is worldly Pow'r,
Transient as the fleeting Hour.
What but Air is Love, is Life,
What but Air, is highest Strife;
What are Prospects, brightly fair,
But light Puffs of empty Air.
Lift thy Thoughts, my Heart! On high,
Search, the Blessings of the Sky,
Seek those Joys, which never Fade,
Joys that need not Fancy's Aid:
Joys as Permanent, as great,
Happy, in a lasting State.
There, shalt thou ecstatic prove,
That th'Almighty is all Love.
Love my Soul, but raise thy Flame,
To those Dwellings, where no Shame
Tints the Cheek, or hurts the Mind,
But where Peace to Virtue's join'd.
Then, shalt thou! enraptur'd prove,
That th'Eternal, is all Love.

Poem XXXIII

Well my Dear! How do you now?
'Pon my Word, I scarce know how:
I tremble, when I think how much,
I venture by each Pencil's Touch.
How know I? But I might have been,
Held in sober Folks' Esteem ;
Had I not these Trifles shown,
Which better I had let alone.
Much I fear, Pierian Spring,
I've proved to be, a dangerous Thing;
And by slight tasting Learning's Stream,
Have spoke, like Children, in a Dream.

Elisabeth Griffith (fl. 1712)

Ti ddyn 'styfnig melltigedig (detholiad)

Ti ddyn 'styfnig melltigedig
Sy'n byw beunydd yn anufydd
Yn cau i'th fynwes megis Difes
Rhag cyngorion Jesu cyfion.
Aur ac arian felfed sidan
Yw dy ddyhead, harddwch drwsiad
A modrwye aur yn dorche
Am dy fysedd, briddyn bydredd
Rwyt ti'n ffaelu, a chyd dynnu
A'th wallt dy hun, . . .
A'th synwyre, golli y gradde
Gwachel fythgen Duw a'i wialen
Drwg yw pob drwg yn ei olwg . . .
Cofia Judas, fal y cafas
Am roi'r cyfion yr Iddewon
Gwerthu ei fistir, tirion cywyr
Wnâth am wobr, rhai dichellgar
Gwan obeithio a wnâth iddo
Ymgrogi ei hun, wrth y rhaffyn . . .
Wyla ddagrau cur dy fronnau
Dryllia'r cloion, sy' ar dy galon
Cymer gysur hwilia'r Ysgrythur
Cannwyll ganaid yw i'th enaid
Y mae yno Eirie yn adde
Dynn'th enaid o gaethiwed
Ceisa'n daerddydd ar dy anwylyd

You stubborn accursèd man (extract)

You man, so stubborn and cursed,
Who lives discontent from the first,
Closing your heart, you churl,
To righteous Jesus' counsel.
Gold, silver, satin and velvet
Are your desire, all that you can get
Of gold rings which encompass
Your fingers, you silly ass,
You stoop to folly and so pull out
Your own hair . . .
But you'll be sniffed out, found out
By God with his rod of justice
Every evil is evil in his eyes . . .
Remember Judas, how he deceived
The Jews' righteous one, whom all believed,
The one worthy of his master,
The pure one, so tender;
Judas got his prize, his petty bribe,
And his own weak hope made him
Hang himself by a rope . . .
Weep tears, and beat your chest
Break open your heart's locks, take rest,
Take comfort, follow the scripture:
It is the candle to lead your nature,
There you'll find the Word which swears
To draw out your soul from its fetters.
Remember at close of day your dear,

Hal weddion yn genhadon
Ni all Duw tirion tyner galon
Lai na rhoddi swcwr iti
Er i'th bechod roi i ti ddyrnod
Mae E'n addo dy reffresio
Mae e'n feddig tirion diddig
Fe lwyr gartha'r clwyfa' eitha'
Nid yw i'th enaid ddyn mor rhated
Ag a gallo'th dowlu heibio.
Rhows o'i fronnau wâd yn ddarne
Wrth dy ennill di ag eraill
Duw sy' serchog a thrugarog
I dy dynnu o'th drybini
Cofia bob pryd, awr ac ennyd
I foliannu o eitha'th allu . . .
Iesu'r haeldad tyn ni atat
Dod ni yn gynnes yn dy fynwes
Ni bydd yno neb yn twyllo
Na'r bydd na'r fall na'r cnawd angall
Ni gawn beunydd fwy llawenydd
Nag all enaid dyn ystyried
Ni gawn o'n bron bob o goron
A swperi gyda'r Iesu
Bendith Duw Iôn a fo rhyngom
Byth yn para, Amen d'weda
Mil a douddeg a saith cant teg
Oed Duw ar led pan y canedd Eliz. Griffith

Elisabeth Griffith (fl. 1712)

Send a prayer as a courier,
For the mild, tender-hearted Lord
Will do no less than give you aid,
Though your sin has marked you,
He promises to extract you,
For he is meek and full of pity,
Your worst wounds will he purify:
For man's soul is not so little worth,
He will give you a second birth.
He gave blood from his own heart
To redeem you and take your part,
Loving God gave you your life,
To extract you from your strife,
Remember him at every hour
And worship him to your utmost power . . .
Jesus, kind father, draw us near,
Place us at your breast so dear,
There no-one will e'er betray,
The frail flesh will have had its day,
We will have more endless rapture
Than human souls could ever picture,
We will each of us have a crown
And we will with Christ sit down
To sup; so let God's blessing be then
Upon us forever and ever, say amen.
For seventeen hundred and twelve years long
Had God been abroad when this poor song
                      was made by Eliz. Griffith.

Mary Robinson [Perdital] (1765-1800)

The Vision (extract)

As lately musing in a lovely shade,
For meditation and contentment made,
The murm'ring streams reach'd thro' the trees,
And verdant poplars, fan'd the gentle breeze,
All dwelt serene within my tranquil breast,
And sweet retirement, lull'd my soul to rest:
Delightful fancy lent her potent aid,
And scenes of wonder, to my sense convey'd . . .

Ann Julia Hatton [Ann of Swansea]
(1764-1838)

Man as He is. Prose made into Poetry

'Tis not that Emma's lips are sweeter,
Or give my feelings higher bliss;
'Tis not because, in love completer,
She better knows than thee to kiss.

'Tis nor because her heart is truer,
Nor will it grieve me should she range;
The fact is, dearest, she is **newer**;
And man you know is giv'n to change.

'Tis true indeed, I love to gather
The honied sweets from evr'y flower;
Believe me, too, I'd sometimes rather
With genius stray in Delia's bow'r.

I love to listen to her reading,
To gaze upon her speaking face;
To hear her voice energic pleading,
And all her heart's emotions trace.

Yet though refinement is a blessing,
And thou volupt'ously dost love;
Though bliss is mine, while thee possessing,
Through grosser paths I long to rove.

Thy white arms fondly round me twining;
Thy fragrant lips my wishes bless;
Yet on thy breast reclining,
Will wish for **coarser arms** to **press**.

For if condemn'd to live on chicken,
Which, seldom ate, I think a treat,
On coarse neck beef I'd fain be picking,
So I might only **change my meat**.

I've seen a housemaid briskly twirling
A mop upon a rough red arm;
Now this has set my senses whirling;
For **she** as well as **thee** can charm.

Tell me, sweet chider, tell sincerely,
Should I wish thee forever stay,
Though now I think you love me dearly,
Would not your passion die away?

Trust me, it would – ah! cease thy scolding,
Were I forever **only thine**;
Some newer lover's flame beholding,
Thy eye no more would beam on mine.

If for variety I'm dying,
'Tis fickle nature you must blame,
At each new Beauty's altar sighing,
Confess with woman 'tis the same.

Nay, weep not, Delia; for thy kisses,
Are treasures that I'll ne'er resign;
And, dear, when change no more a bliss is,
This wand'ring heart will **all be thine**.

Ann Julia Hatton [Ann of Swansea] (1764-1838)

Swansea Bay

In vain by various griefs opprest,
I vagrant roam, devoid of rest,
With aching heart, still ling'ring stray
Around the shores of Swansea Bay.

The restless waves that lave the shore,
Joining the tide's tumult'ous roar;
In hollow murmurs seem to say –
Peace is not found in Swansea Bay.

The meek-eyed morning's lucid beam,
The pensive moon's pale shadowy gleam
Still ceaseless urge – why this delay?
Go, hapless wretch from Swansea Bay.

'Tis not for me the snowy sail
Swells joyous in the balmy gale;
Nor cuts the boat with frolic play,
For me the waves of Swansea Bay.

The glow of health that tints each cheek,
The eyes that sweet contentment speak;
To mock my woes their charms display,
And bid me fly from Swansea Bay.

Haste smiling nymphs, your beauties lave
And sport beneath the sparkling wave,
While I pursue my lonely way,
Along the shores of Swansea Bay.

The frowning mountain's awful sweep,
The rocks that beetle o'er the deep:

The winds that round their summits play,
All bid me fly from Swansea Bay.

Then Kilvey Hill, a long adieu,
I drag my sorrows hence from you:
Misfortune, with imperious sway,
Impels me far from Swansea Bay.

A Man without Deceit

'Shew me on earth a thing so rare,
I'll own all miracles are true.'

Could I but hope at last to meet
The man who never us'd deceit;
Whose lip no falsehood ever stain'd,
Whose tongue no bosom ever pain'd;
And from whose clear and steady eye
No wily glances learn to fly:
Oh! I would journey where the sun
His shining course hath never run;
With untir'd step would gladly haste
O'er burning moor and sandy waste:
I'd brave the tiger's secret hold,
I'd face the serpent's scaly fold,
Could I at last but hope to find
A man with pure and honest mind.

O soul of honour! Soul divine!
With pilgrim step I'd seek thy shrine;
And there with pious hand I'd strew
The virgin lily wash'd in dew;

The *agnus custus*[3] there should shine,
An off'ring fit for truth like thine:
There, softly stealing through the air,
Pale eve should catch my vesper's pray'r;
As soon as morning's star should rise,
My matin hymn should seek the skies;
And thou, Oh man! From falsehood free,
My tutelary saint should be.

Roses Have Thorns

To shun the noontide's scorching hour,
Laurette and I had sought a bow'r,
Where rose and myrtle twining spread,
And round their silken blossoms shed:
There as her hand I gently prest,
And soft reclin'd upon her breast;
Mix'd with her blue eyes' languid ray,
Sweet tender wishes seem'd to play.
I spoke of bliss, and in her ear
Soft whisper'd – "None but love is near;
He guards this bower, no step profane
Will dare approach his sacred fane;"
She heard, and fancy in her eyes
Beheld consenting pleasure rise;
But starting from my circling arms,
Which fondly clasp'd her glowing charms,
From her white hand she threw away
A rose she'd held in wanton play.
Her eyes their sparkling fire resum'd,

---

3. Chaste lamb (Latin).

Her cheek with brighter crimson bloom'd,
As thus emphatical she said,
"See what a **scratch** the thorns have made;
Fair is the flow'r and fragrant too;
But sweet and fair can **mischief** do;
And I, who thought no ill, have found
The fragrant rose can **deeply wound**!"

Resignation

Not yet – not yet, hath my rebellious mind
The bitter lesson to submit been taught;
Not yet my stubborn spirit is resign'd,
I am not meek or humble as I ought.
It is not faded beauty prompts my tears,
Or lack of riches gives me agony –
That causes Sleep that even sickness cheers
To bring to me, but dreams of misery.
Condemn'd to feel a pang that probes the soul
To meet forever Disappointment's blight –
To see long months, nay years before me roll,
Nor gain from hope one cheering ray of light –
In life's sad mystery to wander on
To find despair on all my haunts intrude –
To know that patience never will be won,
To dwell within my heart's drear Solitude!
Oh! Let my groans ascend, and meet thine ear
God of compassion! Pity me – and still
The throbbing of my brain, – teach me to bear
And bend with resignation to thy will.

The Mirror

As yet no wrinkles in thy face appear;
Thy bosom has no stain of yellow hue;
And still meandering as a streamlet clear,
Thy veins disclose a bright and healthy blue.
As yet there's lustre sparkling in thine eye,
Thy dewy lips a crimson tint disclose;
And still unfaded on thy cheek doth lie
The glowing colour of the summer rose.
'Tis thus my mirror most deceitful says
That time to me, but little harm hath done;
Vain as I am, and fond perhaps of praise,
This flattery my belief has never won: -
Credulity alas! Is woman's bane –
By adulation thousands are betray'd –
Deceitful mirror! O, pronounce again,
Unsay the falsehoods thou has lately said!
Tell me that vainly blooms the polish'd mind
When youth's gay rosy hours away have flown.
Tell me that man can seldom – **never** find,
Beauty or charm in **intellect alone**.

Jane Cave (fl. 1770-96)

A Poem Occasioned by a Lady's doubting whether the Author Composed an Elegy, to which her Name is Affix'd

If Lady B_ will condescend
To read these lines which I have penn'd,
Perhaps it may her doubts confute,
And she'll no more my word dispute,
But own I may the Author be,
Of what she did on Sunday see.

You'd hate a base perfidous youth,
Such my disgust to all in truth.
A gen'rous mind is never prone
To claim a merit not her own:
I would disdain t'affix my name
To that which is another's claim.
Of beaut'ous form Heaven made me not,
(Nor has soft affluence been my lot,)
But fix'd me in a humbler station,
Than those at court in highest fashion:
But there are beauties of the mind,
Which are not to the great confin'd;
Wisdom does not erect her seat
Always in places of state;
This blessing Heav'n dispenses round;
She's sometimes in a cottage found;
And tho' she is a guest majestic,
May deign to dwell in the domestic.

Yet of this great celestial guest,
I dare not boast my self possest,
But this would represent to you,
As wisdom does, the muses do,
No def'rence shew to wealth or ease,
But pay their visits as they please.
Sometimes they deign to call on me,
And tune my mind to poetry;
But ah! they're fled, I'll drop my pen,
Nor raise it till they call again.

Thoughts, which occurred to the Author, at-Llanwrtid, in Breconshire, in walking from Dol-y-Coed House to the Well

Sweet, silent, solitary place,
Where I majestic footsteps trace,
Where Reason may ascend her throne,
And meditation reign alone,
Contemplate the works of Nature,
And in the works, the Great Creator,
See the sweet songsters of the day,
And hear them tune their artless lay;
Behold at once the fragrant fields
Which vivid green and pasture yields;
The flowing river gently glide;
Before, behind, on either side,
Four pond'rous hills stupendous rise,
As if to teach my heart and eyes
To send their wishes to the skies:
Thither my thoughts and eyes ascend,
Where wonders still more wond'rous blend:

A vast expanse of azure sky,
Boundless its width, its height how high!
Yet higher still, immensely higher,
Behold yon' orient blaze of fire,
The radiant region of the day,
With matchless majesty display
More of the great unfathom'd All
Than doth the whole terrestrial ball.
My eyes recoil, the rays so bright,
Tho' short the gaze, dissolve my fight:
If such thy power, great work divine,
How might this who bade thee shine!
Ah! what am I? Why, less than nought,
Below the merit of a thought:
Yet thought which doth all thought transcend,
That mighty All may be my friend!

Now to the salutary will
I bend my steps – and hear it tell
Important truths! My heart applies
The admonition as it flies:
'Tis true – how fast the stream is flowing;
Ah me! So fast my life is going.

As is the stream still downwards bending,
So is the grave my steps attending.

This head that thinks – these eyes that see,
In some short time must cease to be.
This well shall flow, – those hills shall rise,
That azure deck yon' splendid skies;
Those verdant meads be cloth'd in green,
That river gently glides between,
And yon' bright orb perform his round,
When not a dust of me is found.

But here I pause – and have a sigh!
While the full tear drops from mine eye.
How big with awe, this solemn theme!
No fancy'd tale, or idle dream.
Not, that I am – is truth more just,
Than that I shall return to dust.

Another year, perhaps a day
May join me to my mother day.
If now my fleeting race were run,
Is the important business done?
More awful thought – is it begun?

But thoughts most awful still arise,
As to the well I cast mine eyes:
For in the flowing stream I see
An emblem of Eternity.
This stream has flow'd, and still it flows,
From year to year, from race to race,
And still behold we no decrease
Such that tremendous, vast expanse,
To which each moment I advance.
When twice ten thousand years are past,
And more than numbers e'er can cast,
Eternity! What wond'rous thing,
Will at that period but begin!
And Oh! My soul! Where shalt thou be,
Through this immense eternity?

An Elegy on a Maiden Name

Adieu dear name which birth and Nature gave –
Lo! At the altar I've interr'd dear Cave;
For there it fell, expir'd, and found a grave.

Forgive dear spouse this ill-tim'd tear or two,
They are not meant in disrespect for you;
I hope the name which you have lately giv'n,
Was kindly meant and sent to me by heav'n.

But ah! the loss of Cave I must deplore,
For that dear name, the tend'rest mother bore,
With that she pass'd full forty years of life,
Adorn'd th'important character of wife:
Then meet for bliss from earth to heav'n retir'd
With holy zeal and true devotion fir'd.

In me what blest my father may you find,
A wife domestic, virtuous, meek and kind.
What blest my mother may I find in you,
A friend and husband – faithful, wise and true.

Then be our voyage prosp'rous or adverse,
No keen upbraidings shall our tongue rehearse;
But mutually we'll brave against the storm,
Remembering still, for help mates we were born.

Then let rough torrents roar or skies look dark,
If love commands the helm which guides our bark,
No shipwreck will we fear, but to the end,
Each find in each, a just unshaken friend.

On Marriage

A married life to speak the best,
Is all a lottery contest,
'Tis an important point to know,
There's no perfection here below.

Man's an odd compound, after all,
And ever has been since the fall;
Says that he loves you from his soul,
Still man is proud, nor brooks controul,
And tho' a slave in love's soft school,
In wedlock claims the right to rule.

Ann Griffiths (1776-1805)

Dyma babell y cyfarfod

Dyma babell y cyfarfod
Dyma gymmod yn y gwaed,
Dyma noddfa i lofryddion,
Dyma i gleifion feddyg rhad;
Dyma fan yn ymyl Duwdod
I bechadur wneud ei nyth,
A chyfiawnder pur Jehofa
Yn siriol wenu arno byth.

Pechadur aflan iw fy enw,
O ba rai y penna'n fyw,
Rhyfeddaf fyth, fe drefnwyd pabell,
I'm gael yn dawel gwrdd a Duw;
Yno y mae'n yn llond ei gyfraith,
I'r troseddwr yn rhoi gwledd,
Duw a dyn yn gwaeddi 'Digon'
Yn yr Iesu, 'r Aberth hedd.

Myfi a anturiaf yno yn eon,
Teyrnwialen aur sydd yn ei law,[4]
A hon senter at bechadur,
Llwyr dderbyniad pawb a ddaw;
Af yn mhlaen Dan waeddi 'Maddeu',
Af a syrthiaf wrth ei Draed,
Am faddeuant, am fy ngolchi,
Am fy nghanu yn ei waed.

Here we find the tent of meeting

Here we find the tent of meeting,
Here the blood that reconciles;
Here is refuge for the slayer,
Here the remedy that heals;
Here a place beside the Godhead,
Here the sinner's nesting place,
Where, for ever, God's pure justice
Greets us with a smiling face.

Sinner is my name, most shameful,
Chief of all in sinfulness;
Yet such wonder! In this temple,
Finding God in quietness;
He fulfils his law completely,
The transgressor shares his feast,
God and humans cry 'sufficient!'
Jesus, Sacrificed, makes peace.

Boldly, I will come before him;
His gold sceptre in his hand,[4]
Points toward this favoured sinner:
Here, accepted, all can stand.
I'll press onward, shouting 'pardon',
Fall before my gracious Lord:
Mine the pardon, mine the cleansing,
Mine the bleaching in his blood.

---

4. See *Esther* 4:9-5:3. Even the Queen can only enter the presence of the King if he extends his sceptre towards her; otherwise, the punishment is death.

O am ddyfod o'r Anialwch
I fynu fel colofnau mwg,
Yn uniawn gyrchiol at ei orsedd
Mae yno'n eistedd heb ei wg;
Amen diddechreu a ddiddiwedd,
Tyst ffyddlon yw, ai air yn un,
Amlygu y mae ogoniant trindod
Yn achubiaeth Damniol ddyn.

Mae bod yn fyw yn fawr ryfeddod

Mae bod yn fyw o fawr Ryfeddod
O fewn ffurneisiau sydd mor boeth,
Ond mwy Rhyfedd, wedi mhrofi,
Y Dof ir canol fel aur coeth;
Amser canu, Diwrnod nithio,
Etto'n Dawel, heb ddim braw,
Y Gwr a fydd imi'n ymguddfa
Y sydd ar wyntyll yn ei law.

Blin yw mywyd gan elynion,
Am ei bod yn amal Iawn,
Fy Amgylchu maent fel gwenyn
O foreuddydd hyd Brydhawn;
Ar rhai o'm ty fy hun yn bena
Yn blaenori uf[f]ernol gad,
Trwy gymmorth gras yr wyf am bara
I ryfela hyd at waed.

O, to come like smoke in columns
Rising from this wilderness,
Straight toward his throne to see him
Seated with unfrowning face;
Without end, without beginning,
Witness to the one in three,
Making known the threefold glory,
True Amen, who sets us free.

[Translation by Alan Gaunt]

What a wonder! to be living

What a wonder! to be living,
once to furnace flames consigned;
greater wonder, after testing,
centred here, like gold refined;
time of bleaching, day of sifting,
yet so calm, without distress,
for the one who sifts the harvest,
is himself my hiding place.

Life is weary, I am stricken,
pressed by foes persistently,
coming round like bees and swarming,
day and night, continually;
even some from my own household
lead the hellish war on good,
yet, by grace, I go on fighting,
even though I shed my blood.

[Translation by Alan Gaunt]

Am fy mod i mor llygredig

Am fy mod i mor llygredig
Ac ymadel ynddwi'n llawn,
Mae bod yn dy fynydd Santaidd
Imi'n fraint oruchel Iawn;
Lle mae'r lleni yn cael ei rhwygo,
Mae Difa'r gorchydd yno o hyd,
A Rhagoroldeb dy ogoniant
Ar ddarfodedig bethau'r byd.

O am bara i uchel yfed
O ffrydiau'r Iechydwriaeth fawr,
Nes fy nghwbwl ddisychedu
Am ddarfodedig bethau'r llawr;
Byw dan ddisgwyl am fy Arglwydd,
Bod, pan ddel, yn effro Iawn,
I agoryd iddo'n ebrwydd
A mwynhau ei ddelw'n llawn.

Rhyfedda fyth, briodas ferch

Rhyfedda fyth, Briodas ferch
I Bwy yr wyt yn wrthddrych Serch;
O Cenwch, waredigol hil,
Rhagori y mae fe ar ddeng mil.

Since I still remain corrupted

Since I still remain corrupted,
leaving you repeatedly,
right to scale your sacred mountain
is high privilege to me;
there the veils are torn that hide you
every cover swept aside,
transient things of earth made nothing,
your great glory magnified.

O, to drink on high for ever,
where salvation's waters rise,
drink, till I no longer thirst for
transient things the earth supplies;
live to watch for my Lord's coming,
wide awake and in my place,
there to open quickly to him
and, in joy, reflect his face.

[Translation by Alan Gaunt]

In endless wonder, bride, declare

In endless wonder, bride, declare
yourself the object of his care;
and he whose ransomed seed you are
excels ten thousand souls by far.

[Translation by Alan Gaunt]

Wele'n sefyll rhwng y myrtwydd

Wele'n sefyll rhwng y myrtwydd
Wrthddrych teilwng o fy mryd,
Er mai o ran, yr wy'n adnabod
Ei fod uwchlaw gwrthddrychau'r byd;
Henffych foreu, &c.
Y caf ei weled fel y mae.

Rhosyn Saron yw ei enw,
Gwyn a g[w]ridog, teg o bryd,
Ar ddeng mil y mae'n rhagori,
O wrthddrychau pena'r byd;
Ffrind pechadur,
Dyma ei Beilat ar y mor.

Beth sy imi mwy a wnelwyf
Ag eulunod gwael y llawr?
Tystio'r wyf nad yw ei cwmni
Yw cystadlu a Iesu mawr;
O am aros, &c
Yn ei gariad ddyddiau f'oes.

See him stand among the myrtles

See him stand among the myrtles,
object worthy of my mind,
though I only partly know him,
over all things, unconfined;
hail that morning,
when I see him as he is.

He is called the Rose of Sharon,
handsome, radiant, fair of face,
he excels by far ten thousand
splendid sights in time and space;
friend of sinners,
here's their pilot on the sea.

What concern to me in future,
ailing idols of the earth?
I proclaim that none among them
rivals Jesus' matchless worth;
O to stay here,
in his love through all my days.

[Translation by Alan Gaunt]

Gwna fi fel pren planedig, O fy Nuw

Gwna fi fel pren planedig, O fy [N]uw,
Yn ir ar lan afonydd Dyfroedd byw,
Yn gwreiddio ar led, ai ddail heb wywo mwy,
Ond ffrwytho dan gawodydd dwyfol glwy.

Gwlad dda, heb wae, gwlad wedi ei rhoi dan Sel,
Llifeirio mae ei ffrwyth o laeth a mel,
Grawn Sypiau gwiw i'r anial dir sy'n dod,
Gwlad nefol yw, uwchlaw mynegu ei chlod.

Jehofa yw, yr un ai Enw pur,
Cyflawnwr gwiw ei addewidion gwir;
Mae'n codi ei law, cen[h]edloedd ddaw i maes,
Nodedig braw o'i rydd anfeidriol ras.

Cen[h]adon hedd, mewn efengylaidd Iaith,
Sy'n galw ir wledd dros for yr India faith;
Caiff Hottentots, Goraniaid dua ei lliw,
Farbaraidd lu, ei dwyn i deuly Duw.

Make me, my God, just like a tree that grows

Make me, my God, just like a tree that grows
securely planted where life's river flows;
with wide-spread roots and leaves that never fade,
and fruits, from showers your godly wounds have made.

A good land, free of sorrow, well-secured
where flowing milk and honey are assured,
and grapes in bunches picked for desert ways,
a heavenly land, that far exceeds all praise.

Jehovah here, for ever stays the same,
fulfils his promises, confirms his name;
he lifts his hand, to beckon race on race,
and prove the worth of free and boundless grace.

Missions of peace, by gospel tongues released,
across the Indian ocean take the feast,
and Hottentots, Coranian hordes, set free,
Barbarian hosts, all join God's family.

[Translation by Alan Gaunt]

Felicia Hemans (1793-1835)

The Cambrian in America

When the last flush of eve is dying
  On boundless lakes afar that shine;
When winds amidst the palms are sighing,
  And fragrance breathes from every pine:
When stars through cypress boughs are gleaming,
  And fireflies wander bright and free,
Still of thy harps, thy mountains dreaming,
  My thoughts, wild Cambria! dwell with thee!
Alone o'er green savannas roving,
  Where some broad stream in silence flows,
Or though the eternal forests moving,
  One only home my spirit knows!
Sweet land, whence memory ne'er hath parted!
  To thee on sleep's light wing I fly;
But happier could the weary-hearted
  Look on his own blue hills and die!

The Rock of Cader Idris
(It is an old tradition of the Welsh bards, that on the
summit of the mountain Cader Idris is an excavation
resembling a couch; and that whoever should pass a
night in that hollow, would be found in the morning
either dead, or endowed with the highest poetical inspiration).

I lay on that rock where the storms have their dwelling,
  The birthplace of phantoms, the home of the cloud;

Around it for ever deep music is swelling,
　The voice of the mountain-wind, solemn and loud.
'Twas a midnight of shadows all fitfully streaming,
　Of wild waves and breezes, that mingled their moan;
Of dim shrouded stars, as from gulfs faintly gleaming;
　And I met the dread gloom of its grandeur alone.
I lay there in silence – a spirit came o'er me;
　Man's tongue hath no language to speak what I saw:
Things glorious, unearthly, pass'd floating before me,
　And my heart almost fainted with rapture and awe.
I view'd the dread beings around us that hover,
　Though veil'd by the mists of mortality's breath;
And I call'd upon darkness the vision to cover,
　For a strife was within me of madness and death.
I saw them – the powers of the wind and the ocean,
　The rush of whose pinion bears onward the storms;
Like the sweep of the white-rolling wave was their motion,
　I felt their dim presence, – but knew not their forms!
I saw them – the mighty of ages departed –
　The dead were around me that night on the hill:
From their eyes, as they pass'd, a cold radiance they darted, –
　There was light on my soul, but my heart's blood was chill.
I saw what man looks on, and dies – but my spirit
　Was strong, and triumphantly lived through that hour;
And, as from the grave, I awoke to inherit
　A flame all immortal, a voice, and a power!
Day burst on that rock with the purple cloud crested,
　And high Cader Idris rejoiced in the sun; –
But O ! what new glory all nature invested,
　When the sense which gives soul to her beauty was won!

Maria James (1795-1868)

Wales

Beyond the dark blue sea,
Beyond the path of storms,
Where wave with wave, in converse loud,
Uprear their forms –

Westward, on Britain's isle,
The rocky cliffs are seen,
With cities fair, and ruin'd towers,
And meadows green.

But cities or towers,
Are not so dear to me
As one lone cot that stood beside
A spreading tree.

Though dim on memory's page
The recollections rise,
As backward, through the vale of years,
I cast my eyes;

Yet well I mind the fields
Where best I lov'd to roam,
Or meet my father when at night
Returning home.

And well I mind the path
That led towards the spring,
And how I listened when the birds
Were carolling.

And well I mind the flowers,
In gay profusion spread
O'er hill and dale, and how I deck'd
My garden bed.

For there the summer sun
Unfolds the cowslip-bell,
And there the cuckoo's voice is heard
In shady dell.

There Snowdon lifts his head
To greet the rising day,
Whose latest glories linger round
The summit gray.

There sleep her sons of fame;
There rest her bards of yore:
And shall the Cambrian lyre
Awake no more?

Cymru, thou wert of old
A land renown'd for song;
But where is now thy soul of fire, –
Thy melting tongue?

'Twas in that tongue that first
I heard the Book Divine, –
The guide through life's bewildering maze, –
A light to shine.

And still the sacred page,
At morn or even tide,
From lips which now are hush'd in death,
Did calmly glide.

I heard Jehovah's praise
In Cymru's native tongue,
And hung upon those artless strains, –
In rapture hung.

'Twas like the gushing streams
In dry and thirsty land,
Or soul-dissolving melody
Of some full band.

'Twas in that tongue that first
I heard the voice of prayer,
Beseeching Heaven to take us all
Beneath its care.

Was ever cause on earth
With interest so replete,
As when a parent's heart draws near
The mercy-seat?

So fervent, such sincere,
Importunate distress, –
"Oh bless them, for the Saviour's sake, –
My Father, bless"

"And if, through cloud and storm,
Life's trembled waves be past, –
Oh grant them this – that safe in heaven
They moor at last."

Land of my fathers! Ne'er
Shall I forget thy name, –
Oh ne'er while in this bosom glows
Life's transient flame!

The Meadow Lark

Bright is the sky, and the breezes are blowing;
Earth in the sunshine is joyous and gay:
See from his nest how the meadow-lark rises, –
Hark! As triumphant he carols the lay.

Not in the covert, far, far in the green wood,
And scarce on the bough, of his warbling we hear;
But where the swain at his labour is plying,
Hastes he with music, the moments to cheer.

Down in the field, where the red-blossom's clover,
At morn and at evening is bent with the dew, –
Lonely his mate, till, as homeward returning,
She hails him: – 'Bob Lincoln!' – sweet Bob, is it you?

Say, – as thy song is a stranger to sorrow, –
Say, does thy bosom ne'er heave with a sigh?
Where dost thou flee when the mower is coming?
Where dost thou hide when the tempest is nigh?

Sure as I hear thee, my heart is misgiving,
That often in silence 'tis thine to endure: –
Sharp is the thorn where the roses are sweetest;
Deep is the spring when its waters are pure.

Oh that like thee, in the way of my duty,
I still may go forward, – nor vainly repine
That others are wiser, or richer, or greater;
Whatever their lot, be contented with mine.

To a Singing Bird

Hush, hush that lay of gladness,
It fills my heart with pain,
But touch some note of sadness,
Some melancholy strain,
That tells of days departed,
Of hopes forever flown;
Some golden dream of other years,
To riper age unknown.

The captive, bow'd in sadness,
Impatient to be free,
Might call that lay of gladness
The voice of liberty; –
Again the joyous carol,
Warm gushing, peals along,
As if thy very breath
Would spend itself in song.

Oft as I hear those tones of thine,
Will thoughts like these intrude;
'If once compared, thy lot were mine,
How cold my gratitude.
Though gloom, or sunshine, mark the hours,
Thy bosom, ne'ertheless,
Will pour, as from its inmost fount,
The tide of thankfulness.'

The Broom

Give me a broom, one neatly made
In Niscayuna's distant shade;
Or bearing full its staff upon

The well-known impress 'Lebanon'.
A handle slender, smooth, and light,
Of bass-wood, or of cedar white;
Where softest palm from point to heel
Might ne'er a grain of roughness feel –
So trim a fix, the stalks confine;
So tightly drawn the hempen line;
Then fan-like spread divided wove,
As fingers in a lady's glove –
To crown the whole, (and save beside,)
The loop, the buckskin loop is tied.

With this in hand, small need to care
If C _ y or J_n fill the chair –
What in the banks is said or done –
The game at Texas lost or won –
How city belles collect their rings,
And hie to Saratoga springs; –
To Eerie's, or to Ontario's shore,
To hear Niagara's thunders roar –
While undisturb'd my course I keep,
Cheer'd by the sound of sweep, sweep, sweep.

See learned doctors rack their brains,
To cure mankind of aches and pains,
When half, and more than half arise
From want of prudence, – exercise.
The body like a garment wears,
And aches and pains may follow years;
But when I see the young, the gay,
Untimely droop, and pine away,
As if the life of life were o'er,
Each day less active than before, –
Their courage fled, their interest cold, –
With firmer grasp, my broom I hold.

Nor is this all; in very deed
The broom may prove a friend in need;
On this I lean, – on this depend;
With such a surety, such a friend,
There's not a merchant in the place
Who would refuse me silk or lace;
Or linen-fine, or broad-cloth dear,
Or e'en a shawl of fam'd Cashmere,
Though prudence whispering, still would say,
"Remember, there's a rainy day."

Hand me the broom, (a matron said,)
As down the hose and ball were laid;
I think your father soon will come;
I long to see him safe at home.
Pile on the wood and set the chair, –
The supper and the board prepare;
The gloom of night is gathering fast, –
The storm is howling o'er the waste.

The hearth is swept, arrang'd the room,
And duly hung the shaker broom,
While cheerful smiles and greetings wait
The master entering at the gate.
Let patriots, poets, twine their brows
With laurel, or with holly boughs;
But let the broom-corn wreath be mine
Adorn'd with many a sprig of pine;
With wild-flowers from the forest deep,
And garlands from the craggy steep,
Which ne'er have known the gardener's care,
But rise, and bloom spontaneous there.

Jane Williams [Ysgafell] (1806-85)

A Celtic Tradition from Cornwall, of a Funeral Among the Small People[5]

>The term of fairy life appears
>Restricted to a thousand years;
>And hence, 'tis said, the envious spite
>With which some fairy elves delight
>To vex those days with care and strife
>Which prelude man's immortal life.
>Though Fancy's eye at eve has seen
>Bright fairies dancing on the green;
>And oft returning, traced at morn
>The rings by frequent footsteps worn;
>Though Fancy's eye has Puck espied
>While many a trick malign he tried;
>Or kinder sprites has seen at night,
>Aid human toils with elfish might;
>Their bounty oft in gifts has known,
>Or proved their wants by trivial loan;
>Their utmost weakness still was hid,
>A sight to prying gaze forbid;
>Till one strange night, revealed at last
>To rustic wight with awe aghast.
>Amid the drifted sands of Hayle,
>The home of many a fairy tale,
>From far St. Ives old Richard came,
>With pilchards laden for his dame;

---

5. Vide *Athenaeum*, October 10, 1846 – FOLK LORE.

Retarded by the burden's weight
He crossed the mystic Towyn late;
From cloudless skies a moon serene
With silvery light illumed the scene;
A deadened bell, with toll suppressed,
Alone disturbed the landscape's rest;
As up the hill his course he wound,
With wondering ears he caught the sound;
And when towards Lelant Church he drew,
Bright lights within it gleamed to view.
Then nameless fears his heart assailed,
Yet hope inquisitive prevailed.
With cautious steps, with movements still,
He ventured towards a window sill –
Peeped in, and dazzled by the light
Saw only all within was bright.
At length, along the centre aisle,
With progress slow, in double file,
He saw a long procession move
Through crowds impressed with sorrowing love;
Their tiny torches – slips of pine,
On all the fair assembly shine;
And flowers of phosphorescent light
Cast radiance from the altar's height.
No coffin, sable robes, or pall,
Obscured this fairy funeral.
They wreaths of tiny roses wore,
And sprays of blossomed myrtle bore.
Six to the bier their shoulders pressed,
Whereon, attired in flowing vest,
A fairy lady, so minute
No human type her form may suit;
So fair – so exquisite her face,
Our language fails to speak its grace;

So lovely, in that sad display,
Like "a dead seraph" there she lay!
White flowers the little corpse o'erspread –
White blossoms wreathed the beauteous head,
And twined among the hair's gold thread.
The bier approached the altar rail –
They rested it within the pale;
While close beneath the altar's shade,
With many a pickaxe small and spade,
A host of little sextons gave
Their toil to shape a little grave.
With all the reverence of love,
Then tenderest hands the corpse remove;
And fondest looks all thronging pressed
To see her, ere her latest rest.
The corpse was lowered, and off they tear
Their wreaths, and breaking in despair
Their flowery branches wildly spread,
And loudly wail, "Our Queen is Dead!"
"Our Queen is Dead!" A sexton's spade
Then dust on that fair body laid;
And thrilling from the host arose
A shriek, so eloquent of woes,
That Richard, from his caution thrown,
Augments its clamour with his own;
That very instant all was rout,
And every fairy light went out.

Elin Evans [Elen Egryn] (1807-76)

Dyhuddiant Chwaer Mewn Trallod ac Iselder Meddwl

Margaret bach, os yw dy galon
'Nawr yn drigfa i helbulon,
Gwawria hawddfyd arnat eto,
Pob peth yma sy'n myn'd heibio.

Gwelsom aml gwmwl terwyn,
A'r olwg arno braidd yn ddychryn;
Ond cyn iddo ddechreu gwlawio,
Awel fach a'i cariai heibio.

Pe caet tithau fyw mewn hawddfyd,
Heb un peth i flino'th ysbryd,
Byddai'n ofid i ti gofio
Fod dy hawddfyd i fyn'd heibio.

Felly, Margaret, sych dy ddagrau,
Da i ni yw cael gofidiau;
Ein gofid dry yn gysur cofio
Mai byd yw hwn sy'n myned heibio.

Ar ein taith trwy ddyffryn trallod,
Cofiwn am y Ganaan uchod;
Cawn mewn hawddfyd yno drigo
Pan â'r byd a'i ofid heibio.

Consolation for a Sister suffering from depression and tribulation

Margaret[6] dear, although your heart is now
The dreary dwelling-place of sorrow,
Prosperity will dawn on you again one day,
For everything on earth will pass away.

We have seen many a tempest-laden cloud,
Whose glowering look with threat was bowed;
But before the downpour came, true to say,
A little breeze would just blow it away.

If you could live in comfort and ease,
Without a thing to spoil your peace,
But one thing would spoil it all one day:
To recall that your ease would pass away.

Therefore, Margaret, dry your tears,
It's good for us to have our pain and fears;
Our grief turns to comfort when we recall one day
That this is a world which passes away.

On our journey through the vale of blighted love,
Let us remember Canaan high above;
For we will one day there make our way
When this world and its cares have passed away.

---

6. Margaret was one of Elen Egryn's sisters, born 10 May, 1812. It is thought that she died at a relatively early age, as did a number of her siblings.

I Gydnabod y Bardd G. Cawrdaf[7] am-Hyfforddiad

Dawnus hyfforddiad union, – a gefais,
    Mi gofiaf d'orch'mynion;
Dysgaist a llywiaist fi'n llon,
Wrth burddoeth raith y beirddion.

Diolch yt a dalaf, – da achos,
    Dy iechyd ddymunaf;
A bydded nodded Duw Naf
Cywirdeg i'r bardd Cawrdaf.

To thank the poet G. Cawrdaf[7] for his instruction

Inspired, honest instruction I got,
   I remember your direction;
You taught and steered me gladly,
By the old bards' pure sagacity.

I pay my tribute to you – a good cause,
   May good health be your due;
Let the Good Lord protect and save
And bless with correctness the bard Cawrdaf.

---

7. 'Gwilym Cawrdaf' was the bardic name of William Ellis Jones, 1795-1848, poet, printer, and lay preacher. As these englynion reveal, he seems to have been responsible for at least some of Elen Egryn's poetic apprenticeship.

Anne Beale (1816-1900)

The Dog Violet

Blue, modest, but deceitful flower,
    We learn of life from thee,
Deluding all thy little hour,
    With semblance fair to see.

For culling thee we seek in vain
    The violet's scented breath,
And cast thee on the sod again,
    Unpitied in thy death.

Like thee, deceitful violet,
    The world's false friends are fair;
We view them, and awhile forget
    That perfume dwells not there.

For there are those on this bright earth
    Most lovely to the eye;
We prove them, and we find a dearth
    Of Christian charity.

The sun unto the mountain height
    May lend his rays of gold,
But when his radiant beams take flight,
    The mount is grey and cold.

So round the lips sweet smiles may dwell,
    The eye, as thine, be blue;
But softest smiles can scarcely tell
    If the deep heart be true.

'Tis not the bland and courtly air
    That proves the inward mind;
But deeds that speak, and hearts that share
    The sorrows of mankind.

These, like the perfumes that exhale
    From thy sweet sister's sigh,
Are wafted far upon the gale
    In blessings ere they die.

To Mrs. Hemans

Lovely and gentle in thy heavenly musing,
    We have been with thee long;
Thou thy pure spirit graciously diffusing
    In the soft breath of song.

Through the dark forest or green meadows roving,
    By the stream sparkling bright,
We have been with thee, thy soft presence loving,
    In fancy's wayward flight.

Now like the sunbeam that in gladness leapeth,
    Over a troubled sea –
Now like the moonlight on a lake that sleepeth,
    Were life's brief joys to thee.

Revelling in nature with the poet's gladness,
    Hopes opened with the leaf;
Brooding o'er sorrow with the woman's sadness,
    Thy life was chastened grief.

For thee the wandering zephyrs gently sighing
    Poetic treasures brought;
From the lone echoes, each to each replying,
    Thy soul new language caught.

On earth the laurel-wreath of fame was twining
    Meekly around thy brow;
May there, upon thee, in the heavens be shining
    A crown of glory now!

Emily Jane Pfeiffer (1827-90)

Peace to the Odalisque

Peace to the odalisque, the facile slave,
Whose unrespective love rewards the brave,
Or cherishes the coward; she who yields
Her lord the fief of waste, uncultured fields
To fester in non-using; she whose hour
Is measured by her beauties' transient flower;
Who lives in man, as he in God, and dies
His parasite, who shuts her from the skies.
Graceful ephemera! Fair morning dream
   Of the young world! In vain would women's hearts
In love with sacrifice, withstand the stream
   Of human progress; other spheres, new parts
Await them. God be with them in their quest –
Our brave, sad working-women of the west!

Glân-Alarch, his Silence and Song (extract)

I am the bard Glân-Alarch, he who sings
Beneath the morning cloud which wraps Crag-Eyrie,
Who basks upon his sun-kiss'd side at noon,
And sleeps with him in silence when his crown –
A beacon fire whose message hath been sped –
Fades on the east where he prolonged the day.
I am Glân-Alarch, he whose day of life
Is likewise hasting to its close, who holds

His course, a waning, lonely light, ere long
To drop as drops the sun, – but in a sea,
If not more silent, one whose murmurous music,
Hath never found a voice in tongue of man, –
And leave his fame to love a twilight hour
Glowing upon the heights he loved to range.

* * *

An ancient bard, – my children, have you thought
What that may mean? A poet with the snows
Of time upon his beard and burning lips,
A nightingale whose song is for the rose,
Belated where his rose has ceased to bloom;
A child who in a cave which darkens daylight
And deadens music, wears away his heart,
And struggles to repress the life that throbs
Too rudely for his mouldering house of clay.

But not in sadness will I quench my song:
For joy still lives, if not for old Glân-Alarch
And pride of strength; what though its fountains rise
From other springs than his, – its droppings reach
Him in his drouth, and there is light in heaven
For him and every poorest thing that breathes,
And bardic fire for me, which when it burns,
Mine ancient house still glows with deathless youth!

Any Husband to Many a Wife

I scarcely know my worthless picture,
    As seen in those soft eyes and clear;
But oh, dear heart, I fear the stricture
    You pass on it when none are near.

Deep eyes that smiling give denial
    To tears that you have shed in vain;
Fond heart that summoned on my trial,
    Upbraids the witness of its pain.

Eyes, tender eyes, betray me never!
    Still hold the flattered image fast
Whereby I shape the fond endeavour
    To justify your faith at last.

Red or White?

In a western city new-born from a withering fire,
Fresh as a phoenix that rises renewed from the pyre,
    I, musing aloft, far removed from the noise of the street,
Looked down from my window and saw where the palaces spread
In stony files o'er the wigwams of red men dead, –
    Ground into dust in the march of the white men's feet.

Then I mixed with the crowd and beheld how the white men strive,
Jostle and fret as the bees ere they swarm from the hive, –
    Marked how with weapons newfangled the fight goes on, –
And asked: "What good or to soul or to body's health
Has come of the change?" And the answer was: "Golden wealth, –
    Golden each step we have made o'er the red man gone."

As I looked in the white hatchet faces I half understood
How "gold" was the word which they said when they
                        thought to say "good"; –
  They had chaffered away the true scale of the value of
                                            life,
They who giving their hand to a brother were 'ware of a
                                            thief,
Having sharpened their wits on the whetstone of unbelief,
  As for "good" they read "gold", they for "peace in
                                 possession" saw "strife".

The red man who out of his tribe nor demanded nor gave
Either quarter or grace, was a child with each brotherly
                                     "brave",
  And as simply plighted the word he as simply kept;
He followed the buffalo thundering over the plain
With a fierce delight, ere he feasted upon him slain, –
  Toyed with the squaw well content with his leavings,
                                              and slept.

Then I laughed: "Dull savage, who fashioned and threw
                                   the spear,
Deft-handed, swift-footed, lynx-eyed, keen of scent, fine
                                   of ear, –
  Whom the white man supplanted as red men supplanted
                                         the beast;
Will the red man or white, with his biliary troubles to cheat,
With his advertised nostrums, his blundering fingers and
                                            feet,
His sensory slowness, strained nerves, and his hurried
                                   heart-beat,
  Arise the more lean when they both shall have finished
                                   life's feast?"

Sarah Williams [Sadie] (1838-1868)

Snowdon to Vesuvius

Brother, across the sea I send you greeting,
I, standing here in calm that is not peace,
Bound to respect these pigmies at my feet,
Do envy you the power to maim and slay,
To thrust aside these fretting human things
That call themselves our masters, and are vile.
Was ever yet a stone that told a lie?
A rock that did betray his nearest friend?
A stream that smiled towards the loathsome dark?
A wind that turned itself i' the hand of God,
And smote where He was blessing? Thus do men.

VESUVIUS

'Tis true, the race is feeble, strangely weak,
Shifting as stormy breezes, varying oft,
And worn to death with just a moment's life.
But all frail things have some peculiar strength,
And man is strong in loving.
                              I have heard
That on this ground he even can meet God,
And stand before Him, interchanging thought
As with an equal.
                    Once on Mount Moriah
The very meekest, gentlest of them all,
Stood thus with God until he kindled so,
His visage was all burning, unconsumed.

And once, upon the Mount of Calvary,
'Twas said the Son of God Himself came down
For love of man, and suffered many things,
Even the pang called death.

SNOWDON

Strange! that a race with such capacities
Should sink so low! 'Tis true the mountain's height
Doth make the valley's depth; but never yet
Was known a mountain that refused to rise;
That, ass-like, supine, did resist the good,
And plant itself dead level.

       But these men
They use not even this, their power of love;
And, after all these centuries of light,
Have still no rule of right for questions vext,
Save springing at each other's throats like dogs.
Nay, I have known them meaner than the dogs,
Snarling and snarling, daring not to fight –
Whole nations, in their puny arrogance,
Vomiting evil words across the seas,
Until the air grew sulphurous with spite,
And cannon came to clear it.

VESUVIUS

       Yet I saw,
Only the last time when mine inward fires
Did grow too strong upon me and burst forth, –
I saw a youth, a careless, laughing youth,
Who, hearing moans for help beneath the wreck,
Did fling himself upon the scorching ash,
And dig and dig, with feet and fingers charred,

All quick with pain acute, dug on and on,
Until he recued thence a stranger lad,
Of whom he knew just this, – that he was man,
And man in need.
                    And I have faith in man,
That some time, surely, he will wake to feel
His brotherhood, deep underlying all,
The kinship that is given him for strength,
The strange, mysterious soul which he alone
Doth hold in common only with his kind.
And if it be so, if the time should come
When men shall all be one, as once 'twas said
They were one man, then, as in those fair days,
The earth shall be subdued, and all our powers,
No more rebellious, shall before him bow,
The worthy subjects of a worthy King.

O Fy Hen Gymraeg!
"Oh for [a word of] mine own old Welsh!"
The proverbial longing of the Welsh in London.

Yes, there is nothing I want, dear,
   You may put the candle by;
There is light enough to die in,
   And the dawning draweth nigh.
Only the want remaineth,
   Gnawing my heart away:
Oh for a word of my mother tongue,
   And a prayer she used to pray!
     O fy hen Gymraeg!

I wish I had taught you to speak it
   While the light was on my brain;
It has vanished now, with the thousand things

That will never come back again.
Only a vision of waters
   Rising towards the flow,
Cometh instead of the countless hills,
   The hills that I used to know.
     O fy hen Gymraeg!

The people are frozen hard here –
   Not you, my darling, not you! –
And the air is thick with its yellow fog,
   And the streets have slime for dew.
There is never a line of beauty
   In all the weary rows,
And the saddest thing of the whole is this,
   That the bareness no one knows;
They are quite contented, and think it fine.
     O fy hen Gymraeg!

Hush thee a moment, dearest,
   A vision is mine just now:
The place where of old we used to play,
   On the edge of the mountain's brow;
And the time, one sunny morning,
   When a preacher came by that way,
And he talked to us with the gentle words
   That hallowed and blessed our play,
     O fy hen Gymraeg!

We gathered us round about him,
   And we told him our boyish dreams;
And I saw the light in his deep-set eyes
   Come flashing in tender gleams.
And we said,"Are our visions folly?
   Should we banish them, and forget?"

And he answered, – how well I can see him now,
With the shade of the mountain across his brow! –
"There is never a longing the heart can feel,
   But a blessing shall fill it yet."
   Gorphwysfa! O Gorphwysfa!*
      Gogoniant!** Amen.

Poet's note:

* Gorphwysfa: The name of his home, common in Wales, – meaning a resting-place.

** Gogoniant!: Glory! The old rallying shout at the open-air preachings; said to have first suggested to Handel the idea of the Hallelujah Chorus.

Sarah Jane Rees [Cranogwen] (1839-1916)

Y Cyflwyniad

Fy Mam! – anwylaf, oraf fam! – i ti,
A chalon serchog, y cyflwynaf fi
Y sypyn bychan, diymhongar hwn
O flaenaf ffrwyth fy awen eiddil. Gwn
Y gweli nad yw wedi tyfu'n llawn,
Y teimli nad yw yn un aeddfed iawn;
Ond blinais yn ei ddisgwyl ef, fy mam:
A rhag i tithau orfod rhoddi cam
I arall fyd, – i'r dieithr fyd a ddaw, –
Cyn derbyn unwaith, i dy anwyl law,
A gweled *peth*, o ffrwyth y gangen hon
A dyfodd yn dy gysgod, ar dy fron,
A phrofi ei flas, – mi benderfynais i
Ei dynu: – wele ef, fy mam, i ti.
Gobeithiais byddai'n well; ond derbyn ef:
Ni thyfodd, gwyddost, ar athrylith gref;
Un egwan, eiddil, yw y gangen bu
Y blaenffrwyth hwn yn tyfu arni hi;
Ond pa mor eiddil bynnag, annwyl fam,
Ni chafodd gennyt ti erioed un cam;
Ah! na, ei magu wnaethoch chwi eich dau,
Fy nhad a'm mam, ei chyson ddyfrhau;
Ac, hwyrach, os y ca' hi eto fyw
Yng ngwlith a gwres y Nef, dan fendith Duw,
Y dyga ffrwythau gwell, o beraidd rin,
O'r rhai y gwesgir *peth* anfarwol win.

Yn awr fy mam, fel *dafn* o foroedd serch
Yw hwn i ti, oddiwrth dy unig ferch.

Dedication – to her mother

Mam! – dearest, best of mothers! – from the start,
To you I dedicate, with a loving heart,
This unpretentious little thing,
The first fruit of my paltry Muse. I sing
Though you'll see that my song is lacking,
You'll feel that it is not full grown;
But, mother, I tired of the waiting:
And lest you take your first step into
The strange other world – which will be our own –
Before once receiving in your dear hand
Or seeing some fruit by this branch made,
Which grew at your breast, thrived in your shade,
And tasting its juice, I decided to pluck it: –
Here it is, mother, it's for you –
I'd fain have it better, but please accept it;
It grew not from a strong talent, as you know,
A feeble, tender branch was this one
On which this first fruit grew;
But however feeble, dear mam,
It never received from you any harm;
Ah no! you two constantly nurtured it,
My mother and father, you always watered it;
And, perhaps, if this branch is allowed to live
In Heaven's blessed dew, survive and thrive,
She will bring forth better fruit, of the purest,
From which some eternal wine may be pressed.

Now, mam, like a drop from love's endless sea
This comes to you, from your only daughter, me.

Myfyrdod Nosawl

Dystawrwydd nos, – O mor fanteisiol yw,
   I wrandaw sibrwd yr ysbrydol fyd!
Anwyliaid nefol, deuwch, d'wedwch ryw
   Ddrychfeddwl newydd i'm hiraethus fryd:
O! rhoddwch dro am danaf, er yn wael!
   Ysbrydion hawddgar, peidiwch cilio draw!
Mae'm calon flin yn llawn o awydd cael
   Rhyw newydd o'r ysbrydol fyd uwchlaw.

Mae myrdd yn disgwyl wrthrych, fel fy hun,
   Yn disgwyl yn ddeisyfgar, ddyfal iawn,
Am gael rhyw newydd; ac y mae pob un
   Na mi, un wael, o haeddiant yn fwy llawn;
Ah! ydyw, y mae pawb yn well na mi,
   Pawb sydd yn disgwyl wrth y Nef a Duw:
Ond, engyl tyner, nac anghofiwch *fi*, –
   Myfi y wael, – myfi y waela'n fyw!

O! pe gwybyddech drymed yw fy mhwn,
   Fy maich o bechod, o euogrwydd blin,
Ac mor ddi-nerth, mor ysig wyf dan hwn,
   Mor wan, mor eiddil wyf o'm rhan fy hun,
Diau y rhoddech imi, heb nacâd,
   Ryw air, ryw newydd, felus air o hedd,
Un wnâi im benderfynu ceisio'r wlad,
   Y nefol Ganaan wlad, tu draw i'r bedd.

Dywedwch im, rai annwyl, – gwyddoch chwi
   Am bethau rhyfedd, gwyrthiau'r byd a ddaw, –
A fu peth tebyg a phe byddai i *mi*
   I ddianc byth o gyrraedd poen a braw?
A ydych chwi yn cofio fod erio'd
   Fath ryfedd wyrth yn ymerodraeth Duw
A phe cawn *i*, yr anheilyngaf fod,
   Fy nghyfiawnhau, fy ngeni i fythol fyw?

Evening Meditation

The silence of night, the perfect time to hear
  The whisper of the spirit world, which seems so near!
My heavenly dears, bring me some
  New ideas, my mind's desire: come!
Pay me a visit, although I'm sick, please stay,
  Amiable spirits, don't shrink away!
My heavy heart is full of eagerness to have
 Some succour from the spirit world above.

Millions like me are longing for an object,
  Waiting and hoping, sad and abject,
For some news; and every single person
  More worthy than I, the sickly one;
Oh, yes, all my betters await a word,
  Everyone waits on Heaven and the Lord:
But, tender angels, don't forget me, –
For I am bad, – the worst that any can be!

Oh! if you only knew how heavy is my load,
  My weight of sin, of tedious guilt,
And I'm so impotent and bruised beneath it,
  So weak, so feeble, lonely on my road,
Doubtless you'd give me, without hesitation,
  Some word of peace, some new word so sweet,
To make me try the spirits beyond to meet
  Beyond the grave, in the heavenly land of Canaan.

Tell me, lovely ones, – you who know
  Of marvellous things, of miracles dear, –
Is it likely that I shall ever go,
  Escape, from all this pain and fear?
Do you recall in your lives ever seeing
  Such a rare miracle in God's domain
That even I, the most unworthy being,
  Might be redeemed, be born again?

Ysbrydion pur, O! rhoddwch fi yn rhydd!
  Mae cadwyn ofn yn rhwymo f'enaid gwan:
Ai gormod im, dywedwch, ddisgwyl dydd
  O'r tonnau geirwon hyn i gaffael glan?
Yw'r gobaith yn rhy ddisglaer, yn rhy dda,
  I *mi* i'w fabwysiadu, fod y Nef
Yn agor im croesawu, ac y gwna
  Dosturio wrthyf, wrando ar fy llef?

Ah! na, bendigaid fyddo enw Duw!
  Mi glywaf lais, – pereiddlais llawn o rin, –
Dystawed pawb yn awr, llais Iesu yw!
  A'm galw mae, fy ngalw ato'i hun!
O rhyfedd iawn! mae'n d'wedyd fod i mi,
  I *mi*, 'r pechadur pennaf, duaf gaid,
Faddeuant llawn trwy Aberth Calfari,
  A theyrnas Nef trwy rinwedd dwyfol waed!

Diolchaf byth, mae bronnau'r nos yn llawn
  Yn awr o sêr prydferthaf fu eri'od;
Mi wela'r llwybr yn olau, olau iawn,
  Yn awr i'r man dymunwn ynddo fod:
Llefara mwy, heb dewi, Iesu da!
  Llefara, O! mae'th eiriau oll yn hedd!
Llefara air yn fynych; hynny wna
  Y cwbl yn deg, yn olau, i'r wlad tu draw i'r bedd.

Pure spirits, oh! set me free once more!
  The chain of fear keeps my weak soul at bay:
Say, is it too much for me to expect a day
  When from these rough waves I reach the shore?
Is the hope too fond, too bright,
  That Heaven should open to my sight,
That it should have mercy on my care,
  Should pity me, and hear my prayer?

Ah! no, blessed be the name of the Jehovah!
  I hear a voice, – the purest voice ever
Let all be silent now, it's Jesus's voice!
  And he's calling me to him, rejoice, rejoice!
Oh wondrous! he's saying that even one such as I,
  Who has the greatest, blackest burden of sin
Shall be redeemed through the sacrifice on Calvary,
  And shall see Heaven through the blood divine!

I give thanks always, for now the breasts of night
  Are full of the most perfect stars that ever shone;
I see the path glitter exceptionally bright,
  Toward the place I long now to be gone:
Speak again, dear Jesus, never cease!
  Speak, for your words are all of peace!
Speak often a word; a word that will amend,
  And me content to the land beyond will send.

Fy Ffrind

Ychydig iawn o flodau teg
   Y byd sydd fwy eu harddwch,
Sydd burach, well eu sawr, na chweg
   Flodeuyn cyfeillgarwch;
Ychydig hefyd, yn ddiau,
   O flodau'r byd presennol,
Mewn bri a harddwch, sy'n parhau
   Mor hir, ac mor ragorol.

Ah! y mae hwn yn rhosyn hardd,
   Yn d'wysog mewn prydferthwch!
A oes rhyw un o fewn yr ardd
   Yn fwy ei fri a'i degwch?
Mae'r blodau eraill sydd gerllaw
   Fel yn ymgrymu iddo;
A phob un genfydd oddi draw
   Fod gwedd urddasol arno.

Blodeuyn anawyl, tyner, yw,
   A swynol ei arogledd;
Ond, er mor ryfedd mae yn byw,
   Er 'stormydd â'u digllonedd,
Yn wir ni wna y dymhestl gref,
   Ar ôl i hwn gael gwreiddio,
Ond gwasgar ei arogledd ef,
   A rhoi gwell lliwiau iddo.

A oes i'w gael ragorach un?
   Fe dd'wedir fod, ond chwilio;
Yn dlysach yn ei liw a'i lun,
   A gwell arogledd iddo;
Ac fod y t'wysog hwn erioed

Sarah Jane Rees [Cranogwen] (1839-1916)

My Friend

Very few of the pretty blossoms
   Of the world are more sweet,
More pure, or smell lovelier than
   Friendship's little floweret,
Very few too, no-one can doubt,
   Of the blossoms of this world
Last so long in loveliness and fame
   And excellence unfurled.

Ah! this is a lovely rose,
   A prince in beauty!
Is there another in the garden
   Fairer or more haughty?
See the other flowers nearby
   Are bowing to him;
And everyone must admit
   That his beauty does not dim.

He's a dear little tender flower,
   His perfume quite enchanting;
Yet his survival is quite strange,
   In the midst of stormy ranting,
Truly the powerful tempest only
   Spreads his perfume anew
Once he is well rooted,
   And gives him a better hue.

Is there anywhere his superior?
   Yes, they say who time seeking have spent,
One lovelier in colour and form,
   And with a sweeter scent;
And they say that this prince has ever

Yn arfer ei gydnabod,
Ac, heb ymddadlu, yn dioed
Ymgrymu i'w awdurdod:

A hwnnw, meddir drwy y wlad,
Yw'r *pen*, neu yw y *brenin*,
Ac nad yw'r eraill flodau mad
Ond deiliaid yn ei ganlyn;
A Chyfeillgarwch, rosyn cu,
Medd rhain, yw'r pentywysog,
Nodedig am ei urddawl fri,
Sydd nesa' i'r pen coronog.

Wel, bydded "Cariad" ynte'n *ben*,
Yn *frenin* cain y blodau,
A deued beirdd y ddae'r a'r Nen
I ganu iddo odlau;
Mi ganaf finnau'r ganig hon
Yn llawen, doed a ddelo,
I d'wysog Cyfeillgarwch llon,
Sydd wedi'm hollol swyno.

Ah! anawyl chwaer, 'rwyt ti i mi,
Fel lloer i'r lli, yn gyson;
Dy ddilyn heb orphwyso wna
Serchiadau pura'm calon:
Mae gweld dy annwyl, siriol wedd
I mi yn hedd a gwynfyd,
A chael munudau o'th fwynhau
Yn haul ar oriau'm bywyd.

Cael edrych yn dy wyneb cu,
Ac agor iti galon
Orlwythog, sydd yn f'ysgafnhau

Been used to bow to him,
And without cavil or question,
   Acknowledge his dominion:

And he, it's said throughout the land,
   Is the King to whom others bow,
The other myriad flowers fair
   Do nothing but follow;
And Friendship, dear rose,
   Is the eldest prince, they say,
Which proudly sits beside
   The crowned head every day.

Well, let "Love" then be the head,
   The perfect King of all the flowers,
And let all the poets of heaven and earth
   Come to sing his praises at all hours;
But I shall sing this little song
   With joy, whate'er may chance,
To the gay prince of Friendship,
   Which has me quite entranced.

Ah! dear sister, you are to me,
   Faithful, like the moon is to the sea;
The purest passions of my heart
   Will forever with you be:
To see your dearest, happy face
   Is peace and bliss to me,
And to rejoice in your company
   Is sunshine in a shady place.

To look upon your lovely face,
   And to open to you a heart
O'erburdened, gives me release

O bwysau o helbulon;
A chael dy gydymdeimlad gwir
Ym mhob rhyw gur a gofid,
Sydd fwy ei werth nag aur y byd,
Ei fawl i gyd, a'i wynfyd.

I seren deg dy wyneb di
Ni welaf *fi* un gymar,
Er crwydro'n hir, – yr un mor fad
Yn wybren gwlad y ddaear:
Mae miloedd eraill, sêr o fri,
Yn gloywi y ffurfafen;
Edmygaf hwy, ond *caraf* di,
Fy Ngwener gu, fy "Ogwen."

Ni wn y medr unrhyw iaith,
Er bod yn berffaith ddigon,
I ddweud, i eglurhau, mewn *rhan*,
Mor gu wyt gan fy nghalon:
Ond *gwyddost* ti fy nghalon oll,
Fy chwaer, heb raid mynegi;
Deallaist lawer gwaith cyn hyn
Mor gu'r wyf yn dy garu.

Mae'm calon oll yn olau i ti,
A gwn y gweli yma
Dy annwyl ddelw di dy hun
O'r bron yr un eglura':
Wel, dyna i gyd, bydd yma o hyd,
Nes llifo'm bywyd allan;
A phleser cu fy mywyd i
Fydd syllu arni'n mhobman.

From my troubles' cruellest dart;
And to have your sincere sympathy
   'Gainst every blow and care,
Is worth more than all the wide world's gold,
   All its bliss and praises fair.

I see no parallel anywhere
   To the sweet star of your beauty,
Though I've travelled far, – so many
   Are in this earth's sky:
Thousands of other honoured stars,
   Glitt'ring on the horizon;
I admire them all but I *love* you,
   My dearest Venus, my "Ogwen."

I don't think any language can,
   Though it be quite perfect,
Express, explain, even in part,
   How dear you are to my heart:
But you know my heart entire,
   My sister, no words are due;
You have shown that you understand
   How dearly I love you.

My heart is all exposed to you,
   And I know that you see in it
The lovely image of yourself
   Which is clearer minute by minute:
Well, be assured that it will always be here,
   Until life itself flows from me;
And then the sweetest pleasure of all
   Will be to look upon you everywhere.

Diwedd y flwyddyn

Mae blwyddyn arall bron, ymron terfynu,
A minnau o hyd ymlaen, ymlaen yn nesu;
Mae llawer blwyddyn bellach wedi ei threulio,
A'm hoes, fy unig oes, yn myned heibio:
'Rwy'n teimlo'n awr fy mod yn teithio i waered
Yn gyflym iawn, – O ryfedd mor gyflymed!
Y dydd – y mis – y flwyddyn, yn prysuro,
Fel ar adenydd buain, cyflym, heibio;
A mi yn meddwl am eu llon roesawu,
Y maent yn pasio heb yn wybod imi:
Os mynnir canu ar eu genedigaeth,
Rhaid gwneud yn union, neu bydd cnul marwolaeth
Yn galw'n bruddaidd iawn i lan eu beddrod,
Ac felly y mae cwbl y byd yn darfod.

Pa beth? – A ydyw amser yn cyflymu
Yn gynt nag oedd, i gau, i ddirwyn 'fyny?
A oes rhyw Allu mawr yn tynnu arno?
A roddwyd, tybed, enw newydd iddo?
A ydyw amser, – ydyw'r oll presennol,
Yn nesu 'mlaen yn agos i'r tragwyddol,
A nerthoedd mawrion hwnw'n sugn-dynu,
Yn gwneyd i rodau amser oll gyflymu?
'Rŷ'm fel yng nghyrraedd llanw Tragwyddoldeb,
Mae'r cwbl yn myn'd, yn myned mewn prysurdeb,

Ond o mi fynnwn i pe gallwn *aros*!
Mae'r dydd yn troi, – mor fuan daw y cyfnos!
Mae gwaith i'w wneud, a minnau o hyd yn methu,
Yn *meddwl* gwneud, ac amser yn cyflymu,
Yn *penderfynu* gwneud yn dda, a brysio,
A'r dydd, a'r mis, a'r flwyddyn, yn myn'd heibio; –

Sarah Jane Rees [Cranogwen] (1839-1916)

The end of the year

Almost, almost done, another year,
And I go forward, forward, drawing near;
Many a year is now left high and dry,
And my life, my only life, is passing by:
I feel now that my journey's a descent
A rapid one, – Oh strange how downward bent!
The day – the month – the year, all onward brings,
Hast'ning past, as if on speedy, tiny wings;
While I am contemplating them with joy,
They fly past, making of my mind a toy,
If one must sing happily at their birth,
One must do the same now, or the knell of death
Will sound with sorrow from the brink of their grave,
And thus does all in this sad world its ending have.

What? – Does the speed of time increase,
As it draws near the end of its lease?
Is there some great Power which pulls at it?
Perhaps a new name is given to it?
Is it true that the whole of the present,
While toward eternity it follows the current,
With its great powers sucking ardently,
Speeds on time's wheels, which turn more quickly?
It's as if we're in reach of the tide of Eternity,
And everything goes speeding on at a gallop,
But oh how I long to be able to say "stop"!
But no, too quickly the twilight falls for me!

There's work to be done, but time pays me no heed,
I think of doing, but time goes on with speed,
I decide to do, I plan, and I make haste,
While the day, the month, the year, speed past; –

Y dydd yn dechreu marw yn y boreu,
Yr wythnos yn diflannu yn ei goreu,
Y flwyddyn, fel pe byddai mewn rhedegfa,
Am gyrraedd pen ei thaith yn gynt na'r un ddiwetha'!

Pa beth sy'n bod? – I bl'e mae'r cwbl yn myned
Fel hyn, – yn troi, – yn gyrru, mor ddiarbed?
A oes dim *aros* rywbryd, dim *gorphwyso*?
Daw dydd 'r ôl dydd, a genir blwyddyn eto;
Ond i fy ngolwg i mae'r cwbl yn fyrach,
Y cwbl yn llai, mae popeth yn gylymach:
Wrth yrru'n chwyrn fel hyn, rhaid daw y terfyn
Heb fod yn hir, mae'n sicr o fod gyferbyn;
Ac yna – beth, fy Nuw, O! beth fydd *yno*? –
Llonyddwch mawr, a'r cwbl yn gorffwyso?
A yw chwyrn rodau amser cyfnewidiol,
Tu hwnt i'r terfyn, wedi peidio'n hollol?
A oes blynyddau yno'n byw a marw?
A oes i'r Cefnfor hwnnw drai a llanw?
Oes i'r Cyfandir hwnnw ryw derfynau, –
I'w haul a'i leuad rai cyfnewidiadau?
O f'Arglwydd Dduw, mor eang yw'r tragwyddol!
Mor annirnadwy ydyw'r annherfynol!
Mor amhlymiadwy ydyw'r Cefnfor hwnnw,
Na fu, nad oes, o'i fewn ond bythol lanw!
'Rwy'n teimlo f'hun yn cael fy nhynnu iddo!
Pa beth, O! beth a fydd fy nhynged ynddo?
'Rwyt Ti'n ei blymio, ydwyt, i'w waelodion!
O dyro imi gael dy wir adnabod,
A llechu byth yn ddiogel yn dy gysgod!
Ac yna i'r tragwyddol ymollyngaf
Yn dawel iawn, ac ynot ymddiriedaf!

Each morning the day begins to die,
And the week just disappears, goes powering by,
The year, as if it were running a race,
Eager to reach its end, it speeds apace!

What is going on? – Where is everything going
Like this, powering onward, unstoppable, turning?
Is there no rest sometimes, no respite?
Day follows day, a new year comes to light;
But to my eyes everything seems restrained,
Everthing's smaller, quicker, contained:
As it drives forward like this, before long it's sure
The end will be reached, the eternal cure,
And then – what, my Lord, will be thy behest? –
A great stillness, and everything at rest?
The eager wheels of changeful time will
Beyond this boundary, be completely still?
Do the years there live and die?
Does the tide there have a neap and high?
Are there boundaries to that Continent, –
Does its moon change from waning to crescent?
Oh my Lord God, how boundless is Eternity!
How incomprehensible is that place to me!
How impossible to plumb that Ocean's deeps,
Whose tide is high and brooks no neaps!
I feel myself being pulled towards it!
What, oh what will be my fate within it?
You plumb its very depths, entirely!
Oh grant that I may know you fully,
And shelter always in your shadow!
I'll release myself into the eternal now
Quietly, trusting always in you!

Fy Ngwlad (detholiad)

Fy ngwlad! Fy ngwlad! Fy annwyl Gymru lonydd!
Mor gu i mi yw'th fryniau a'th afonydd!
Mor las, mor deg, mor brydferth, yw dy wybren!
Mor lon dy haul, mor loyw dy ffurfafen!
Mor bur, mor fwyn, mor dyner yw dy awel!
Ah mae dy bopeth di mor annwyl ac mor dawel!

Ond O! pa fodd, fy annwyl Gymru dirion,
Mae canu clod dy ferched di a'th feibion,
Dy annwyl blant a fagwyd ar dy liniau,
Dyfasant hyd dy gymoedd di a'th fryniau?
Fy annwyl wlad, y rhain yw'th degwch mwyaf!
Fy Nghymru fad, hwy yw'th ogoniant pennaf! . . .

Mae rhai, efallai, yma a thraw'n bradychu
Eu gwlad a'u hiaith, ac eraill, rai, 'n eu gwadu;
Ac weithiau, hwyrach, clywir ambell un
Yn erlid, er cywilydd iddo'i hun,
Yn gwadu unrhyw linell berthynasol
A Chymru wen, eu meib a'i merched haeddol;
A myn mai estron ydyw ef o Sais neu Wyddel,
Ac fod ei waed yn goch, ac fod ei ben yn uchel,
Ac felly yn y blaen, – yn brolio yn ddiddiwedd,
Yn ceisio gwadu'r cwbl f'ai iddo yn anrhydedd!

Wel, croesaw i'r rhai hyn i droi eu pennau allan,
I fyned gyda brys; fydd yma neb yn cwynfan
Eu colled ar eu hôl . . .

Ond os oes *rhai* i'w canfod yn bradychu,
Eithriadau ŷnt; ffyddloniaid yw y Cymry,
Yn caru eu gwlad, eu hiaith, yn caru ei gilydd,
Yn caru rhyddid gwir, yn caru crefydd . . .

My Country (extract)

My country! Oh my country! My beloved, silent Wales!
How inexpressibly dear to me are your hills and vales!
How blue, how fair, how lovely are your skies!
How gay your sun, how bright your horizon lies!
How pure, how mild, how tender is your breeze!
Ah! everything of yours is dear, still, and at ease!

But oh! how can I, my gentle land,
Praise the offspring raised by your caring hand,
The daughters and sons raised at your knee,
Who grew up in your every hill and valley?
My dear country, these are of all your crown!
My diverse land, they are your glory, your own! . . .

There are some, perhaps, who here and there betray
Their land and language, and others who deny;
And sometimes, there is one of evil name
Who attacks Wales, to his own eternal shame,
Denying any connecting, familial link
With lovely Wales; who'd have us think
He was a stranger, an Englishman or Irish,
And that his blood is blue, as blue as he would wish,
And so on, – blabbing and boasting to the last,
Denying the very things that would on him honour cast!

Well, such men are welcome to turn their faces away,
To leave abruptly; no-one here will regret the day
Of their leaving . . .

Yet if there are a few who are untrue,
They are exceptions; the Welsh, give us our due,
Are faithful to their land, their language, and each other,
They love true freedom, and the church, our mother . . .

Pa beth a dalaf finnau i ti, fy ngwlad,
Am roddion fyrdd, a charedigrwydd rhad? . . .

Mi allaf ddiolch, gallaf, ar fy ngliniau,
A chynnig iti fy ngwasanaeth goreu:
Ond beth f'ai hynny oll yn amgen na *chydnabod*
Fy nyled bwysig iawn? – Ah mae ei *thalu*'n ormod
O waith i mi, tra'n fyw! gan hynny, wele fi,
Fy ngwlad, am dreulio 'mywyd i'th wasnaethu di.

What can I pay you back , my country,
For all your gifts, your generosity? . . .

I can give thanks, oh yes, down on my knees,
And offer you my heartfelt, best service;
But what would that be other than to vouch
My pre-eminent debt? – Ah to *redeem* it were too much,
Too great a task for me! So, to acknowledge my due,
My country, I shall spend my life in service unto you.

Catherine Prichard [Buddug] (1842-1909)

Blodyn yr Eira

Blodyn gwyn yr eira glân,
Ydwyt destun cu i'm cân:
   Mae dy hedd yn ymdywynnu,
   Mae dy wyneb fel goleuni;
   Heb frycheuyn du na chrychni,
Arian wedd yr eira mân.

Gwyn a glân wyt, flodyn cain,
Gwynnach nac un lliain main:
   Megis alaw yr aderyn
   Cyntaf glywir yn y gwanwyn,
   Ydwyt tithau, deg flodeuyn,
Swyn rhyfeddol sydd i'r rhain.

Blodyn glân yr eira gwyn,
Testyn cân o bridd y glyn;
   Rhwymau tynion rhew ac eira,
   Anian ynnot ymagora'n
Fywyd newydd wedi hyn.

Cranogwen

'Rwyf bron a'th addoli, anfarwol Granogwen,
   'Rwyt wedi fy synnu, a'm swyno yn lân,
Y mae dy athrylith a'th awen ddisgleirwen,
   Yn twymo fy enaid – yn ennyn fy nghân.
Dy ryfedd huawdledd a'th ddwys dduwiolfrydedd,
   A'th ddoniau gwahanol enillodd fy serch:
Pwy bellach faidd wadu nas gall arucheledd
   A mawredd meddyliol babellu mewn merch?

Snowdrop

White flower of the snow, so perfect,
You are for my song the lovely subject:
   There radiates from you a sense of peace,
   Like light itself your shining face;
   Without a black spot or a defect,
You silver cheek of the snowflake, delicate.

Beautiful flower, you are clean and neat,
Whiter than the finest linen sheet:
   Like the first bird who sings
   Full of joy in the spring,
   To me too you bring,
Fair flower, a strange enchantment.

Pure flower of the snow so pale,
Subject of song from the soil of the vale;
   The bonds of ice and snow in which you lie,
   Will loosen soon, your tender nature will untie,
To bring forth strong new life, by and by.

Cranogwen

I almost worship you, deathless Cranogwen,
You've amazed me and charmed me for so long,
Your genius and your dazzling skill with the pen ,
Quicken my soul – and inspire my own song.
Your rare eloquence and intense piety,
Your many different gifts have won my admiration:
For who today can claim that superiority
And intellectual greatness can't exist in woman?

Brwydr Dirwest a Bacchus

Ymarfogwn, ferched dirwest,
    Wele ni mewn rhyfel fawr;
Nid oes orffwys cyn cael concwest,
    Nid oes rhoddi arfau i lawr:
Ymgafaelion medd'dod creulon,
    Cymru annwyl sydd yn brudd;
Dirwest dyr y rhwymau tynion –
    Yn ei llaw fe ddaw yn rhydd.

Cadarn yw y ddiod feddwol,
    Dyn yn unig sydd yn wan;
Byddin gref yn llu dirwestol
    Sydd am ddwyn y llesg i'r lan;
Merched glân ardaloedd Cymru
    Lusgir yn y llu i'r llaid;
Dirwest wen a'u cwyd i fyny,
    Gweithiwn, gweithiwn yn ddibaid.

Ysgafn iawn yw rhwymau dirwest,
    Dim ond *peidio* yfed mwy:
Dyna'n unig ydyw'r orchest,
    Peidio, felly ni cheir clwy':
Peidio, ferched, dyna'r rhyfel
    Drosodd, heb ddim tywallt gwaed,
Peidio, dyna froydd tawel,
    A dynoliaeth ar ei thraed.

Peidio profi, *peidio* edrych,
    Dyna dd'wed y Gair yn groch;
Gwylio rhag yr eilun wrthrych,
    Pan yr ymddangoso'n goch:
O! mor goch yw ein haelwydydd,
    Gan y gwaed dywalltodd hwn,

Catherine Prichard [Buddug] (1842-1909)

The battle of Temperance and Bacchus

To arms, sisters of temperance!
We are in the midst of a great fight;
We must win through perseverance,
No peace 'til victory's in our sight:
Caught in the claws of the demon drink,
Our dear Wales is shamed and in need;
Temperance will unchain her, link by link –
By its hand she will be freed.

Intoxicating drink is strong,
Only man himself is weak;
Our strong army, the temperance throng,
Bring the needy to the shore they seek;
Pure women from all parts of Wales
Are dragged down into the dirt;
Temperance will raise them, it never fails:
Let us work to protect them from hurt.

The bonds of temperance are light,
Drink no more and the deed is done:
That alone means you've won the fight,
Abstain, and you'll harm no-one:
Abstain, sisters, and that's the contest
Over, with no drop of blood shed,
Abstain, and the vales will be at rest,
And human beings resurrected.

Abstain from tasting, *abstain* from looking,
That's what the Word says, loud and plain;
Guard against the false idol's glimmering,
When it shows up like scarlet rain;
Oh our poor hearths are ne'er at peace,

Bacchus greulawn – deyrn anedwydd,
   Rhwymwn di o dan dy bwn.

Mae yr arfau yn ein dwylaw,
   Ferched annwyl, gloywn hwynt;
Peidio yw eu henw hylaw,
   Peidio yfed, dyna'r pwynt;
Peidio cymryd, *peidio* rhoddi,
   Laddai fedd'dod yn y fan,
Bacchus druan foddai'n fuan,
   Ac ni welai byth mo'r lan.

Mefus a Hufen

Am y mefus melus cochion,
'Rwyf yn diolch o fy nghalon:
Buont i mi'n iachawdwriaeth,
Well nac unrhyw feddyginiaeth.

Hefyd am yr hufen melyn,
'Rwyf yn diolch yn ddiderfyn,
Ond tu hwnt i'r moethau amheuthun,
Am y cariad sy'n eu canlyn.

Melus fefus yn fy nghlefyd,
Peraidd hyfryd hufen hefyd,
Ond melusach cydymdeimlad,
A phereiddiach cywair cariad.

Darfod wnaeth yr aeddfed ffrwythau,
Darfod wna pob peth fel hwythau:
Ond yn aros mewn eneiniad
Mae diddarfod ffrwythau cariad.

But red with the blood spilt by Bacchus,
Boorish Bacchus – yet his unhappy rule will cease
When he and his burden are tied up by us.

In our hands are the weapons to kill shame,
Dear sisters: let us sharpen them;
A*bstinence* is their point and name,
Abstinence will the vile flood stem;
From drink we demand total *abstinence*,
This would kill drunkenness in a trice,
Poor Bacchus would drown a long way hence,
And far from this shore would sink his vice.

Strawberries and Cream

For the strawberries so sweet and red,
I thank you from my heart well-fed;
They were simply my salvation,
Better than any medication.

Also for the yellow cream,
I give you thanks, it was a dream,
But beyond this gorgeous luxury,
Thanks for your love, the dearest delicacy.

Sweet strawberries for my disease,
And luscious cream with them agrees,
But sweeter than both is the sympathy,
And the purer tone of your love's empathy.

For the ripest of fruits have their day,
As everything like them will decay:
But in our souls there will endure
The endless fruits of love which all ills cure.

Yr 'Hen' Ann Griffiths

Ann Griffiths. Pam yn hen?
   Nid oedd ond ieuanc oedran,
Rhyw chwech ar hugain oedd pan aeth
   I'r bedd o Ddolwar Fechan!
Bydd rhyw ieuenctid byth
   Ar fynwent Llanfihangel,
Nes daw ei chysegredig lwch
   I ateb yr archangel!

'Old' Ann Griffiths

Ann Griffiths. Why 'old'?
   She was young, our Ann,
When she went, barely a woman,
   To her grave from Dolwar Fechan!
Some air of youth will hover ever
   Over the graves of Llanfihangel,
Until her sacred ashes rise
   To answer the archangel!

Alice Gray Jones [Ceridwen Peris] (1852-1943)

Manion am y Merched (detholiad)

Cadw tŷ sydd fater dyrys,
Canu cân sydd yn ddifyrrus.
Ond gall gwraig sy'n ddoeth a diwyd
Cadw tŷ, a chanu hefyd.

Cyfarchiad dechrau blwyddyn – 1929

Merched Cymru! Blwyddyn Newydd
   Dda fo i chwi, lon, ddifraw.
Dyma flwyddyn y blynyddoedd –
   Mil naw cant, dau ddeg a naw!
Merched oll yn meddu pleidlais,
   Pan yn un-ar-hugain oed!
Ple mae proffwyd y dyfodol?
   Fu'r fath beth a hyn erioed?

Ferched ieuanc – byddwch effro –
   Gwyliwch beth a wnewch yn awr,
Cofiwch hyn – bydd ôl eich gweithred
   Ar ddeddflyfrau Prydain Fawr!
Merched, meddir, yw'r mwyafrif –
   Chwi sydd felly wrth y llyw,
Gwyliwch, trwy eich difaterwch,
   Ddrygu'ch gwlad, a digio Duw!

Alice Gray Jones [Ceridwen Peris] (1852-1943)

One or two details about women (extract)

Housework's a slog and it never seems done,
Whereas singing a song is just so much fun.
But as a woman who's wise can tell
You can keep a house and sing as well.

A New Year Greeting – 1929

Women of Wales! Let the New Year
Be good, happy, carefree, all that's fine.
For this is the year of years –
Nineteen hundred and twenty nine!
All women now possess the vote
When they're twenty-one years old!
Where's the prophet of the future?
Who could have such a thing foretold?

Young women – have your wits about you –
Be careful; of what you do be certain,
Remember this – the effect of your action
Will be on the statute books of Britain!
Women, they say, are the majority –
You, therefore, are at the helm,
Guard then lest your apathy displease
The Lord and do mischief to the realm.

Cofio hen aelwydydd Cymru,
  Ddeffry ynom hiraeth prudd –
Mamau duwiol, pur, dirodres –
  Tadau enwog am eu ffydd:
Cofio'r weddi daer esgynnai
  Hwyr a bore'n ddi-nacâd,
Dyma'r hen aelwydydd annwyl
  Roddodd urddas ar ein gwlad.

Ferched Cymru! byddwch wrol,
  Mynnwch degwch, mynnwch hedd –
Llwyr ymlidiwch demtasiynau,
  Trwy nerth Crefydd – nid y cledd;
O! hoff wlad y Diwygiadau –
  Pryd cawn eto eu mwynhau –
Gwlad a'i chân i gyd yn foliant,
  Gwlad a Duw'n ei dyfrhau.

Alice Gray Jones [Ceridwen Peris] (1852-1943)

Remember the old hearths of Wales,
Which awake in us a sad *hiraeth* –
Remember our pure, humble mothers –
And fathers, renowned for their faith:
Remember the fervent prayers that rose
Night and morn to God our guide,
Here they are, the dear old hearths
Which gave our country its pride.

Women of Wales! Be valiant,
Insist on fairness, insist on concord –
Through the Word – not the sword;
And flee from all worldly temptation.
Oh! Dear country of Revivals –
When shall we relish them once more? –
A land whose song is full of praises,
A land whose faith springs from the core.

Cân Gwraig y Gweithiwr

Nid yw fy nwylaw'n wynion,
　　Na phrydferth, esmwyth, chwaith,
Lled arw ŷnt a ch'ledion,
　　Oherwydd cyson waith;
Ond nid oes llaw yn cwyno,
　　Na grwgnach yn fy mron,
Wrth gofio'm cartref cryno,
　　A'm teulu bychan, llon.

Ai'r plant i'r gwely'n brydlon,
　　A minnau i olchi awn,
A dillad bach claerwynion
　　Yn barod iddynt gawn;
Rhown fotwm ar gôt David,
　　A chlem dan esgid Sam,
A thrwsiwn ffrog goch Enid –
　　Trafferthion dyddiol mam.

Ac O, 'roedd pawb o'm cwmpas
　　Mor llon a deryn bach,
A minnau heb un pwrpas
　　Ond cadw'm plant yn iach,
A gwylio ar eu camre
　　A chadw'u geiriau'n lân,
Fel hyn, o hwyr i fore
　　Ceid siriol wên a chân.

Ond tyfu oll a wnaethant,
　　A ffwrdd â hwy o'r nyth,
Ac nid oes obaith deuant
　　Yn ôl i chware byth!
Mae'r bocs i drwsio'r tegan,
　　A hoelio pedol Sam,
Yn hollol lonydd weithian –
　　Dim angen dyfais mam!

Alice Gray Jones [Ceridwen Peris] (1852-1943)

Song of the Worker's Wife

My hands are none too white,
   Nor lovely nor tender either,
They're rough and ugly to your sight,
   Because of the constant labour;
But my hands are not complaining,
   There's no whinging in my breast,
When I recall my tidy house, containing
   My happy little family, like a nest.

The kids would go early to bed,
   And I'd set to doing the wash,
The little snow white clothes all aired,
   I'd get them up so nice and posh,
I'd sew a button on David's shirt,
   And put a nail in Sam's shoe,
And I'd mend Enid's red skirt –
   Those chores that all mothers do.

And oh! they were all around me
   Like glad little chicks in a throng,
And my single purpose was to see
   My children happy, fit and strong,
To keep an eye on their progress,
   To care for them all day long,
To keep their language spotless:
   I was happy, all smiles and song.

But, alas, they've all grown up,
   And all have left the nest,
They'll no more come home to sup,
   And their old toys are all at rest!
The workbox for mending their things,
   And for putting a nail in Sam's shoe,
Is now quite useless – a bird without wings;
   A mam's initiative unwanted, no more for her to do!

Manion – Aelwydydd Dedwydd

Rwyf wedi penderfynu cael *First* am gadw tŷ.
D.D. a fynnaf *gyntaf* ar ôl fy enw'n gu;
Ac yna tair llythyren sydd fwy eu gwerth na gem,
Ynglŷn â'm henw beunydd bydd T, ac G, ac M,

Wrth gwrs am warchod gartref yn rhwydd caf G.B.A.,
Am fwyd fy mwrdd mi fentraf bydd gennyf B.M.A.,
Bydd llond fy nhŷ o heulwen, a'i lond o awyr ffres,
'Rwy'n penderfynu graddio yn Dr. of T.S.

D.D. = Dim Dyled
G.B.A. = Gartref Bob Amser
T.G.M. = Troed Gorau Mlaen
B.M.A. = Bwyd Mewn Amser
Dr. T.S. = Doctor of Tymer Serchog

Alice Gray Jones [Ceridwen Peris] (1852-1943)

More details – happy hearths (extract)

I've decided to get a *First* for keeping house all day
Most of all I want to get an N.D. after my name;
And then three letters more valuable than a gem,
Linked to my name forever: a B, an F, and an A,

Of course for all my hard work I'll easily get an N.O.D.,
And for all the food I cook I'll gain an instant M.O.T.,
My house will be full of sunshine and fresh air, you see,
Since I've determined now to graduate as a Dr. of G.T.

N.D. = No Debt
N.O.D. = Never Out of Doors
B. F. A. = Best Foot Ahead
M.O.T. = Meals On Time
Dr. of G.T. = Doctor of Good Temper

Ellen Hughes (1862-1927)

Tydi, aderyn bychan, mwyn

Tydi, aderyn bychan, mwyn,
Sy'n pyncio'n bêr o lwyn i lwyn,
Wyt fel rhyw gennad nefol llon,
Yn ymlid prudd-der cas o'm bron!
Yr wyt mor llawn o nwyfus hoen,
Pwy dybiai'th fod ym myd y poen,
Mewn byd lle rhua'r storm di-hedd,
Mewn byd mae angau du a'r bedd?

'Does gennyt 'sgubor, cell, na thŷ,
Yn noddfa it mewn gaeaf du;
Newyn, hyll-dremu arnat wna,
Anhawdd yw pigo'r bwyd o'r iâ:
'Does neb ofala mewn un man,
Ai marw o newyn fydd dy ran,
Ond canu 'rwyt o hyd, o hyd,
Er oered i ti yw y byd!

Nid rhyfedd chwaith, mi wela 'n awr,
Gofala Crëwr nef a llawr
Am roddi iti damaid bach,
O ddydd i ddydd i'th gadw'n iach;
Fe'th borthir ganddo Ef ei hun
Yn annibynnol ar bob dyn,
Wel, gelli ganu, – seinia'n bêr,
Gân ddiolchgarwch i dy Nêr.

Mae'th ddiolchgarwch cynnes di,
Yn cywilyddio'm calon i,
Dymunwyf finnau tra f'wyf byw
Ddyrchafu moliant i fy Nuw;
A cheisio credu bellach wnaf,
Os ydyw gofal tyner Naf
Am adar bychain fel tydi,
Nas gall ef fy anghofio fi.

Ellen Hughes (1862-1927)

Oh bird, so tiny and so sweet

Oh bird, so tiny and so sweet,
Who hops from bush to bush so neat,
A messenger from regions blest
Who rids of pain my anguished breast!
You are so full of passionate life
Who'd think you lived in a world of strife,
A world where savage storms do rage
A world where rule the grave and age?

You have no barn, nor house, nor cell,
To shelter you from winter fell;
Starvation glowers, a rabid hound,
As you peck your food from frozen ground.
No-one watches o'er your fate
As the threat of death does not abate,
And yet you sing, all day you sing
From the frozen world your voice does ring.

But now I see, it's not so odd,
The one who cares for you is God,
He gives you food to keep you alive
From day to day he ensures you survive;
He feeds you from his own kind hand,
Not helped by mankind through the land;
Well may you sing the purest chord:
Sound out thanksgiving to your Lord.

Your song of thanks, so true and warm
Fills up my heart with bitter shame,
For I too desire as long as I live
Wholehearted praise of Him to give ;
And from now on I will be sure
That if the Lord shows tender care
For sweet little songbirds just like you,
He'll always protect and love me too.

Elizabeth Mary Jones [Moelona]
(1878-1953)

Y Delyn ar yr Helyg

Mor swynber gynt oedd seiniau
Dy delyn, Gymru lân,
Os weithiau lleddf ei nodau
Doedd dim anurddai'r gân.
Bysedd dy garedigion
Chwaraeai'r tannau tyn,
Ac oddi allan i Gymru gu,
Oedd d'elyn di bryd hyn.

Ond heddiw, llaes yw'r tannau
Mae'th delyn ar y coed,
Pwy gân dy fwyn ganiadau
A'th sathru di dan droed?
O'th fewn mae'th elyn heddiw
O'th aelwyd cwyd dy frad
Gwlad ddieithr wyt i'th blant dy hun
Pwy chwery'th delyn fad?

Doed ysbryd rhai o'th ddewrion,
Yn ôl i'n dyddiau ni,
I ddysgu'th blant afradlon
I'th werthfawrogi di,
Myn eto weld dy delyn
Yn nwylo'th wadwyr ffôl,
Myn glywed ei phereiddiaf dant
Myn gael dy blant yn ôl.

The Harp on the Willow

How sweet and pure in bygone days
Were the sounds of your harp, dear Wales,
Though often mournful were the lays,
None brought dishonour or disgrace.
The eager fingers of your friends
Would play the tight-drawn strings,
And at that time your foes would bide,
Not within your bounds but outside.

Yet the strings are slack today,
Your harp hangs without sound,
Who will now sing your gentle lay
While treading you to the ground?
Today your enemy's within
The traitor is reared in your lap,
You're strange to your very own children
Who will play your lovely harp?

Let the spirit of your heroes come
Back to inspire us now,
To teach your prodigal children
Once more their mother to know,
Demand again to hear your harp sing
In the hands of the fools still denying,
Demand to hear plucked its purest string,
Demand the return of your offspring.

Eto

Ar gangau gwyw yr helyg
Mae'm telyn fechan i,
Â chalon archolledig
Y cefnaf arni hi.
Pa bryd symudir culni
A rhagfarn rhyfedd dyn?
Pa bryd y gwêl wrthuni
Ei hunanoldeb blin?

Mae'm telyn ar yr helyg,
Oes rhywun ofyn pam?
Sut medr merch roi miwsig
A hithau'n cael fath gam?
Y dyn, medd ef ei hunan
Yw'r bod o werth, bid sifir,
Ni oes i'r wraig un amcan
Ond ceisio boddio'i gŵr.

Pa bryd ca' merch ei hawliau?
Pa bryd daw'r fôt i'n rhan?
Nyni wna drefn ar bethau,
Nawr anhrefn sy' mhob man.
Ond O! Ar ffordd ein llwyddiant,
Cyndynrwydd dyn a roed,
A dyna pam mae'm telyn fach
Yn segur ar y coed.

Again

On the willow's withered bough
My little harp hangs low,
And a bleeding, wounded heart
Of which I want no more a part.
When will man's stupidness
And prejudice ever move?
When will we to him prove
His tiresome selfishness?

My harp is on the willow,
Does someone ask me why?
How can a woman music play
When she's gravely wronged today?
Man, in his own opinion,
Is the only human to rate,
For woman has no ambition
But to try to please her mate.

When will woman gain her rights?
When will we win the vote?
Now chaos reigns, we see no light
But come the day, we'll steer the boat.
But oh dear! on the way to success
We find man's stubbornness,
And that's why my harp still hangs low
From the branches of the willow.

Eiluned Lewis (1900-1979)

Departure

Now there is nothing can hold me,
I have come to the end;
Nothing can stay my going,
No lover, nor voice of a friend;
No blossom of dreaming elder,
Loosened by summer gales,
Nor murmur of winding rivers,
Nor all the sweetness of Wales
Can keep me, or hold me longer –
Since here lies my way,
And now on my lips already
I taste the cold spray,
And hear overhead in the rigging
The comfortless cry
Of the gulls in our wake, in the wind
Homeless as I.

The Birthright

We who were born
In country places,
Far from cities
And shifting faces,
We have a birthright
No man can sell,
And a secret joy
No man can tell.

For we are kindred
To lordly things,
The wild duck's flight

And the white owl's wings;
To pike and salmon,
To bull and horse,
The curlew's cry
And the smell of gorse.

Pride of trees,
Swiftness of streams,
Magic of frost
Have shaped our dreams:
No baser vision
Their spirit fills
Who walk by right
On the naked hills.

December Apples

I have come home, my golden dreams are spent,
My songs unsung, yet still I am content,
Content as that one apple on the tree
Which no one thought to pick; it still grows free
And swings so lightly on the topmost twig.
So when its brothers go, both small and big,
To fill the cider press or lie in rows
In darkling lofts, yet still the apple blows
All day secure, when birds are tempest-tost;
Outlives its own sweet leaves, braves the first frost,
Sees the torn clouds at morning, and at night
The clustered stars in orchards blossom-bright;
Outrides the storm, the boughs that strain and creak,
And feels the winter sunshine on its cheek.
Until at length (Ah, must it come to this?)
The greedy thrush will come with sharpest kiss,
Eat out my apple's heart at break of day
And wake December with the songs of May.

Dilys Cadwaladr (1902-1979)

Bara – detholiad

Na ddeuai Rhywun balch i rodio'r tir
   Gan lamu'n llawen tros yr erwau llwyd, –
Rhywun na faliai am ofergoel hir,
   Rhywun a werthai enaid am ein bwyd!

Mae'r cnawd yn pydru ar sgerbydau'r plant,
   A bronnau'r gwragedd fel orennau gwyw.
Pa gellwair oerllyd yw murmuron sant?
   Heb fara, ar ba beth y byddwn byw? . . .

Yr hwn a rydd im faeth a gaiff y galon
   Sy'n llusgo yn y llaid pan gerddwyf i;
A chaiff ei thalu'n llôg i'r Temtiwr rhadlon
   Sy'n gwneud anialwch o'n credoau ni . . .

Mi glywaf sfin fy llygaid trwm yn troi
   Fel sfin y môr yn troi mewn ogofâu.
Mi daerwn fod Sant Jean yn dyfal gnoi
   Rhyw feddal gil, a rhythu ar ein gwae.

Mae'r fenyw fawr o'm blaen yn siglo'n araf,
   A'i chnawd yn frau fel burum dan ei gwisg.
Mi fynnwn daro'r pen pan siglai ataf,
   A'i gadael fel gneuen bwdr o dan y plisg.

Mae'r dwylo mawr yn hongian wrth ei hochor,
   A theimlaf ruthr y nerfau dan fy nghroen.
Mae'r bysedd chwyddog, swrth yn cau ac agor
   Fel genau un ar dranc tu hwnt i boen.

Bread – extract

If only Someone proud would walk our land
Striding in joy across the acres grey, –
Someone o'er whom superstition held no sway,
Someone who, for our food, his soul would pay!

The flesh is rotting on the children's bones,
The women's withered breasts, like fruit, are dead.
There's a grim joke in what the saint intones,
For what are we to live on, without bread? . . .

He who gives me food will receive my heart
That's dragging in the dust and craves relief;
The heart that yields to the kind Tempter's art
Who makes a barren waste of our belief . . .

I hear the turning sound of my heavy eyes
Like the sound of the sea churning in caves afar.
I'd swear that Saint Jean is hard at work, so wise,
Chewing a soft cud, and staring at our despair.

The large woman in front of me slowly reels,
Her flesh brittle as yeast under her apparel.
I'd like to strike that head when near me it keels,
And find it like a rotten nut under the shell.

The large hands hang down limply by her skirt
And I feel the nerves jump beneath my skin.
The fingers close and open, swollen, inert,
Like the jaws of someone dying, beyond pain.

Pa beth i ni yw geni, byw a thranc?
  Fe'n gwrth-hiliogwyd megis haid ystlumod
A gwyd o'r bedd yng ngrym annuwiol wanc
  Gan geisio'r maeth a'u deil ar dir eu difod.

Fe droes pob serch a phob tosturi mwy
  Yn friw deganau doe ar lawr y byd.
Ac ni phlyg neb ei ben o weled clwy'
  Y truan a fu'n wylo'i ffawd cyhyd . . .

Mae'n rhaid ein hachub, cans dieuog ydym,
  Bob truan sy'n ymgrymu yma'n awr.
Nid ni, rai bach, a wnaeth y peth esgymun
  A'n troes o feibion Duw yn llwch y llawr . . .

Boed anadl einioes yn ein ffroenau eto,
  A ni a godwn yn eneidiau byw;
Ac er i'r bara droi yn gerrig heno,
  Eilwaith bydd llwch y llawr yn feibion Duw.

Medi 1945

Birth, life and death? These we no longer heed:
They sterilised us like a flock of bats,
Rising from the grave gripped by a godless greed
To eat the food that keeps them down like rats.

All love and all compassion now have turned
To broken trinkets spread on the floor of the world.
And no-one bows his head to see the wound
Of a wretch who has so long his fate bewailed . . .

We must be saved since we are innocent,
Every wretch who, kneeling, here is bent.
It wasn't us, the paltry ones, who dealt the awful wound
Which made God's sons no more than dust on the
                                                ground . . .

Let the breath of life come to our breasts again
And we shall all rise up as living souls
And though the bread tonight is turned to stone
Once more the dust on the ground will be God's sons.

September 1945

Jean Earle (1909-2002)

Old Tips

Over the years, a tip would take on time's finish,
A greening over –
Seen from far off, a patina
As on bronze memorials. It was a feature
Of place and weather, one of the marks of home
To my springloaded people.

Autumn in the allotments; sunlit on high,
The town shadowed. All the pits asleep.
Sometimes, cows off a neglected farm
Would stray across a very old tip –
Lie around on the strange, wispy grass,
Comforting their udders.
Old tips breathed out a warm, greenish smoke
After rain,
Suggesting thin, volcanic pastures.

Some tips were famed as wicked, secreting runnels
Of dark, treacle death; swallowing houses
Helpless at their feet.
But most were friendly –
We children ran out of school
Visiting the one that rose
Close to our playground.
We scrambled towards the top –
To shriek the dandelion flaring in the grit
And that abandoned crane,
Pointing to the annual sea.

Jean Earle (1909-2002)

Piccalilli

Overheard on a bus –
"Between him dying and the funeral,
I papered the house . . .".

What was in her bosom,
Raging? At a peak time,
Did she go herself to choose patterns
Or send out for some?

A friend rescues old photographs
Off junk stalls. Fades of dead people,
Priced by the frames.
"Pity for them!" she says,
Making space on her wall.
One faintly-laughing group
Centres a baby, that's no more now
Than a tentative smudge –
Protective clasp, though,
Dark as ever, across its white frock.
All buttons sharp. The dog's eyes
Anxiously surviving.

My neighbour runs a vase
For invalid flowers,
The ragged and terminal.
Quiet, a little water, subdued light –
As we'd wish for ourselves.
Through her garden in heatwave
She moves like an ambulance.

Such quirks are collectable –
One goes about

Delving their origin: like trying pickles
To guess the recipe. Certain of salt,
Vinegar. Elusive in the brine,
Often unnameable,
The burning spices . . .

Quaker's Yard Junction, 1950

Dirty, slow up-train
Tumbles off blackboys, white-eyed, red-lipped,
Logs under arm.

Pigeons clocked out of baskets.
Everyone gathers –
Even the man with nystagmus,
His second home the ticket office shadows,
Juts up his face . . .

And they are gone, silvery. An old engine
Butts at the water-stocking.
Bogie-bolster rusts and rusts away,
The siding dandelions
Blaze for place.

Now, the immaculate spark
Engineers ride about in – coasting like silk.
We glimpse their dinner, flashed on a cloth.
And then the four-fifteen – a fuss-pot!
Colliers bundling whippets
To Pontypridd races.
Schoolchildren, banging doors.

Waste off the footplates breathes
To meet pinks in the station borders.
Clove scent and oiled rags . . .
Trucks noisily travelling. Lewis-Merthyr,
Powell Dyffryn, Ebbw Vale, Cory's . . .

About this time, the line dog
(Lives at the ganger's hut, was in a film
So does not speak to us)
Officially rounds sheep off the track,
Back to the mountain.

Over the bridge, to fetch milk
From the village. Waiting the signals' click
Against sunset.
Emerald and red
Sequins the echoing bottles . . .
Stars the long mind.

Solva Harbour

Always one hill brilliant and one dark,
In memory – sharing the long curve
To sunset. Seas leap and fall
With a white sigh around two rocks,
Markers and exclaimers
Under whatever sky,
As we are ourselves

When we return, to breathe upon
Fading light. Is such remembering
A life form? Will it revive

Peripheral presences?
Floaters in the iris,
Vague to a central vision
Dazzled with happiness . . .

Forms we would now acknowledge, name
As witnesses: whether or not aware
On that day, how we sat stunned
In our own silence, like the boats
In the emptied harbour,
Waiting for inflowing tide
To move them again.

There was a girl running to swim
In the evening: she would be old now.
We scarcely noticed her pass
But the years insist, she was beautiful.
We would recreate her
Out of the mindless joy
Through which we sensed her . . .

She: and the flowers in our colours,
The seabirds. All we did not heed
Being on that day our own
Adamant life. In a sunned mirror,
Brighter than experienced . . .
Though it blows up for storm
And the harbour's grey.

Lynette Roberts (1909-1995)

Poem from Llanybri

If you come my way that is . . .
Between now and then, I will offer you
A fist full of rock cress fresh from the bank
The valley tips of garlic red with dew
Cooler than shallots, a breath you can swank

In the village when you come. At noon-day
I will offer you a choice bowl of cawl
Served with a 'lover's' spoon and a chopped spray
Of leeks and savori fach, not used now.

In the old way you'll understand. The din
Of children singing through the eyelet sheds
Ringing 'smith hoops, chasing the butt of hens;
Or I can offer you Cwmcelyn spread

With quartz stones from the wild scratchings of men:
You will have to go carefully with clogs
Or thick shoes for it's treacherous the fen,
The East and West Marshes also have bogs.

Then I'll do the lights, fill the lamp with oil,
Get coal from the shed, water from the well;
Pluck and draw pigeon with crop of green foil
This your good supper from the lime-tree fell.

A sit by the hearth with blue flames rising,
No talk. Just a stare at 'Time' gathering
Healed thoughts, pool insight, like swan sailing
Peace and sound around the home, offering

You a night's rest and my day's energy.
You must come – start this pilgrimage
Can you come? – send an ode or an elegy
In the old way and raise our heritage.

Low Tide

Every waiting moment is a fold of sorrow
Pierced within the heart.
Pieces of mind get torn off emotionally
In large wisps.
Like a waif I lie, stillbound to action:
Each waiting hour I stare and see not,
Hum and hear not, nor care I how long
The lode mood lasts.

My eyes are raw and wide apart
Stiffened by the salt bar
That separates us.
You so far;
I at ease at the hearth
Glowing for a welcome
From your heart.
Each beating moment crosses my dream
So that wise things cannot pass
As we had planned.

Woe for all of us: supporting those
Who like us fail to steel their hearts,
But keep them wound in clocktight rooms,
Ill found. Unused. Obsessed by time.
Each beating hour
Rings false.

The Shadow Remains

To speak of everyday things with ease
And arrest the mind to a simpler world
Where living tables are stripped of a cloth;

Of wood on which I washed, sat at peace:
Cooked duck, shot on an evening in peacock cold:
Studied awhile: wrote: baked bread for us both.

But here by the hearth with leisured grace
I prefer to speak of the vulgar clock that drips
With the falling of rain: woodbine tips, and yarrow

Spills, lamp, packet of salt, and twopence of mace
That sit on the shelf edged with a metal strip,
And below, brazier fire that burns our sorrow,

Dries weeping socks above on the rack: that knew
Two angels pinned to the wall – again two.

Fifth of the Strata

And the sea will insist
Persuade a path to follow,
Longs eagerly to cover
The green valley pastures:
To flow forward along
The sunken ribbed coomb
And dry river-bed . . . endlessly.
And it will succeed
Tomorrow follow
All gravel roads
And rise slowly around
The Dragon's scaled Fort;
To leave nothing of Wales
But white island shining
The crest of Snowdon
Glittering with dark wintry-ice.

Find no woe in this:
For this is tomorrow.
And before tomorrow
England will be
For thousands of years
Lying below us
A submerged village
Like weeping Halkin;
When other and better banks
Dry from ocean beds,
Built of crystalline rock
And sharp shell and shale
Will arise for our freedom
For *our* feet to follow:
And this shall be always,
As it is never.

Curlew

A curlew hovers and haunts the room.
On bare boards creak its filleted feet:
For freedom intones four notes of doom,

Crept, slept, wept, kept, under aerial gloom:
With Europe restless in his wing beat,
A curlew hovers and haunts the room:

Fouls wire, pierces the upholstery bloom,
Strikes window pane with shagreen bleat,
Flicking scarlet tongue to a frenzied fume

Splints his curved beak on square glass tomb:
Runs to and fro seeking the mudsilt retreat;
Captured, explodes a chill sky croon

Wail-iṅg . . . pal-iṅg . . . a desolate phantom
At the bath rim *purring burbling trilling soft sweet*
Syllables of sinuous sound to a liquid moon

Till window, wide, frees thin mails of plume,
Fluting voice and shade through cloud's moist sleet:
A curlew hovers and haunts the room.

Margiad Evans (1909-1958)

The Nightingale

The orchard in the valley first
the green infection took,
the birds forgot their brown highways,
the leaf forgot the root.

The butterflies on breathing wings
went by like sighs of light –
trembled the air's transparency –
articulated flight.

The mountains in the faded mists
with opening souls rejoice.
All night they heard the nightingale
in his full-moon of voice.

Nature and the Naturalist

Nature and the Naturalist
met by moonlight in his breast.

Nature said, anatomy
is the coarsest part of me;

intensely as an insect pries
you search me with your glass-hung eyes.

Margiad Evans (1909-1958)

Folds of the microscope disclose
the chambers of the star and rose.

You tear apart with bladed eye
the dove-tailed feathers of the sky.

Come, said Nature, shining clearly,
stare no more we shall be weary

of each other and our part
in each other's heart.

I am the world, you, mine inhabitant,
you are the world, I, the participant

in it with you and you see me.
I do not see: look then on me

with courageous faith, she said,
nature needs faith like a god.

My actions dress you as they dress
the universe; but clothed the less

is visible of what bright sort
we are; see me with thought.

half close the lenses of your sight,
an instrument, and not a light

the student mind can be. Prostrate
your science. Be initiate.

To my sister Sian

'Do you remember Sian? How dearly do you remember?'
    (*Autobiography*)

Nature and Time are against us now:
no more we leap up the river like salmon,
nor dive through its fishy holes
sliding along its summer corridor
with all the water from Wales, nor tear it to silver
shreds with our childish arms when it bolted our path for
                                          the day,
nor wade wearing our bindings
of string weed, white-flowering from our nakedness;
nor lie in the hot yellow fields with the cows.

We go home separately Sian.
Strangest of all changes, that you have one door,
I another! Dreamily I write to our childhood,
sisters with a brotherly friendship, one loyal to both.
There hang the black woods still with candles of daffodils
lighting the draught of the wind, and our parted language
speaks to each of us of the keepers' cot in the brackeny
                                            corner
and the stream bed where the water had faded to rock –
Easily we keep our secrets now, for no-one cares
if we dare the red floods together, two little fools in the
                                            darkness
whose souls flew high above danger, whose bodies
death had a hundred times in its reach.

Forever we
did not end, but passed over our paths,
I following you, dabbling our hands in the birds' nests,

darting through ghost walk and haunted graveyard
when the year was dead in the church tower.
We had one home together. That put us beyond all danger:
that set us forever, that and our unfathomable friendship
                                                      with trees,
fields and horizons. Two children
solitary, pilgrimy, silent, inscrutably wishing
forever dallying with lostness, whether our choice
was through the jay woods, or over the mushroom
                                                      mountains,
or the old cider orchards.

Our secrets
were eternal and will always be. Forever dallying
with lostness, at last we were lost and all paths
were the path of our unforgettable double childhood.
All our secrets were one – secrecy.
The memory of what we kept secret is gone, but the
                                                     secret is true.
All the places were us, we were all the places,
and the inscrutable innocent altars of nature.
I see two children slipping into a wood
speechlessly happy. Two lives lived have not changed it.
For our ways, our fields, our river, our lostness
were children. So we were our country.

Brenda Chamberlain (1912-1971)

I dream too much, over and over

I dream too much, over and over: I
wander far from home, and am unable
to find the way back
through farmland and empty barns:
lost, among alien people, in unbounded landscape

Against night-hauntings, an evocation:
narcissi, eucalyptus, fritillary
Poseidon! Hygaea!

Now, on a shimmering sweet siren day

Now, on a shimmering sweet siren day
Of soft summer O lazy passionate season
After snow has melted thawed melted blossomed
Into red petals of prodigious roses I ask
Where you are where you are where you are

On the back porch, your old raincoat
Crumpled and cracked from its travels
Hangs above army boots grey with dust
From Saint Pierre and Miquelon

Come again, black days of rain and no sun
I have had enough summer. The Chinese poets
Point far away over drenched grasses
Towards the distant snow mountains

A year ago today we were together
Do you remember O memory retain
A white horse passing in the mist
And how your hands were stained
With the juice of a purple fish

Seal cave

Far down, in the pool below me,
At the base of yellow rock walls,
A monster barks.
It is the bull seal,
Blowing, threshing and flowing,
Nine feet of smooth-packed flesh.
Green as oil, he comes
Out of the secret cavern,
The mammalian bedroom,
Into open water's emerald waves,
And is aware, through their invincible
Rise and fall
Of how I admire his performance.
Though he turns an aquiline profile
And hoods his eyes with heavy lids,
He is nonetheless aware.

From the pulsating
Jewel-coloured sea, from white foam-lace,

Rises a gentle stone-grey head, whiskered, soft-eyed.
Dappled, white-breasted, vulnerable,
Gleaming like a fish, it is a cow of his harem.
Hola, hola, hola, seal cow!
She dives down the entrance tunnel, into the pool;
Her mottled back, where it touches the surface
Becoming iridescent as mother-of-pearl.
Those brown beseeching eyes would have me go to her,
Would drag me down.
Those almost human hands extended,
Then folded inwards to the breast,
Say come, come, come,
To caverns where whale-bones lie
Bleached and growth-ringed.
Mother seal, seal cow,
Your eyes almost compel me to a salt death.
Your eyes are so full of knowledge,
It would be no surprise
To find you had understanding
Of how it is I am a lonely woman
Living on a lonely strand:
Of how it is, that when in the Spring I am crowned,
It is but with seatangle and shells.

Evening has come. It is cold on this sunless rock
Past which waves hurry in tumult.
The moon rises in the wind-whipped sky
Over the flood pouring relentlessly past.
The sea is cold: the moon is cold.
O virginal Spring moon!

Women on the strand

Our eyes surf-dimmed from gazing,
We gather in yellow age
To send out prayers
Over the black waters
That our menfolk may come again
Grinding their boats upon the screaming shingle.
But the sea's a woman, desiring them.
Has she not bones enough yet
That she must beggar our hearths?

Children, born in salt spray,
Storm-birthed in winter dawns,
Little owls, sorcerers,
Flowers of our love,
Turn your eyes from empty waves,
Watch peat flame instead.
Your fathers fish for supper
In watermeads of death.
And the sea's a woman, desiring them,
And we are old, where she is ageless.

Talysarn

Bone-aged is my white horse;
Blunted is the share;
Broken the man who through sad land
Broods on the plough.

Bone-bright was my gelding once;
Burnished was the blade;
Beautiful the youth who in green Spring
Broke earth with song.

Shipwrecked Demeter

Shipwrecked Demeter,
if it is indeed she,
a new Demeter
gold-incrusted, bronze-breasted,
shipwrecked, veiled, intact of face,
Demeter the mourning mother
(if it is she or another unknown
goddess) raised by Turkish
sponge-fishers, off Asia Minor,
has conserved force from the seabed
where the dark centuries held her,
and with salt-burned gaze
gives, under an older sun, solace

Dead ponies

There is death enough in Europe without these
Dead ponies on the mountain.
They are the underlining, the emphasis of death.
It is not wonderful that when they live
Their eyes are shadowed under mats of hair.
Despair and famine do not gripe so hard
When the bound earth and sky are kept remote
Behind clogged hairs.

The snows engulfed them, pressed their withered haunches
                                                          flat,
Filled up their nostrils, burdened the cage of their ribs.
The snow retreated. Their bodies stink to heaven,
Potently crying out to raven and hawk and dog;
Come! Pick us clean; cleanse our fine bones of blood.

They were never lovely save as foals,
Before their necks grew long, uncrested;
But the wildness of the mountain was in their stepping,
The pride of Spring burnt in their haunches,
They were tawny as the rushes of the marsh.

The prey-birds have had their fill, and preen their feathers:
Soft entrails have gone to make the hawk arrogant.

Eluned Phillips b. 1915?

Y Perthi Coll

Mae'r enwau'n dal y glust fel miwsig cain
clychau San Llawddog adeg gŵyl a miri;
Parc Iago, Parc yr Asyn a Pharc Main;
Parc Sticil, Parc y Gog a Pharc y Gelli;
caeau yn lesni o garpedi drud
a'u perthi'n cuddio reiat o syndodau;
dryw bach a'i geg ar agor yn ei grud
ym môn y gwlydd, a'i ffydd ym manna'r gwyrthiau.
Digrifwas Jac-y-jwmper a'i wyllt sioe
yn taenu gwrid ar ruddiau y fioled:
pob llun yn dal ei liw yn ffrâm ein doe
i hongian ym mharlyrau hen gymuned.
Mae'r caeau heddiw fel cyfandir cyfan
heb gysgod dan warchodaeth gwifren drydan.

The Lost Hedges

The old names play on the ear like the fine
Music of Saint Llawddog's bells at festival;
Parc Iago, Parc yr Asyn and Parc Main;
Parc Sticil, Parc y Gog and Parc y Gelli;[8]
Fields all carpeted with costly green
And their hedges hiding a riot of marvels;
A baby wren with its beak open in his crib
Under the chickweed, his faith in the manna of miracles.
Funny boy Jacky Jumper and his wild show
Spreading blushes on the cheeks of the violets:
Every picture still bright in the frame of our yesterday
To hang in the parlours of an old community.
The fields today are like a continent entire
Unsheltered, beneath the watchful electric wire.

---

8. 'Parc' is the usual word for 'field' in the dialect of North Pembrokeshire. Thus: James's field, Donkey's field, Narrow field, Stile field, Cuckoo's field, Copse field.

Joyce Herbert (b. 1922)

Death of an Old Country Woman

Propped on four pillows
she watched herself passing
through veiled green fields.
Her look stopped
at the bed's end.

Gathering
the last of her life
into a strong sound,
'Goodbye', she said,
imperiously, as from a throne.

The Childless Woman

All the almond trees are anchored,
buds will bloom.
In my brick box I wander
from room to room.

Steam coats the windows,
leaves must be shed:
nothing will break from the almonds
when they are dead.

Blood spins round my bones,
the kitchen sink runs dry.
The matrix of my love is barren
and so am I.

Poppies

They spread the blades
of their listening petals
flat for the sun.

Tudor caps of their seedboxes
like felt in the hand:
purple of their ruffs
running blotched on their paper petals,
the stillness of them.

They are for ease,
would take you into tented splendours
dyed the colour of blood:
standing by them you hear them wait
while their seedboxes shrink, explode
their gritty black dust.

The flowers stare past you,
female, opulent. They resent disturbance,
can appear suddenly and sag without warning.
They are secretive, theatrical,
and strong as precious stones.

At the house of Ann Frank

I am not the first, nor the last
who will question this building.
Many have simply stood in it,
looked at their hands, and wondered.

I came to put my fingers on it,
to face the walls, stand in the shadows.
I could not track them where they ate and slept,
where she sat.

Instead I breathed their voices
that quarrelled, caressed, laughed,
stopped like a millwheel checked, and the water
running away to earth.

This was not a house for growing,
where custom could quietly settle,
travel to a family's heart,
comfort with known presences.

This was the refuge of the children of Israel,
the place where the whips came down.

When I stood there among bullets

I heard the old river Prysor far down in the valley . . .
                                                     – Hedd Wyn[9]

Like glass the river splinters over stones.

Below,
the metal water
breaking in the mind,
stays far down
behind mist,
small sounds moving
under mist.

Rain, mist, the watersheets falling,
grasscoloured wet air,
stones leaving strong heels
scattering after galloping sheep
which buck and skid,
curving from your nets of care
that creep the mountain always.

Wintergrass like khaki,
dropping water and seeds.
Furnaces probe like tides
the river's long breathing.

---

9. Hedd Wyn was a young poet from Trawsfynydd who won the so-called 'Black Chair' at the National Eisteddfod of 1917, but he was killed in action before the Eisteddfod took place. 'A sfin 'rhen afon Prysor' is a quotation from his poem, meaning 'And the sound of the old river Prysor'.

Flames flinging metal through.

The water talks like small bells in summer,
moving the grasses,
bending them gently
as a ewe nudging her lamb.

I see you crossing the broken land
surely, wet wool against your ear,
sheepshanks flopping on your shoulder.

Carrying the dead
from the screaming fires of the Somme,
you walk through my head
when I think of Trawsfynydd.

When you thought of it
you heard,
far down, coming like a sharp tune
the long trickle of Prysor in summer.
A sfin 'rhen afon Prysor:
the winter growl of it, savage in fog,
and sheep calling from all the mountains round.

Everything fell over the edge
when metal drove fire through your flesh.

Alison Bielski (b. 1925)

wild leek, Flatholm Island

tenaciously clinging to bleak foreshore
you thrust ugly stems through lifting mist

your pungent leaves cascade over pebbles
while purple flowers glory in light

rare exile rooting under shifting stones
when wrenched from warm earth you adapted

to cold were tended in northern borders
by monks who knew your herbal secrets

ignored today you escape to outcrops
flight ravaging gulls and Severn tides

yet staunchly preserve your identity
determined to thrive on harsh limestone

hunting the wren[10]

we come to hunt the wren
we come to kill the king
in forest trees one leaping spark
flies on thunder wing

---

10. Hunting the wren: This Pembrokeshire custom took place on Twelfth Night.

small goldcrested wren
we come to snatch away
that crimson flame upon your head
our dying sun's last ray

and beat beat green bushes
slashing as we sing
the first to strike a wren down
is king king king!

in ancient druid courts of law
their confidence you won
were hated for your whispers
when verdict was begun

king royal hedge king
revered throughout the year
your ivied nest is sacred
St. Lawrence fire will sear

with rash and burning weals
each one who robs the wren
except on this midwinter day
beware our Lady's hen!

we capture you alive
trap your fluttering flame
inside an oak-bark house
we come to kill and maim

to hide you in a locked room
with windows tightly sealed
so that we can see you
suffocate and bleed

Alison Bielski (b. 1925)

you hammered on a battle drum
to save King William's life
we thrash you now with poles
and wound you with this knife

we come to kill the wren
wide crimson cloth we fold
and decorate your coffin
with ribbons blue and gold

one evening in Gethsemane
your rattling song was guide
to angry Roman soldiers
who moved to Jesus' side

we wrap white silk around you
and stab you as you lie
one bottle of fine spirits
beside you while you die

your family is cursed to live
inside a damp-walled home
we offer you to pagan gods
who watch with eyes of stone

we come to shut the cutty wren
inside his lantern prison
so martyrdom begins for you
who once betrayed St. Stephen

four slender branches
are strapped to your bier
you ride on young men's shoulders
when twelfth night is here

oak wreath green above you
as moss from Bethlehem
you carried to a crying child
to cover each cold limb

so groaning and stumbling
with imaginary weight
this torchlight procession
moves on from door to gate

and chalking on each threshold
of opened house and tavern
from sweetheart and drunkard
we carry our great burden

before dawn approaches
call on those newly-wed
sprinkle with well-water
each warm marriage-bed

bird you were a siren
lured men to dripping arms
changed to a wren escaping
one knight who knew your charms

we came to hunt the wren
now we have killed the wren
and drunker with each step
we sing our surging hymn

mimic ancient prophecies
throw lyrics to sea wind
a torn poet lies rotting
disfigured lame and blind

fishermen beg your body
for talisman at sea
one year without shipwreck
we will not set you free

on seaweed boat in Menai's tide
you perched, young boy took aim
hit you between sinew and bone
to gain his lion name[11]

now give us beer and money
to lay this wren to rest
coin for a plucked feather
from our victim's breast

soon Bran's bird lies buried
in the dunghill heap
and we are all so drunk
we stagger home to sleep

we went to hunt the wren
we went to kill the wren
hiding from robin's noose
we found him once again

short days lengthen into light
sun regains lost power
bird's fire transmuted
grows fiercer every hour

now resurrected wren
your poet's song lives on
oak tree soul soars upward
shedding flesh and bone

---

11. Lleu Llawgyffes, fourth branch of the *Mabinogi*.

leaving blood-stained ribbons
your house rotting in rain
a poet flies in springtime
we cannot kill the wren

sacramental sonnets (a selection):

snowbound in Dyfed

no water as the great freeze locks its grip
so struggling home with one new loaf of bread
that bald announcement echoes while I slip
and stumble on the uncleared frozen road
scraping my balcony I scoop cold snow
into a plastic bucket with small trowel
heat white-filled saucepans on the cooker's glow
to wash essential clothes in steaming bowl
I boil snow coffee carry coloured mugs
hearing the helicopter's rattling drone
promising food supplies then surging plugs
celebrate electricity's return
upon my desk this sonnet waits complete
calming the chaos of our snowbound street

regeneration

nearing this island in one blackened cloud
an ancient eagle skims over our hill
clawing a clustered branch of scarlet fruit
stains water with pulp and eats its fill
plunges into the lake's turbulent heat
splashing and shaking off age and decay
emerge as a youthful-plumaged bird
surveys light skyline soars towards new day
below grey cliffs we crowd the Celtic shore
our baptism no myth but rite of love
flowing water covers our old despair
no eagle circles but one gentle dove
renewed reborn we smooth each drying limb
sunrise bathes ripples in first crimson gleam

love's illusion

your serpent train wriggles towards the hill
at home again I find a loving presence
on cups and plates wild flowers opening still
quickly made bed holding that faint essence
of every movement made during your stay
until you packed each neatly folded garment
my mind begins to paint from memory
a water-colour without temperament
months later when we meet to touch and kiss
excitement frames this likeness lavishly
soon I am used to gentle tenderness
counting small faults as failings jar on me
flesh conquers spirit and I smash my dream
we are too human never what we seem

the undefined

stripped and then packaged in my paper robe
I lie prone on this table ringed by eyes
as camera doctor nurse and scanner probe
identity but not my hidden mind
watching these opaque organs which appear
pulsing in monochrome upon lit screen
I see even the detailed spine is there
and am intrigued by my precise machine
normality is hospital's ideal
as proof of health yet the creative act
must be expressed by the unusual
mind that links image word and artefact
inside flat metal plates that slide away
I long to find one poem's clear X-ray

walking with angels

archangel Michael paced out Skirrid's ridge
claiming another isolated shrine
for men had raised a chapel near the edge
of that raw fissure slashed to make a sign
on first Good Friday all Gwent's mountains shook
with earthquake tremors through that savage day
but when hewn stones enclosed altar and book
Michael knelt in gold candlelight to pray
curiously we stare where smothered walls
clutch contours underground hide secret acts
of persecuted catholics who crawled
and struggled through September gales to mass
sceptical dare we doubt each past event
walking with angels on blue hills of Gwent?

Christine Furnival (b. 1931)

Englyn: Spring

The foxy autumn leaf long fallen,
    The fleecy winter snows long fled:
  – Now creeps the old red beast towards the white
                                    new-born one
And summer fattens off the spring-tide dead.

Needles

The shadows draw out across the grass
Dark and thin,
The children run into the late evening
Their little heels hammering over them:
And the chased sunlight, too, runs about with them:
All this will come under the hammer, soon.

I won't get up, yet, to cluck like a hen,
But sit at the window and watch through to the lawn.
From within the spent holly
A shriek escapes the throttle of a bird –
A sound I've never heard since living in the town,
And could in any case never pretend to understand.
Here comes the ancient, fat-cheeked Easter moon
Pinned to the sky like a badge on a dark school uniform.

I may think, right now, it will be long
Till I forget all this:
Sundown,
The grass new-mown,
The old huntress peering at the running children:
But I've already forgotten too many Easters,
Too many have flown, –
Till today I sit at my foremothers' workbasket in the room,
Glance between stitches at the scene,
And must find a needle not coated with rust.
Some are short, some long,
Some sharper than serpents' tooth or tongue,

And the long shadows go on running out like generations.

The Welsh Love-Spoon

Returning from a visit to Wales
he brought back a love-spoon –
a wooden love-spoon picked up in a craft-shop,
construed by a slim historical pamphlet.

At first he'd intended to give it to her,
but in the end it intrigued him too much:
those wooden spheres running up and down in their
prison,
the way the carpenter had at once captured and released
them –
pulled them from a block of wood as a sculptor pulls a
statue from stone –
all this somehow reminded him of his games and labours
with words.

So he kept the thing on his desk
where he could pick it up and balance it whenever he so
                                                      willed,
and make the little balls chase each other at his pleasure,
or – when he wanted – stop dead.

And on some days when he had gone out
she would wander into his study;
and she would pick up the love-spoon
which somehow reminded her of his absent body.

Rhiannon

How welcome it is, how sweet that the old stories do
                                                    not always tell
of smoking citadels and beauty that drove men mad,
of big-headed, dirty old gods (-and goddesses); of
                                                 dispiriting visits to hell
and those entire sewer-networks of curses where pacific
                                               citizens end up dead;
yes, in the catastrophic hour, how extremely refreshing
                                               and good

it is to encounter those rare, important – even royal – top
persons
who are more intent on living than making ready to die;
who speak some funny lines and act with individual
                                               wisdom,
and are so endearing that we feel a captivated envy
of the ease they bring to being beautiful and good. –
                                             Rhiannon

was such a lady, daughter of Hefeydd the Old – who
                                                  herself aged
slowly, with strong, comely grace – right from the moment
she unveiled herself to Pwyll, Prince of Dyfed
to those days when, widowed and re-married,
she rose, with a smile, to homelessness and some malign
                                                  enchantments.

She was witty & forthright – as when she told her diffident
young suitor
she loved only him – and idiot who should have spoken
                                                  his mind before;
forbearing, too, at times, – a stoic who could say 'poor
                                                  creatures'
to those who perjured truth to make her suffer.
Light-hearted common-sense she brought to being out of
                                                  work and poor.

In fact, she found it hard to put a foot wrong –
yet dodged self-righteousness; was earthy, gay and real;
took in her generous stride a life clear and resilient as
                                                  bird-song
as, bedded, widowed and beggared in wet Wales
she always soldiered on.

Christine Furnival (b. 1931)

A Visit to Caldey Island Abbey
(To my daughters)

You will come here again. The steep
Celibacy in your and every heart will call you back.

And the hermit's loneliness which seems today a little comic
Another year will float your well-spring, salve and Ithaca.

Laugh, then, a little now – but never in scorn. Yes,
They make sensuous perfumes here – 'Island Madrigal'
                                                  and 'Gorse',

'Fern', 'Pot-pourri' – and no doubt some warm
Nights when the small town gleams on the opposite bay

And – as they seemed odd to you, to them seems gay –
                                                  and their God's
Grey seals slide freely into the ocean, and his huge

Black fisher cormorants dip, catch and exalt – no doubt a
                                                         yen
For coastal arcane weighs within each monk. – But listen

Ponder. And wait. You will return, transported here one
                                                         year
By the abbey's endemic bell-toll, fast-anchored by its vibrate
                                                         centre.

('Caldey' is derived from 12th Century Norse 'keld', a spring, and 'ey' an island.)

Nest Lloyd (b. 1934)

Iâr

"Rhyw hen iâr mewn ffrog grimplîn."

I

Llithro llaw
yn ofalus araf
o dan ei chynhesrwydd
meddal
a hithau'n clwcian
yn ddiddig ar ei nyth;
brasgamu 'nôl
yn wyllt
a gwaed
yn rhybudd coch
ar fraich.

II

Ofn plentynnaidd
o groesi'r clos
rhag ei hymosodiad
pigog, dibryfôc.
Chwilio'i nyth
yn y drain,
ym môn clawdd,
ar ben tas wair,
a'i chael mewn
rhyw hen dwll annisgwyl

Hen

"Some old hen in a crimplene frock"

I

Sliding a hand
slowly, carefully
under her warmth
her softness
while she clucks
contentedly on her nest;
jumping back
wildly
with blood
a red warning
on my arm.

II

A childish fear
of crossing the yard
lest she attack,
pecking, unprovoked.
Searching for her nest
in the thorns,
at the base of a hedge,
on top of a haystack,
and finding it
in some unexpected hole

ym mur
hen furddyn,
fel trysor cudd.
Ei llygaid
crwn, maleisus,
coch
yn slei
gilwylio.

III

Gweld ei
gwingad olaf
a hithau'n crogi
wrth ei choesau
wrth iet
ar ôl gwthio'r
gyllell
lan ei gwddf.
Ei gwaed
yn llifo
fel misglwyf merch.
Ei chorff yn ymdonni'n
gynddeiriog
y gwaed
yn ewyn coch
ar draeth pridd.

IV

Ei diberfeddu
a rhyfeddod
wyau anaeddfed
ei chroth yn

in the wall
of an old ruin,
like hidden treasure.
Her eyes
round, malicious,
red
slyly
half-looking.

III

Seeing her
last shudder
as she hangs
by her legs
from a gate
after the knife
thrust
up her throat.
Her blood
flowing
like a woman's period.
Her body quivering
crazily
the blood
a red tide
on a beach of earth.

IV

Removing her entrails
and the miracle
of the unripe eggs
from her womb

fach, mwy a mawr
ar ford y gegin fach.
Symbolau bywyd.

V

Anghofia
dy ddarlun llyfr plant
o greadur dof
yn crafu am weddillion
yn y llwch a'r baw.
Mae'n perthyn i'r
eryr, yr alarch a'r fwltur;
ffyrnig, ffrwythlon
eiddig am fyw.

small, bigger, biggest
on the back kitchen table.
Symbols of life.

V

Forget
your child's picture book image
of a tame creature
scratching for leftovers
in the dust and dirt.
She's related to the eagle,
the swan and the vulture;
fierce, fruitful,
eager for life.

Merched Llanio[12]

Lleng o Sbaenwyr
Yn sythu yng nglaw
Ceredigion,
Hiraethu am haul,
Dioddef diflasdod ymarferiadau
Milwrol
Mewn gwlad elyniaethus,
A'r corsydd a'r coed
Yn sibrwd bygythion
Yr Ordoficiaid anhydrin.

Ond 'roedd yn y 'vicus'
Fenywod.
Petrusa'r athro
Rhag cyffroi merched ffeministaidd
Trwy ddefnyddio gair megis
'puteiniaid'.
'Roedd 'na briodasau anghyfreithlon . . .'
mentra'n ofalus
ac ychwanegu
'Gwgid ar yr arfer.'

Pwy oeddynt,
Y gwragedd gefnodd
Ar gynhesrwydd y llwyth
A mentro i Dir Neb
Y clwstwr hofelau
Y tu allan i furiau'r gaer.
Eu cymunrodd inni:
Crair o bren cerfiedig,

---

12. Mae Llanio'n safle is-gaer Rufeinig yng ngogledd Ceredigion.

The women of Llanio[12]

A group of Spaniards
Freezing in the rain
Of Ceredigion,
Longing for sun,
Suffering the boredom of military
Exercises
In a hostile country,
While the hedges and trees
Whispered the threat
Of the unmanageable Ordovicans.

But there were in the camp
Women
The professor hesitates
Not wanting to annoy the feminists
By using a word like
'prostitutes'.
'There were illegal marriages . . .'
he ventures, carefully
and adds
'The practice was frowned upon.'

Who were they,
The women who turned their backs
On the warmth of the tribe
And ventured into No Man's Land
The cluster of hovels
Outside the walls of the fort?
This is our inheritance from them:
A carved wooden relic,

---

12. Llanio is the site of a minor Roman fort in northern Ceredigion.

Carn cyllell efallai,
Ar lun pen merch
A gwallt tynn, cordeddog.
Hwn, a'r enw Sarn Helen.

Islais o hanes y fenyw
O ganol imperialaeth Rhufain.

A knife handle perhaps,
In the shape of a girl's head
With tight, braided hair.
This, and the name Sarn Helen.

Just a whisper of woman's history
From the midst of Rome's empire.

Sally Roberts Jones (b. 1935)

Narcissus

Coming at length to the pool, and seeing there
That perfect image on unmoving glass,
Over his head the branches weave and pass,
Light dapples gold on grass, the flowing air
Ripples about him now unfelt. His stare
Fixed on the stagnant water, narrows in,
Blocked at the surface. String as that dusty skin,
His fellow answers him, moves as he moves, is bare
To him as he is bare. The dance they weave
Spins on a single point, and both entranced
Lean to the centre, meet, and join, and leave
Both in a single breath the bond they danced.
Now in the dusk a single body drifts,
Foul, in the muddy pond where no air lifts.

To the Island

They say it's unwise
To arrive at the end of a voyage
There, in the place that you always meant to go;
That arriving is ending,
The island like many another,
All cursed with the heat and the flies;
That the people are bad,

Vicious or sullen,
Living too well in their dirt.

They say – let them say:
Who never arrived, never sailed.
Illusion is truth
Observed in the eye of a god,
And that is a country for gods,
For the open eye
Seeing the shapes desired
Beneath the dust.

And the island is here,
The voyage as much of itself
As the rock and the sun:
That will never be reached,
And is always the land where we live.

Community
(Mr. Rogers, buried April 26, 1972)

There has been a death in the street.
Drawn curtains, collection for wreaths –
The historians call it Cymortha,
Assume that it vanished
In the steam of industrial birth.

We're the size of a village: forty houses,
A shop. Over fences the women gossip,
Watch weddings and growings – observe
The proper and ritual tact
Of those who must live with their kin.

No blood ties, it's true; our bonds
Are accent and place – and desire
For much the same ends. We are not
Political animals; held
An Investiture feast for the children,

And praised all that pomp. On Sundays
Expediency pegs out the washing:
If God is not mocked – well, He knows us –
I suppose it was like this before
When Piety lay in the clouds, an oncoming thunder.

There has been a death in the street;
We are less by that much. Statistics
Cannot say what we lose, what we give:
Questionnaires for the Welfare Department
Tell industrious lies.

We adapt. To the chimneys, the concrete,
The furnace, the smoke, the dead trees.
Our fields are the names of roadways,
Our flocks and our language are gone:
But we hold our diminished city in face of the sun.

Gillian Clarke (b. 1937)

Catrin

I can remember you, child
As I stood in a hot, white
Room at the window watching
The people and cars taking
Turn at the traffic lights.
I can remember you, our first
Fierce confrontation, the tight
Red rope of love which we both
Fought over. It was a square
Environmental blank, disinfected
Of paintings or toys. I wrote
All over the walls with my
Words, coloured the clean squares
With the wild, tender circles
Of our struggle to become
Separate. We want, we shouted,
To be two, to be ourselves.

Neither won nor lost the struggle
In the glass tank clouded with feelings
Which changed us both. Still I am fighting
You off, as you stand there
With your straight, strong, long
Brown hair and your rosy,
Defiant glare, bringing up

From the heart's pool that old rope,
Tightening about my life,
Trailing love and conflict,
As you ask may you skate
In the dark, for one more hour.

Shearing

No trouble finding them. Their cries
rise with the wind along the lane
spiced with hawthorn and golden chain.

A shovel turning snow, the blade
slides under the filthy fleece
to sugar-almond flesh,

turning the wool's silver, spreads it
in the dirt of the barn, whole,
wide as a double quilt.

In the orchard the ewes grieve.
Warm winds herd them, begin
to heal their nakedness.

A sheepdog with silver eyes
listens for cries and silences
under trailing electric flexes.

At tea-break we rest, the smells of wool
like wet Burberries going home from school
delayed in woods by a pool of sticklebacks,

that space between two activities
where something is lost and somebody's
footsteps are following you home.
And innocently, helping Nanna,
I pass tea to the thin, dark man
in the blue boiler-suit and move on,

take out my camera for a picture
of shearing-day, Hywel, Nanna,
and helpers from neighbouring farms.

Next day, still in my camera not smiling,
he died in a noose in his own barn
leaving Hywel his moon-eyed dog.

The wind got up and it was colder,
though wool still curded hawthorn lanes,
chaining the farms to each other.

Lunchtime Lecture

And this from the second or third millennium
B.C., a female, aged about twenty-two.
A white, fine skull, full up with darkness
As a shell with sea, drowned in the centuries.
Small, perfect. The cranium would fit the palm
Of a man's hand. Some plague or violence
Destroyed her, and her whiteness lay safe in a shroud
Of silence, undisturbed, unrained on, dark
For four thousand years. Till a tractor in summer
Biting its way through the longcairn for supplies
Of stone, broke open the grave and let a crowd of light
Stare in at her, and she stared quietly back.

As I look at her I feel none of the shock
The farmer felt as, unprepared, he found her.
Here in the Museum, like death in hospital,
Reasons are given, labels, causes, catalogues.
The smell of death is done. Left, only her bone
Purity, the light and shade beauty that her man
Was denied sight of, the perfect edge of the place
Where the pieces join, with no mistakes, like boundaries.

She's a tree in winter, stripped white on a black sky,
Leafless formality, brow, bough in fine relief.
I, at some other season, illustrate the tree
Fleshed, with woman's hair and colours and the rustling
Blood, the troubled mind that she has overthrown.
We stare at each other, dark into sightless
Dark, seeing only ourselves in the black pools,
Gulping the risen sea that booms in the shell.

Letter from a Far Country (extract)

. . .-Dear husbands, fathers, forefathers,
this is my apologia, my
letter home from the future,
my bottle in the sea which might
take a generation to arrive.

. . . As I write I am far away.
First see a landscape. Hill country,
essentially feminine,
the sea not far off. Bryn Isaf
down there in the crook of the hill
under Calfaria's single eye.
My grandmother might have lived there.
Any farm. Any chapel.

Gillian Clarke (b. 1937)

Father and minister, on guard,
close the white gates to hold her.
A stony track turns between
ancient hedges, narrowing,
like a lane in a child's book.
Its perspective makes the heart restless
like the boy in the rhyme, his stick
and cotton bundle on his shoulder.

The minstrel boy to the war has gone.
But the girl stays. To mind things.
She must keep. And wait. And pass time.

. . . It has always been a matter
of lists. We have been counting,
folding, measuring, making,
tenderly laundering cloth
ever since we have been women.

The waves are folded meticulously,
perfectly white. Then they are tumbled
and must come to be folded again.

Four herring gulls and their shadows
are shouting at the clear glass
of a shaken wave. The sea's a sheet
bellying in the wind, snapping.
Air and white linen. Our airing cupboards
are full of our satisfactions.

The gulls grieve at our contentment.
It is a masculine question.
"Where" they call "are your great works?"
They slip their fetters and fly up
to laugh at land-locked women.
Their cries are cruel as greedy babies.

Our milky tendernesses dry
to crisp lists; immaculate
linen; jars labelled and glossy
with our perfect preserves.
Spiced oranges; green tomato
chutney; Seville orange marmalade
annually staining gold
the snows of January.

(The saucers of marmalade
are set when amber wrinkles
like the sea if you blow it.)

Jams and jellies of blackberry,
crabapple, strawberry, plum,
greengage and loganberry.
You can see the fruit pressing
their little faces against the glass;
tiny onions imprisoned
in their preservative juices.

. . . In that innocent smallholding
where the swallows live and field mice
winter and the sheep barge in
under the browbone, the windows
are blind, are doors for owls,
bolt-holes for dreams. The thoughts have flown.
The last death was a suicide.
The lowing cows discovered her,
the passing-bell of their need
warned a winter morning that day
when no-one came to milk them.
Later, they told me, a baby
was born in the room where she died,
as if by this means sanctified,
a death outcried by birth.

Gillian Clarke (b. 1937)

Middle-aged, poor, isolated,
she could not recover
from mourning an old parent's death.
Influenza brought an hour
too black, too narrow to escape.

More mysterious to them
was the woman who had everything.
A village house with railings;
rooms with good furniture;
fine linen in the drawers;
a garden full of herbs and flowers;
a husband at work; grown sons.
She had a cloud on her mind,
they said, and her death shadowed them.
It couldn't be explained.
I watch for her face looking out,
small and white, from every window,
like a face in a jar. Gossip,
whispers, lowing sounds. Laughter.

. . . Watching sea-roads I feel
the tightening white currents,
am waterlogged, my time set
to the sea's town clock.
My cramps and drownings, energies,
desires draw the loaded net
of the tide over the stones.

A lap full of pebbles and then
light as a Coca Cola can.
I am freight. I am ship.
I cast ballast overboard.
The moon decides my Equinox.
At high tide I am leaving.

. . . I hear the dead grandmothers,
Mamgu from Ceredigion,
Nain from the North, all calling
their daughters down from the fields,
calling me in from the road.
They haul at the taut silk cords;
set us fetching eggs, feeding hens,
mixing rage with the family bread,
lock us to the elbows in soap suds.
Their sculleries and kitchens fill
with steam, sweetnesses, goosefeathers.

On the graves of my grandfathers
the stones, in their lichens and mosses,
record each one's importance.
Diaconydd, Trysorydd.
Pillars of their society.
Three times at chapel on Sundays.
They are in league with the moon
but as silently stony
as the simple names of their women.

We are hawks trained to return
to the lure from the circle's
far circumference. Children sing
that note that only we can hear.
The baby breaks the waters,
disorders the blood's tune, sets
each filament of the senses
wild. Its cry tugs at flesh, floods
its mother's milky fields.
Nightly in white moonlight I wake
from sleep one whole slow minute
before the hungry child
wondering what woke me.

School's out. The clocks strike four.
Today this letter goes unsigned,
unfinished, unposted.
When it is finished
I will post it from a far country.

Llŷr

Ten years old, at my first Stratford play:
The river[13] and the king[14] with their Welsh names
Bore in the darkness of a summer night
Through interval and act and interval.
Swans move double through glossy water
Gleaming with imponderable meanings.
Was it Gielgud on that occasion?
Or ample Laughton, crazily white-gowned,
Pillowed in wheatsheaves on a wooden cart,
Who taught the significance of little words?
All. Nothing. Fond. Ingratitude. Words
To keep me scared, awake at night. That old
Man's vanity and a daughter's 'Nothing',
Ran like a nursery rhyme in my head.

Thirty years later on the cliffs of Llŷn[15]
I watch how Edgar's crows and choughs still measure
How high cliffs are, how thrown stones fall
Into history, how deeply the bruise
Spreads in the sea where the wave has broken.

---

13. Avon/afon: river (Welsh).
14. Llŷr: Lear.
15. Llŷn: N.W. peninsula of Wales.

The turf is stitched with tormentil and thrift,
Blue squill and bird bones, tiny shells, heartsease.
Yellowhammers sing like sparks in the gorse.
The landscape's marked with figures of old men:
The bearded sea; thin-boned, wind-bent trees;
Shepherd and labourer and night-fisherman.
Here and there among the crumbling farms
Are lit kitchen windows on distant hills,
And guilty daughters longing to be gone.

Night falls on Llŷn, on forefathers,
Old Celtic kings and the more recent dead,
Those we are still guilty about, flowers
Fade in jam jars on their graves; renewed
Refusals are heavy on our minds.
My head is full of sound, remembered speech,
Syllables, ideas just out of reach;
The close, looped sound of curlew and the far
Subsidiary roar, cadences shaped
By the long coast of the peninsula,
The continuous pentameter of the sea.
When I was ten a fool and a king sang
Rhymes about sorrow, and there I heard
That nothing is until it has a word.

Clywedog

The people came out in pairs,
Old, most of them, holding their places
Close till the very last minute,
Even planting the beans as usual

That year, grown at last accustomed
To the pulse of the bulldozers.
High in those uphill gardens, scarlet
Beanflowers blazed hours after
The water rose in the throats of the farms.

Only the rooted things stayed:
The wasted hay, the drowned
Dog roses, the farms, their kitchens silted
With their own stones, hedges
And walls a thousand years old.
And the mountains, in a head-collar
Of flood, observe a desolation
They'd grown used to before the coming
Of the wall-makers. Language
Crumbles to wind and bird-call.

Anorexic

My father's sister,
the one who died
before there was a word for it,
was fussy with her food.
'Eat up,' they'd say to me,
ladling a bowl with warning.

What I remember's
how she'd send me to the dairy,
taught me to take cream,
the standing gold.
Where the jug dipped
I saw its blue-milk skin
before the surface healed.

Breath held, tongue between teeth,
I carried in the cream,
brimmed, level,
parallel, I knew,
with that other, hidden horizon
of the earth's deep
ungleaming water-table.

And she, more often than not half-dressed,
stockings, a slip, a Chinese kimono,
would warm the cream, pour it
with crumbled melting cheese
over a delicate white cauliflower,
or field mushrooms
steaming in porcelain,

then watch us eat, relishing,
smoking her umpteenth cigarette,
glamorous, perfumed, starved,
and going to die.

The King of Britain's Daughter[16] (extract)

Day after day
a starling comes to my hand,
both of us small birds at a window
he, with a dark rainbow
in every feather, takes seed
and crumbs from me,
touches my hand like rainfall

and I tell my name until
he holds its two syllables
of water in his throat
two pearls to bear across the sea
on a prevailing westerly.
I throw him into the wind
calling 'Branwen, Branwen'
to the far horizon.

---

16. The giant Bendigeidfran, also known as Brân, son of Llŷr, was king of the island of Britain. Matholwch, king of Ireland, married Branwen, daughter of Llŷr. For a year she was happy, until the Irish Court became troubled by an old grievance against Wales. Matholwch's brothers demanded vengeance and Branwen was driven from the King's chamber to work in the kitchens. There she reared a starling and taught it to speak her name, and it flew to Wales to find her brother. When he knew of her sorrow, Bendigeidfran set off in a rage across the Irish Sea with a fleet of ships. In the ensuing battle all but seven men were killed. Branwen was brought home to Wales, where she died of grief. (Poet's note) The story of Branwen is told in the *Mabinogi*.

Jane Edwards b. 1938

Gwreiddiau

Ti'n drist, medda fo.
Y felan,
medda fi.
Fy mai i, medda fo.
Y lle 'ma,
medda fi:
Pob ffordd
yn arwain
allan.
Dihangfa, medda fo,
dyna ydi mynd am dro.
Adnabod,
medda fi,
Syllu ar betha cyfarwydd
Gwybod am ffinia
Bod yn rhan.
Ti'n siarad am Fôn, medda fo,
Bro mebyd,
medda fi,
Hiraeth, medda fo
Gwae
medda fi,
Pwn cael fy nghau a ngwasgu
fy nhagu a'm mygu gan
wreiddiau.

Roots

You're sad, says he.
Depressed,
I say.
My fault, says he.
It's this place,
I say:
Every road
leads
away.
An escape, says he,
that's what a walk's for.
Recognition,
I say,
Looking at familiar things
Knowing the limits
Being a part of it.
You're talking about Môn, he says,
Native patch,
I say,
Homesickness, says he
Pain
I say,
The burden of being closed in and squeezed
strangled and choked by
roots.

Christine Evans (b. 1943)

Second Language
For Carys P., Carys T., Elena, Manon, Nia and Teyrnon

I watch their faces rise to meet me
from the green depths of a culture
older than I can fathom. They glide
as if weighted by dreams or water

through my lessons, taking notes,
assiduously handing in assignments
in good time, browsing gravely
through all the books I offer, *thanking* me –

and all the time I feel I could be
beguiling selkie people to the land
to the bright amnesiac desert air
where I burn off my life without blossoming.

Five girls and a boy riding a name out of myth
whose language fills the mouth like fruit
who have grown in the delicate light
of an old walled garden that was once the world.

Manon, whom I see in jet and amber
accepting tribute, was the first
tangled in the word-lures, drawn out
to stand beside me with her colours brittling.

She claims she heard no echoes, never sang
in her own language. Now the others hover

offering in devout, tentative palms
iridescence from the inside of their minds.

In their calm faces I can find no clues
that they are still at ease in their own skins
that dredging for this voice has drowned no other
and my teaching has not made them strangers.

Tide

> First, seepage, then, flux:
> as the great heart pumps and sucks
> every inlet whispers.

Myxomatosis

Once set, he had to keep on
killing rabbits that summer on the island,
a moment's sharpness in his hands
seeming kinder than three days' long dying
in that heat. But though they crouched
so openly for death
they screamed stronger than babies
and struggled like wet cats. Bucks
fought drunkenly but the very young
with no resistance in them were the worst.

He had to try to smash their pain
with sticks and stones, inexpert jabs
edge-handed, at the tender nape.
Swinging them head-down against
a wall acted out atrocity he'd glimpsed
on some old news film of Vietnam.

In the end, taught himself a trick:
blunt to the sharp, starved arch
of the backbone, the swollen, suppurating head
he felt noose-fingered for the small hot pulse
and stopped it. Each corpse

he laid carefully aside to be stripped clean.
For a few weeks, even from the sea
the island breathed a foulness
until, two days before he left,
the weather broke. Warm rain
softened the dead flesh, washing it out
with its swarming crews
leaving only scattered vertebrae
the small white cogs of suppleness
to find their new connections in the earth
or wait, numb as shells
for moonless winter nights
to smooth them out completely.
The Friday that he left, he was fourteen.

Llŷn

Skies tower here, and we are small.

Winters, we sleep on a flap of land
in a dark throat. We taste the salt
of its swallow. Huge cold breaths
hurtle over, cascade down
till we feel the house hunch.

Along the northern edge, the rocks
go on holding on
but taught obedience by ice, the clays
of the southern shore slide palely under.

Christine Evans (b. 1943)

When morning comes at last
houses sit up with pricked ears
on reefs of land the black tide
leaves, or sidle crab-wise
to the lane, their small squashed faces
giving nothing of their thoughts away.

In summer, flowers loosening with seed
reach out to fingerstroke
cars passing in the long sweet dusk.
Hay-meadows sigh. Pearl-pale
in the bracken on the headland
shorn ewes step delicate
and wary as young unicorns.

The sea we look out over is a navel
the wrinkled belly-button
of an older world: after dark
like busy star-systems, the lights
of Harlech, Aberystwyth, Abergwaun
wink and beckon. The sun's gone down
red as a wound behind Wicklow.
A creaking of sail away
Cernyw and Llydaw wait.

Once, here was where what mattered
happened. A small place
at the foot of cliffs of falling light;
horizons that look empty.
If we let ourselves believe it,
fringes.

(Cernyw and Llydaw = Welsh names for Cornwall and Brittany)

Nesta Wyn Jones (b. 1946)

Dawns y Sêr

Os mynni weld byth bythoedd,
Sylla ar sglein y sêr.

Ynddynt mae patrymau
Hŷn na'n hamserlen ni
Yn iasau oesol.
O graffu,
Gwelwn hen oleuadau
Sy'n gasgliadau
   Yn gyfanweithiau cyfnewidiol;
Cytserau pefriog
Yn taflu golwg pŵl
I oleuo ein nosau ni.

Bod a darfod.
Bydoedd di-ben-draw
Yn anfon pelydr, ar hap,
Cyn chwalu'n chwilfriw
– a hyn fyrddiynau, fyrddiynau chwil
Yn ôl – ymlaen
Ymhell – yn agos
I ffwrdd – tuag atom
Yn affwysedd y gwacter mawr
A'u patrwm
Fel gemau gwasgaredig
Yn llonyddwch effro
Ar nenfwd sgrin ein synhwyrau.

Sylla i fyw fy llygaid.
Hwn yw'r byth bythoedd
Sy'n syfrdan ar fy ngwefus.

Dance of the stars

If you'd like to behold forever-and-forever,
Then gaze at the gleam of the stars.

In them are patterns,
Older than our timelines,
Perpetual pulsations.
Looking hard we see ancient luminaries
That are compilations,
    Shifting compositions;
Scintillating constellations
Casting a faint glance
To illuminate our nights.

Persisting and perishing.
Worlds without end
Sending a ray, at random,
Before disintegrating
—and this, myriads, reeling myrians
Of years ago—yet to come
Far off—close by
Away from us—approaching
In the great void's abyss,
Their patterns
Like scattered gems
An attentive stillness
On our senses' ceiling screen.

Gaze deep into my eyes.
This is the forever-and-ever
Dumbfounded on my lips.

[Translated by Joseph P. Clancy]

Ffarwél y twrch daear

Rwyt ti wedi mynd, y melfed,
I'r bur hoff bau
   Ar draws yr afon
    I'r gweryd
I ble bynnag y bydd tyrchod yn mynd
I fagu adenydd
Ond – dyma dy law.

Esgyrn bach gwynion ar bincws melfed y mwsog,
Ewinedd hirion Mandarin,
Cefn llaw fach sgwâr
Yn blethwaith o esgyrn cywrain,
Asgwrn braich,
Asgwrn ysgwydd . . .

Llaw fach brysur y pridd
Bellach yn fodfedd helaeth o
Lonyddwch.

Onid fel hyn y daw i'n byd
Ysgerbydau anweledig,
Llygod, ystlumod, tyrchod,
Wedi eu lapio mewn modfeddi o flew,
Pob un yn berffaith
Yn ôl y patrwm?
Miloedd ar filoedd o esgyrn ifori
Yn gwau o'r golwg yn y cysgodion
Heb i ni eu gweld –
   Heb ddod i'n golwg ni,
    Ni, yr esgyrn dwylath.

Nesta Wyn Jones (b. 1946)

Goodbye to the mole

You've gone, my velvet one,
To that dear and lovely country
Over Jordan
To the Grave –
Wherever moles go to grow wings.
But look, here's your hand!

White on a pincushion of moss,
Little bones on velvet,
With the long Mandarin nails,
Small square back of a hand
Like wickerwork of accurate bones,
Arm bone,
Shoulder bone …

Little hurrying hand of the soil
Now just a broad inch
Of quiet.

Don't the invisible skeletons
Of mice – bats – moles –
Come like this to our world,
Each wrapped
With its inch of fur
Perfect
In its own fashion?
Thousands and thousands –
Ivory bones
Out of sight in the shadows,
Warp and weft –
      On us (the six-foot skeletons)
      They don't impinge.

[Translated by Tony Conran]

Mêl Taid Cyplau
*(Ar ôl gweld dau grwybr gwenyn ar y wal mewn
tŷ bwyta yng Nghorris yn addurn i ddieithriaid
– un yn wyn a newydd, a'r llall yn dangos
prysurdeb hafau a fu.)*

Beth ŵyr y rhain amdanynt
Nac amdanom ninnau
A brofodd y mêl hwnnw gynt
Pan oedd cwch gwenyn
Yn wynder a grynai yng ngwres yr haul?

Crwybr gwenyn . . .
Pob cell dan ei gloyw sêl –
Melyster y cof
Yma, fesul hecsagon, yn y gwêr brau.

Hen fêl.
Hen wenyn.
Hen flodau.
Hen hafau . . .
Diferion difyrrwch.

Su cysurlon eu hadenydd
A ddychwel yn dryloywon drwy niwl y blynyddoedd.
Gwelaf draed yn glanio,
Yn dringo print du petalau
Ac yna'n ailymddangos
Wysg eu cefnau
Yn llwch melyn drostynt –
Dwyn yr aur o dywyllwch.

Taid's Honey
*(After seeing two honeycombs on the wall of a restaurant in
Corris as decoration for visitors, one white and new, the other
showing the activity of summers past. 'Taid' and 'Nain' are
North Welsh for 'Grandfather' and 'Grandmother'.)*

What do they know of them
Or of us, for that matter,
Who tasted that honey
Once, when a beehive
Was a whiteness that shimmered in the warmth of the sun?

Honeycomb…
Every cell, brightly sealed —
The sweetness of memory, hexagon by hexagon,
Here, in the fragile wax.

Long-ago honey.
Long-ago bees.
Long-ago blossoms.
Long-ago summers…
Trickles of delight.

The comforting hum of their wings
Comes back, transparent, through the mist of the years.
I see feet alighting,
Climbing the black print of petals
And then reappearing.
Backwards,
Covered in yellow dust —
Bearing gold out of darkness.

Gwrando ar eu grŵn
Nes i frychni haul ddisgyn eilwaith
Fel paill dros fy nhrwyn . . .
Suant heibio
I ddirgrynu yng nghalonnau llond gweirglodd
                                          o flodau . . .

Yn y bwtri oer yn nhŷ Nain
Mae aroglau llefrith cynnes
Heb ei hidlo
Yn hufennu ymylon bwcedi'r cysgodion,
Aroglau myniawyd y bugail
Yn amlinell ddu yn erbyn ffenest glir,
Cyrtans lês diamser yn siffrwd –
Ac aroglau mêl,
Hen fêl,
Yn diferu yn araf
I lawr
O grwybr y gorffennol.

Listening to their droning
Till freckles fall once more
Like pollen across my nose…
They murmur past
To throb in the hearts of a meadowful of flowers.

In Nain's house, in the cold pantry,
There is the sense of warm milk,
Unfiltered,
Creaming the rims of shadowy buckets.
The scent of geraniums,
Black silhouettes against a bright window
    — Timeless lace curtains whispering —
And the scent of honey,
Long-ago honey,
Slowly trickling
Down
From the honeycomb of the past.

[Translated by Joseph P. Clancy]

Blodeuwedd

*(Y ferch a wnaed o flodau
– erwain, banadl, a deri).*

Meddylia di am wlad
Heb gaeau na therfynau
A honno'n llawn o flodau . . .

Blodau mân, brau i bellteroedd
Yn ymestyn am yr haul
Ar goesau main –
Milddail a chlychlys a phys llygod,
Brenhines y weirglodd, hefyd,
A'r haul yn drwm o aroglau neithdar
A sïon pryfed.

Dyna pryd
Y daeth Gwydion i gerdded yn y gwlith
A dotio atyn nhw
Nes i'w harddwch droi'n golofn niwlog
Ac anadlu o'i flaen o
Yn ferch oer, dlos.

Yna, ryw fin nos, pan oedd y blodau golau
Yn llachar a llonydd fel ysbrydion
Yng ngwyll y gwyfynnod,
Llithrodd dylluan wen druan
Fel atgof haf –
Hedfan yn fud o dywyllwch eithaf y goedwig
I glwydo ar silff fy ffenest
A'i dau lygad di-syfl
Yn herio'r inc i lifo dros y memrwn.

Blodeuwedd

*(The woman made of flowers –
meadowsweet, broom, and oakleaves).*

Imagine a country
Without meadows or boundaries
Full of flowers...

Pale, frail flowers for miles
Reaching for the sun
On slender stems—
Yarrow and harebells and vetches,
Meadowsweet, also,
And the sun heavy with the scent of nectar
And the buzz of insects.

It was then
That Gwydion came to walk in the dew
And doted on them
Until their beauty became a misty column
And breathed before him
A cold, beautiful maiden.

Then, one evening, when the light flowers
Shone still like spirits
In the twilight of the moth,
A poor white owl glided
Like a summer memory,
Flying silently from the utter darkness of the forest
To perch on my window sill
Its eyes unblinking,
Challenging the ink to flow across the parchment.

[Translated by Joseph P. Clancy]

Ymwrthod â geiriau
(yn ninas Manceinion)

Does dim defnydd i chi, bellach.

Gosodaf chwi yn oleuadau glas ar adeiladau –
Tyrau bach crwn, glas uwchben archfarchnad anferthol
A lle i un fil ar bymtheg o deiars i barcio bob dydd.

Rhoddaf chwi'n ddyddiad ar arhosfan bws: un naw tri dim
Ac yn dŵr eglwys, a adawyd yn addurn pan symudwyd hi.

Gosodaf chwi yn bont Fecano goch dros gamlas,
Yn goed sy'n ymestyn bysedd i'r nos mewn Parc Eco.

Eich gosod ynghlwm wrth draed blinedig y farchnad
A pheri i chwi wrando ar waedd y sawl sy'n gwerthu
Big Issue.

Ewch, cerddwch yn eich dillad gorau i'r Opera
Neu sefwch yn stond wrth gadwyni'r hanner-cerflun
Sy'n tynnu, tynnu wrth angor y ddaear.
Dawnsiwch ar ôl y tramiau –
Prynwch flodau –
Gwyliwch, gwyliwch wynebau'r byd yn mynd heibio
Cyn cripian yn flinedig i olrhain, ar reiliau,
Drefn o-chwith y diwrnod.

Daliwch drên o Bicadilly . . .
Ewch! Ewch o 'ngolwg i.

Cerwch adra!

Nesta Wyn Jones (b. 1946)

Renouncing words
(in Manchester)

You're no use any more.

I place you like blue lights on buildings –
Little, round, blue turrets above an enormous supermarket
With room for sixteen thousand tyres to park every day.

I put you as a date on a bus stop: nineteen thirty
And on a church tower, left behind as a decoration when
                               the church was moved.

I place you as a red Meccano bridge over a canal,
As trees extending fingers into the night in an Eco-park.

I place you at the tired feet of the market
Making you listen to the cry of the *Big Issue* seller.

Go, walk in your best clothes to the Opera
Or stand stock-still by the chains of the half-statue
Which tugs, tugs at the earth's anchor.
Dance in the wake of the trams –
Buy flowers –
Watch, watch the world's faces going past
Before crawling wearily to trace, along rails,
The topsy-turvey order of the day.

Catch a train from Piccadilly . . .
Go! Get out of my sight.

Go home!

Hen Baentiad

*(Snow at Louveciennes, neu ran ohono,
gan Alfred Sisley 1839-1899)*

Hi ydi hi.
Yn cerdded drwy'r eira rhwng y muriau
Dan goed sy'n drwm gan eira –
Hi ydi hi.
Sgarff am ei phen,
Sgert laes ddu,
A basged siopa ar ei braich . . .

Mae hi'n cyrraedd at y drws yn y mur . . .
Ie, hi *ydi* hi!
      Gwaeddaf!
      Rhedaf drwy drwch yr eira –
      Gwaeddaf!
Ond mynd y mae hi
Heb droi i wenu
Na chodi llaw . . .
      Mae cymylau eira yn drymion uwchben
      A'r coed afalau yn gwyro dan eu beichiau . . .
Cerdded y mae hi
(Heb fynd, ychwaith)
Cerdded yn ddistaw yn yr eira gwyn
Ei thraed yn prin symud . . .
Petrusaf –
Ai cysgod yw hi?

  Cysgod cant oed.
  Blotyn o ddu
  Yng nghanol anhrefn pwrpasol
  Du ac oren
  Rhyw artist a fu.

An old painting
(Snow at Louveciennes, or a detail of it,
by Alfred Sisley 1839-1899)

It's her.
Walking through the snow between the walls
Beneath trees heavy with snow –
It's her.
A scarf on her head,
A smooth black skirt,
And a shopping basket on her arm . . .

She's reaching the door in the wall . . .
Yes, it's *her*!
> I cry out!
> I run through the snowdrifts –
> I cry out!

But go she must
Without turning to smile
Nor waving goodbye . . .
> The snow clouds are heavy up above
> And the apple trees are bending under their
> > load . . .

She is walking
(And yet not leaving)
Walking silently in the white snow
Her feet barely moving . . .
I hesitate –
Is she a shadow?

A hundred-year-old shadow.
A black mark
In the midst of the purposeful
Black and orange anarchy
Of some artist from the past.

Capel Celyn[17]

Fe aeth dydd o haf dan y dyfroedd . . .

Dydd o haf yng Nghae Fadog
A'r cymylau'n gwibio'n uchel
Uwch canghennau pendrwm y coed.
Ninnau'n blant ar fuarth dieithr,
Dan ehediad gwenoliaid,
Yn chwarae cuddio
O gwmpas ydlan a beudy a chutiau moch.
Canlyn Dafydd bach o gwmpas ei waith, am sbel,
Ac yna blino, a dilyn ein trwynau
Yma a thraw, ar antur.
Naid, toc, dros y ffos grimp
Â dyrnaid o flodau melyn
I'r tŷ
At Dodo Nel
A'n dilynai i dywyllwch y gegin
Dan chwerthin
Am mai chwyn oedden nhw, medde hi.

Eistedd ar glustog anghyfarwydd
I wrando ar sgwrs ffermwyr, ymddiddan perthnasau,
A chlywed tipian cloc
A su cacwn yn y gwres
Pan ddoi ysbaid dawel, ar dro,
A rhyw sisial gloyw ym mrigau'r coed . . .

Fe aeth dydd o haf ar ddifancoll,
A chwmwl isel sy'n sgubo'r dyfroedd.
Does yma ond cŵyn y don
Yn torri
Ar draethell anadferadwy.

Nesta Wyn Jones (b. 1946)

Capel Celyn[17]

A summer day has gone beneath the waters…

A summer day in Cae Fadog,
The clouds flitting high
Above the trees' heavy-handed branches.
And we, children in a strange farmyard,
Under a flight of swallows,
Playing hide-and-seek
Round hay barn and cowshed and pigsties.
Trailing after Dafydd Bach at his chores, for a time,
And then growing bored, and following our noses
Here and there, at loose ends.
A jump, soon, across the dried-up ditch
With a fistful of yellow flowers
Towards the house
And Dodo Nel
Who followed us into the darkness of the kitchen
Laughing
Because, she said, they were weeds.

Sitting on an unfamiliar cushion
To listen to farmers' talk, relatives' voices,
 And hearing the ticking of the clock
And bumble bees's hum in the heat
When a quiet spell came, now and then,
And a shimmering whisper in the treetops…

A summer day has gone for good,
And a low cloud sweeps the waters.
There's nothing here but the wave's lament
Breaking
On an irretrievable strand.

[Translated by Joseph P. Clancy]

---

17. Capel Celyn was the village drowned in the construction of a dam at Tryweryn, near Bala, in the early 1960s.

Cwch

Ar ehangder y môr
   cwch
  yn siglo, siglo
  heb angor, heb rwyf
yn ddi-baent,
yng ngolau'r lleuad.

Sgriffiadau a tholciau ar hyd-ddo i gyd
Bu ei bren yn froc môr
a wyngalchwyd gan wylanod
ar ryw draeth anhygyrch
cyn i fysedd y llanw ymestyn amdano
a'i hawlio eilwaith
i siglo, siglo
yn ddi-baent, yn ddi-bwynt
ar donnau.

Cymylau llonydd.
Lleuad.
A'r môr yn ganfas gloyw.
                    Dim yn symud
                     ond sigl y cwch
                  sy'n nesu
              nesu
               fel ysbryd
             at ymyl y llun
           cyn llithro
          fel cysgod
       ohono.

Boat

On the sea's expanse
    a boat
  swaying, swaying
  anchorless, oarless
unpainted,
in the moonlight.

Scrapes and bumps all over it
Its wood was flotsam
whitewashed by seagulls
on some remote shore
before the fingers of the tide reached for it
and possessed it once again
to sway, sway
paintless, pointless
on the waves.

Still clouds.
A moon.
And the sea a bright canvas.
                    Nothing moves
                      but for the boat's sway
                  which gets closer
                closer
              like a ghost
            to the edge of the picture
          before slipping
        like a shadow
      out of it.

Glenda Beagan (b. 1948)

Blodeuwedd

Lust was the loom
I was woven on
the man who webbed me
knowing nothing
human. Frost
were the eyes
that pulled me
into life for Lleu,
but when he was gone
I was lonely for Gronw
and how was that wrong?

I am glad to be free
to flit among
dank trees. Smells
are meanings for me;
scuttlings speak.
Out of coppiced hazels I skim
into blue light, the moon fingering
me. My feathers are glad to be
dipped in wind. After my catchings
I sit on a bough and clean myself.
So how is this punishment?

Vixen

motherhood peels me bare
like a willow wand
some small child scrapes in the road
or throws in the pond

motherhood aches me pale
I bleed with my child's wound
and hurt with his friend's unfriendliness
I climb with his bruise

motherhood grows me brave
now no mere woman nor wife
the vixen who fights for her cubs
will fight for her life

Shaman

To find a speech, a tongue
to fit interstices
of this land worn close as a skin.

To climb among the blackthorn, cold
cupping of bud white
on black twigs; a scent

is there thin and shining
as cowslips in floodweather, under
skies of dark geese, deep eddies

of cloud. Here, the high bank
crumbles; fragile roots are prinked
with gobbets of red earth.

What is the sound this land makes
at the far reach of March,
with the lengthening sun, a cleanness

of fresh sap? The speech
of the shaman is locked in the water web
where rivers meet; slowdeep

valley wanderer of the wide meander,
still chuckling mountain freshet,
spate river, riding on pebbles,

not mud, blending watery selves,
distinct as people, below Rhydyddauddwr.
Incompatible are they; slow sluggish

dark flow, quick moody swift
young sprinter to the sea? It was
like this a millennium earlier

at the crossing place. Hear heavy wains,
the whinny of horses, the voices in the dusk;
chill calls, that Norman French nasality,

Tegeingl mingling Mercian – vowels broadening,
lengthening, but never merging with the plaited water
nor interweaving on a loom of water.

The threads remain; sharp, several, sure.

Marged Dafydd [Meg Elis] (b. 1950)

Y Milwr
(i Manon)

Syllu
a ffens rhyngoch.

Iaith,
gwlad,
carolau
yn eich clymu.

A gwn,
taflegryn,
ffens y comin
yn rhagfur rhyngoch.

Brechfa
Llandwrog
a'r Rhondda'n cwrdd.

Ac uwchben mae'r cwmwl.

The Soldier
(for Manon)

Looking at each other,
a fence between you.

Language,
land,
carols
connect you.

And gun,
missile,
the Common's fence
a barrier between you.

Brechfa
Llandwrog
and the Rhondda meet.

And above hangs the cloud.

Einir Jones (b. 1950)

Gwraig I

Gwraig
a chanddi gorff
fel torth.
Bara gwyn
yw ei chnawd.

Burum
wedi ei roi
yng nghwpanau ei dwylo
yn troi o fod yn ddim
ac yn llenwi.

Blawd gwyn.
A rhoi y burum yn y pant
sydd yn ei ganol.

Gadael iddi
sefyll.
Cadach gwyn amdani
wrth y tân;
codi yn ara deg
yn grwn
yn llond y bowlen.

Tylino,
crasu yn y popty
hithau'n caledu,
ac yn sadio
yn gynnes,
codi chwant
gyda'i hanadl.

Woman I

A woman
with a body
like a loaf.
Her flesh is
white bread.

Yeast
placed
in the cups of her hands
turns from nothing,
into fullness.

White flour.
Placing the yeast in the hollow
in the middle.

Letting her
stand.
A white cloth around her
by the fire;
rising slowly
roundly
filling the bowl.

Kneading,
baking in the oven
she's hardening,
and solidifying
warmly,
her breath
provoking desire.

Dwylo yn dod
ac yn rhwygo crystyn,
cloddio i ganol y
cnawd
efo cyllell
finiog.

Ei bwyta
i gyd

a thaflu'r
briwsion
i'r adar.

Gwraig II

Yr oedd ganddi freichia,
bronna,
bol
a chlunia
fel gwely plu.
Fe fedrai suddo i mewn iddi
pan fynnai
a thynnu
plancedi,
cynfasa,
clustoga
ac eiderdown ei chorff
drosto yn dynn
fel plentyn yn y nos
yn cuddio dan 'dillad:

Hands coming
and tearing a crust,
digging into the centre
of the flesh
with a sharp
knife.

Eating her
all up

and throwing
the crumbs
to the birds.

Woman II

She had arms,
breasts,
a belly
and knees
like a feather bed.
He could sink into her
when he wanted to
and pull
blankets,
sheets,
pillows
and the eiderdown of her body
over him tightly
like a child in the night
hiding under the bedclothes:

weithia
dim ond weithia
y bydda fo'n teimlo
fel pry
wedi tresmasu
a ffeindio ei hun
yng nghell pidyn y gog
yn sownd;
yn cael ei sugno
yn ara deg
i mewn 'w chorff.

Y fam fawr
yn cynnwys ynddi'i hun
fel y frenhines
wedi un daith
ddigon o egni
i gynhyrchu
llin
cyfan;

yn chwyrnu yn dawel
dan y plancedi
gan ei ddal yn dynn
fel tedibêr
yn feis
ei breichia
a fynta
heb falio mwy
am falio
yn ymlacio,
ac er gwaethaf siarad
pobol ddoeth, wybodus
fusneslyd
y byd hwn
y cysgu yn braf
tan y bora.

sometimes
just sometimes
he would feel
like an insect
which had trespassed
and found himself
in a Venus Flytrap,
stuck;
being sucked
slowly
into her body.

The great mother
containing within herself
like a queen
after a journey
enough energy
to produce
a whole
tribe;

snoring quietly
under the blankets
holding him tight
like a teddy bear
in the vice
of her arms
and him
not caring any more
about caring
relaxing,
and despite the talk
of all those people who were
wise, knowledgeble
busybodies
he slept soundly.

Angau

Mi rydan ni yn cysgu efo angau bob nos;
yn troi ato fo cyn cloi llygaid
ac yn rhoi sws nos da;

mi wnaiff o hyd yn oed
afael yn eich llaw
a'i gwasgu'n gynnes;

mi wnaiff o anadlu
yn eich clust chwith
(y glust bethma)
a rhoi sws i'ch gwddw chi;

mi wnaiff o redeg ei law i lawr
eich corff
yn ara deg.

Gwyliwch o
pan fydd o'n dechrau datod
rhubannau'r gïau.

Trowch eich hun i ffwrdd;

a chysgwch
yn anniddig
tan y bora.

Death

We sleep with death every night;
we turn towards him before shutting our eyes
and give a goodnight kiss;

he will even
hold your hand
and squeeze it warmly;

he'll breathe
in your ear the left one
(the whatyoucall one)
and give you a kiss on the neck;

he'll run his hand down
your body
slowly.

Watch him
when he begins to undo
the sinews' ribbons.

Turn yourself away;

and sleep
uneasily
till morning.

Byji

Mae trio deud wrth rhywun
be ddaru chi 'deimlo
ar ennyd fach eneiniedig
yn eich hanes chi'ch hun
fel trio dysgu byji
i siarad.

Sefyll
(ne ista)
am hydoedd
wrth gell
y cnawd
a deud yr un profiad
yn union yr un geiria
drosodd
a throsodd.

Wel, o'r diwedd
a chitha wedi hen laru ar y profiad
ar yr un hen eiria
ar dôn y llais
ac yn barod i regi y rhigwm
ac yn meddwl yn eich meddwl
(y syniad yn ffurfio yn ara
fel cneuen
ond mor sydyn â'r ystum
o'i thorri),
"Reit, 'dwi'n rhoi fyny,
'dwi'n mynd o'ma."

Ac mi ddeudith yr hen fyji druan
yr union beth
oeddech chi'n crefu arno i'w ddweud.

Budgie

Trying to tell someone
what you felt
at one tiny little moment
in the history of yourself
is like trying to teach a budgie
to talk.

Standing
(or sitting)
for ages
by the cage
of the flesh
and telling the same experience
in precisely the same words
over
and over again.

Well, at last
When you're completely fed up with the experience
With the same old words
With the tone of your voice
And ready to curse the rhyme
And thinking to yourself
(the idea forming slowly
like a nut
but as sudden as the gesture
of breaking it),
"Right, I'm giving up,
I'm out of here."

And the poor old budgie will say
The exact same thing
You were begging him to say all the time.

Efallai nad ond
i gau eich ceg chi
am ei fod o wedi blino,

ond be bynnag ydi'r rheswm
mae o'n gwneud i chi deimlo
fel dofwr llewod,
ac mi rydach chi'n cario 'mlaen
am sbel bach eto.

Sgwennais i 'Rioed

Sgwennais i 'rioed gerdd dda.
Cerdd y medrwn edrych yn ôl arni
pan fydda hi'n goelcerth
a honno'n dal
heb ei difa.

Er i mi dynnu fy 'sgidia
mwd oedd dan draed
a gwynt oedd y llais.

Yn y tywod
'doedd gen i ddim syniad
lle i agor craig.

Yn y nos,
'fedrwn i ddim
ond palfalu
fel pawb arall.

Perhaps only because
He wants to shut you up
Because he's tired,

But whatever the reason
He makes you feel
Like a lion-tamer,
And you carry on
For a little while longer.

I never wrote

I never wrote a good poem.
A poem I could look back at
and see that it was a bonfire
which burnt and burnt
and didn't go out.

Though I took off my shoes
there was mud underfoot
and the voice was the wind.

In the sand
I had no idea
where I could open a rock.

In the night,
I couldn't do anything
but grope
like everyone else.

'Fedrais i erioed arwain
tyrfa gyfa
o bryfed genwair,
heb sôn am bobol,
allan o'u poen
a'u trybini.

Mi ddringais
i ben uchaf mynydd
ond mi roedd y niwl yn rhy dew
i mi weld bawd fy nhroed
hyd yn oed.

A dyma fi'n stopio
ac yn gweiddi crïo
ac yn y waedd honno
pan oedd fy ngwyneb
i hylla
pan nad oedd ots gen i
sut olwg oedd arnai
a phan oeddwn i wedi rhoi i fyny
bob dim

mi welais
sut beth
oedd y gerdd.

Einir Jones (b. 1950)

I never could lead
a whole horde
of worms,
not to mention people,
out of their suffering
and their troubles.

I climbed
to the top of the mountain
but the fog was too thick
for me even to see
my big toe.

And then I stopped
and howled with tears
and in that howl
when my face was ugliest
when I couldn't care less
what I looked like
and when I'd given up
everything

I saw
what sort of thing
the poem was.

Y Goeden Geirios Gynnar

Amser.

Gobled y goeden yn wag.
Amlinelliad goleuni ar frigau'r gwydr
yn siap gloyw.

Amser.

Tywalltiad sydyn o flodau
yn sblincian yn fân
a goglais

gan godi'n stribedi
yn llinynnau igam-ogam
o'r ochrau brau.

Amser.

Ffroenau'r awel
yn llawn o'r ewyn.
Pinc
yn brothio,
swigod o liw
yn bostio
ar rimyn yr awel
fain.

Amser.

Tawelodd y tawch.
Diffoddodd y cyffro.
Suddodd y goleuni
yn ôl ar ei golyn.
Syrthiodd.

Amser.

Â'r bwrlwm bywiog
wedi egru'n ddail.

The Early Cherry Tree

Time.

The tree's goblet empty.
The outline of light on the glass branches
a glowing shape.

Time.

A sudden outpouring of flowers
minutely glittering
and tickling

rising up in strips
zig-zag lines
from the tender sides.

Time.

The breath of the breeze
full of blossom.
Pink
frothing,
coloured bubbles
bursting
on the sharp edge of the
breeze.

Time.

The vapour cleared.
The energy quenched.
The light sank
Back on its hinge.
It fell.

Time.

The fizzing frenzy
Sours to leaves.

Lili

Hen flodyn hyll ydi Lili.

Mae hi'n ymddangos o'r gwyrdd
yn sydyn
fel amnaid angau,
ac yn casglu rheinciau
o bryfed
yn ei bol.

Pan blygo'r nos i'w mynwes
bydd y rhain yn hishiad
fel chwrligwgan
o'i mewn
fel pys mewn tun,
neu bres mewn bocs dyn dall.

Mae ei hwyneb trwm a chnawdol
yn atgoffa rhywun
am dai rhai gwragedd rhydd eu moes,
a'r golau coch
yn wincian
o'i chanol noeth
di-fai, di-liw.

Cynhesrwydd swrth didaro
sydd iddi
hi.
Ar eirch a phethau felly
mae'n gloywi'n bwdr wyrdd-olau
yn y tywyllwch
ar ganol dydd.

Lily

A lily's an ugly old flower.

She appears from the greenery
all of a sudden
like death beckoning,
and she gathers scores
of insects
in her belly.

When night bends over her bosom
these buzz and hiss
like a whirligig
inside her
like peas in a tin,
or coins in a blind man's box.

Her heavy, fleshy face
reminds you
of the houses of some women of easy virtue,
with the red light
winking
from her naked middle,
faultless, colourless.

A sultry apathetic warmth
comes from
her.
On coffins and suchlike
she glows light green and rotten
in the darkness
at midday.

Drewdod pur
sy'n chwant am ddiweirdeb,
yn ffals a gloyw
yn hoyw gynnes
mewn gwyrddwyn oer,
yn dalp o harddwch
marw.

Lladd-dŷ

Diferion gwaed
o lori y machlud
wrth ddrws lladd-dŷ yr awyr
yn disgyn yn araf
o yddfau cymylau'r hwyr
cyn tatshio
a goferu
hyd y coed drain.

Blobiau
crynion
o be fu yn fyw
yn sownd
fel mwclis
ar linyn main
y drain.

Brefu
torcalon;
yr hogi yn codi dincod.
Yr haul yn mynd i lawr
ar ddiwedd dydd
ar ddiwedd haf
ac ogla'r gwaed
yn codi cyfog gwag
yn y gwynt.

A pure stink
that's a longing for chastity,
false and bright
warm and gay
in a cold green-white,
a heap of dead
beauty.

Slaughter-house

Drops of blood
from the sunset lorry
by the slaughter-house door the sky
dropping slowly
from the throats of the late clouds
and splashing
brimming
over the thorn trees.

Round
blobs
of what was once alive
stuck
like a necklace
on the thin wire
of the thorns.

The lowing
of heartbreak;
the sound of sharpening sets teeth on edge.
The sun going down
at the end of the day
at the end of the summer
and the smell of blood
drawing an empty retch
from the wind.

Menna Elfyn (b. 1951)

Cân y di-lais i British Telecom

'Ga i rif yng Nghaerdydd, os gwelwch . . .'

'Speak up!'

'GA I RIF YNG NGHAER-'

'Speak up – you'll have to speak up.'

Siarad lan, wrth gwrs, yw'r siars
i siarad Saesneg,
felly, dedfrydaf fy hun i oes
o anneall, o ddiffyg llefaru
ynganu, na sain na si
na goslef, heb sôn am ganu,
chwaith fyth goganu, llafarganu,
di-lais wyf, heb i'm grasnodau
na mynegiant na myngial.

Cans nid oes im lais litani'r hwyr,
dim llef gorfoledd boreol
nac egni cryg sy'n crecian, yn y cyfnos.
Atal dweud? Na. Dim siarad yn dew
dim byrdwn maleisus, na moliannu.

Ac os nad oes llef gennyf i
ofer yw tafodau rhydd fy nheulu,
mudanwyr ŷm, mynachod,
sy'n cyfrinia mewn cilfachau.

Song of the voiceless to British Telecom

'Ga i rif yng Nghaerdydd, os gwelwch . . .'

'Speak up!'

'GA I RIF YNG NGHAER-'

'Speak up – you'll have to speak up.'

'Speak up' is, of course,
the command to speak English.
I sentence myself to a lifetime
of sentences that make no sense.
No pronunciation, no annunciation,
inflection. I am infected
with dumbness. I can neither lampoon,
sing in tune; much less can I
intone. My grace-notes
are neither music nor mumble.

I am not heard at Evening Prayer
nor at triumphal Matins,
nor am I that voice in the dusk
that is husky but vibrant.

An impediment, then? No. No thick tongue,
no chip on my shoulder, a compulsion to please.
And if I am without speech
what of the fluency of my people?

Ym mhellter ein bod hefyd
mae iaith yr herwr
yn tresmasu, ei sang yn angel du,
gyrru'r gwaraidd – ar ffo.

Wrth sbio'n saff, ar y sgrin fach
gwelaf fod cenhedloedd mewn conglau mwy
yn heidio'n ddieiddo;
cadachau dros eu cegau,
cyrffiw ar eu celfyddyd,
alltudiaeth sydd i'w lleisiau,
a gwelaf fod yna GYMRAEG rhyngom ni.

A'r tro nesa y gofynnir i mi
'siarad lan',
yn gwrtais, gofynnaf i'r lleisydd
'siarad lawr',
i ymostwng i'r gwyleidd-dra
y gwyddom amdano, fel ein gwyddor.
Ac fel 'efydd yn seinio'
awgrymaf, nad oes raid wrth wifrau pigog,
bod i'r iaith 'wefrau perlog',
a chanaf, cyfathrebaf
mewn cerdd dant,
yn null yr ieithoedd bychain;
pobl yn canu alaw arall
ar draws y brif dôn,
er uched ei thraw,
Gan orffen bob tro
yn gadarn, un-llais,
taro'r un nodyn – a'r un nwyd,
gan mai meidrol egwan ein mydrau.

'A nawr, a ga i –
y rhif yna yng Nghaerdydd?'

We are mutes, Trappists,
conspirators in a corner.
The usurper's language pierces
to the very centre of our being,
a minister of darkness before whose tread
our civility must give ground.
From the safety of my television
I see nations forced into a hole,
possessors of nothing but their dispossession,
mufflers over their mouths,
their captive craft under curfew.
There is an injunction against their speech,
and I perceive it is Y GYMRAEG that we share.

So the next time I am commanded
to 'speak up'
deferring to the courtesy
that is our convention,
with like courtesy I will require the operator
to 'pipe down';
and like 'sounding brass'
I will suggest the superfluousness of barbed wire,
since our language has berylled wares.
I will sing and make contact
in *cynghanedd*, as the small nations do,
a people in counterpoint
to the leit-motif, dominant
though its pitch be,
ending each time on the same
obstinate monotone
with the same passionate concern
though mortally muted our metrics.

'A nawr, a ga i –
y rhif yna yng Nghaerdydd?'
[Translated by R. S. Thomas]

Y gneuen wag

Nid oedd fy nghorff eto'n wisgi
na gwinau fel y gollen hardd,
eithr coeden ifanc oeddwn
am fwrw cnau i ddynoliaeth,
a'u cnoi fyddai'n galed, unplyg,
a'u cadernid ym masgl eu cymeriad;
cyn amser rhoi, tynnwyd y gneuen
a'i thorri'n ddwy o'm mewn,
ac nid oedd yno ond crebachlyd ffrwyth
i'w daflu'n ôl i'r afon â dirmyg,
gan fy ngadael yn goeden ddiolud
ynghanol cyll ysblennydd.

Eucalyptus

*(Clywais fod arogl yr eucalyptus yn llenwi strydoedd Baghdad
yn ystod Rhyfel y Gwlff a bod olew'r goeden yn cael ei
ddefnyddio fel tanwydd am nad oedd trydan yn y ddinas).*

Cyn ei gweld yn Lisboa
nid oedd ond enw i mi,
ffisig gwella annwyd
fu'r losinen esgus
at rhyddhau'r frest
o'i thrydar.

Ond heddiw, llumanau yw'r petalau
sy'n cynnig gŵyl
i bawb yn ddiwahân,
coed hynaws
sy'n ffafrio na gwerin na gwlad.

The empty shell

Though my body was not ripe-shelled
or brown like the fine hazel,
still, as a young tree I wanted
to cast nuts for humanity –
the bite of them hard and true,
strength the character in their shells.
But before time, the nut was plucked,
broken in two inside me;
nothing but fruit shrivelled
and despised, thrown back to the river,
leaving me poverty stricken
in the midst of splendid hazels.

[Translated by Tony Conran]

Eucalyptus
*(I heard how the scent of the tree filled Baghdad
during the Gulf War, its oil being used to cook
with in the absence of electricity).*

Before I saw it in Lisboa
it was only a name to me –
the best medicine for a cold,
a pretend sweet
to free the chest
of chirping.

But today, those petals are banners:
they give the same
festival to everyone –
genial trees, that favour
no one people or land.

O'u gwraidd cyfyd gwres
olew yn ogleuo byd,
yn iro mewn cawg
faeth i deulu.

A'r eucalyptus euraid
fu'n ffrwtian yn ddi-feth
islaw ffrom yr holl ffrwydradau,
bu'n amgáu bwyd,
yn creu bwrdd bendithiol.

Onid i hyn y parhawn â bywyd;
o bryd parod i brydwedd,
rhythmau dŵr i'n gwddw,
mydrau maeth ar bob min?

A'r diferion a ollyngwyd
yn ffawd garedig dros anffodusion
gan ledu eu sawr –
mwy o rin sydd i'r rhoi
a'i ddogn yn rhoi digon.

A'r nos mor oer ag abo
eiliw o'r eucalyptus
sydd i'w glywed mewn cilfachau,
yn hel cyfrinachau
yng nghanol rhaib a rwbel.

Yr olew syml:
fu'n dal anadl cynhaliaeth
gan lathru goleuni
dros fywydau gloywddu.

Menna Elfyn (b. 1951)

Warmth rises from their roots –
oil lighting the world,
grease in a bowl
and a family fed.

The golden eucalyptus
spluttered, and did not fail.
Though all round hell exploded
it still compassed food,
creating a table of blessedness.

And isn't it for this we go on living
from ready meal to love-feast –
rhythms of water to our throat,
metres of nourishment on each lip?

Drops that once were released
as a kindly fate
for the unfortunate,
spread their odour –
richer in the giving,
and in every share of it, giving enough.

In a night cold as a corpse
it's the eucalyptus
that they smell, those hide-outs
and gathered fellowships
amid rape and rubble.

The simple oil
once kept me breathing,
now over blackened lives
shines like light.

[Translated by Tony Conran]

Siapiau o Gymru

Ei diffinio rown
ar fwrdd glân,
rhoi ffurf i'w ffiniau,
ei gyrru i'w gororau
mewn inc coch;
ac meddai myfyriwr o bant,
'It's like a pig running away';
wedi bennu chwerthin,
rwy'n ei chredu;
y swch gogleddol
yn heglu'n gynt
na'r swrn deheuol
ar ffo rhag y lladdwyr.

Siapiau yw hi siŵr iawn:
yr hen geg hanner rhwth
neu'r fraich laes ddiog
sy'n gorffwys ar ei rhwyfau;
y jwmpwr, wrth gwrs,
        ar ei hanner,
gweill a darn o bellen ynddi,
ynteu'n debyg i siswrn
parod i'w ddarnio'i hun;
cyllell ddeucarn anturiaethydd,
neu biser o bridd
craciedig a gwag.

A lluniau amlsillafog
yw'r tirbeth o droeon
a ffeiriaf â'm cydnabod
a chyda'r estron
sy'n ei gweld am yr hyn yw:

Menna Elfyn (b. 1951)

The shapes she makes

I was defining her
on a clean slate,
fleshing out her frontiers,
badgering her to her borders
in red ink;
when a foreign student said,
'It's like a pig running away';
laughing done with,
I believe her;
the northern snout
hoofing it faster
than her southern rump,
fleeing her slaughterers.

She's made of shapes, you know:
the slack old mouth, agape
or the lazy, lolling arm,
resting on its oars;
the jumper, of course,
       half-done,
wrapped around a bot of wool and the needles,
or else, she's a pair of scissors
ready to ribbon herself,
an adventurer's double-hafted knife,
or an earthen pitcher,
hollow and cracked.

She's polysyllabled pictures,
this inleted landmass
I swap with acquaintances
and with the foreigner
who sees her for what she is:

    ddigri o wasgaredig
    sy
    am
    fy
    mywyd
        fel bwmerang diffael yn mynnu
              mynnu
                ffeindio'i
            ffordd
          yn
        ôl
        at
    fy nhraed.

Pomgranadau

Bob hydref deuent at bomgranadau
a'u rhannu rhyngddynt, yn ddarnau,
mwynhau eu llygaid gwangoch
a'u celloedd yn llawn cellwair
a'r byd o'u cwmpas, yn gwirioni
derbyn aelodau'n arllwys eu llifeiriant,
cynulliad, addewidion llawn
oeddynt, ar wahân, cyn eu rhyddhau, o'u conglau.

Un dydd, cawsant gerydd
am eu bwyta mor gyhoeddus,
'ffrwyth i'w rannu yn y dirgel yw,'
meddai'r surbwch wrth eu gwylio;
gruddiau ffrwythau'n gwrido
nes torri'n wawch o chwerthin mewn dwrn.

comically scattered
who is,
on my life,
    like an unerring boomerang which wills
            wills
        its
      way
    back
  to
my
feet.

[Translated by Elin ap Hywel]

Pomegranates

In autumn, always pomegranates
to break between them, portions
relished for their rose-red eyes,
cells flowing with foolery
in a world infatuated.
They take each flood-drenched limb
brimful of promises,
prise each seed from its corner.

One day they were told off
for feasting so openly,
'They should do it in private,'
scowled someone sourly at the sight
of fruit's flushed cheeks bursting
to screams of laughter in their fists.

Un hydref, ag ef wrth ei hunan
rhythodd ar y ffrwythau
fu'n serchus hyd at benrhyddid,
celloedd arall a welodd, coch ei lygaid,
collodd awydd eu torri â chyllell ei hiraeth.

Meddyliodd am y cynrhon a'u cynllwyn.

Safodd yno'n syn
ac yn lle delwedd
ar lun angerdd
gwelodd –

gryndod a'i henw'n grenêd.

Diwinyddiaeth Gwallt

Deuthum ger dy fron â phlethiadau syml
yn forwyn goeslas, yn Fair na faliai
bod eu cadwynau'n glymau dan rubanau.
Un oedd fy nghorun, â'r gwallt a lithrai

dros sedd galed cysegr, yn ffrwst rhaeadrau,
a'u diferion yn tasgu wrth droi a disgyn
dros lintel dal cymun, ac yswn am ei deimlo
a'i blethu'n gywrain, llanw'r awr wrth estyn,

at ryfeddod genethig. Yn hafau o gyfrwyau
a garlamai ar fy ôl wrth gipio fy anadl,
rhedeg hyd y gelltydd a'r gwylltiaid o walltfeydd
yn herwa dros fochau nes troi'n destun dadl,

Then one autumn alone
he stared at the fruit
that had been such easy love,
saw other cells, the red of their eyes,
lost all his taste to slice them
with need's knife.

He thought of the conspiracy of the maggot,

stood dazed,
and where had been
the symbol of desire
he saw –

a quivering grenade.

[Translated by Gillian Clarke]

The Theology of Hair

I came before you with simple plaits,
a long-legged maid, a lass who couldn't care less
that her sheaves were all bound up with ribbons,
for wasn't the hair on my head like the hair which foamed

over the hard pew-back with a rustle like rivers,
drops shivering as it arced and fell
over the communion shelf, and I ached to touch it,
to twine it in patterns, to fill up that hour by reaching out
                              to a girlish wonder.

It made me think of summers full of imaginary ponies
galloping after me, taking my breath away
as I cantered over hills, and the banditti-like bangs
outlawed their way over my cheeks. There were arguments,

minnau'n ffoli ar ei egni. Eurwallt y forwyn
yn llithrig ysgathru 'nghnawd, a'i flys ar ryddid,
a weithiau trown yn ufudd mewn dull breninesgar
gan blannu dros glust, hanner llygad gwyddfid.

Pa aflwydd a ddaeth iddo? Hyd heddiw – tresi penrhydd
yw cyffro brwd ieuenctid nes plyga'n lled amharchus,
ai'r fforestydd dirgel ynddo oedd achos mawr y drysu
gan awdurdodol rai a'i drodd yn drwch anweddus?

Ac eto, Ysbryd Glân, oni roddaist in ei ddathlu:
y pennad gwallt. Yn gorun llawn. Yn dlysni,
I'w drin yn ddethol. Yn grychiog gnwd gusanau
pa anfoes oedd – dychmygion am gefnoethi

dros groen? Troi rhai ar dân? Ai atalnwyd llawn
i'w docio'n grop? Llyffethair ar lywethau
rhag disgyn ar fron. Rhag codi angerdd a'i hagor
gwalltdrylliad fu. Cael ynys neb ei gwefrau.

Coron Merch
(i Maura Dooley)

Coron geneth oedd y llen ar ei chorun,
fe godai gwallt ei phen,
i weled ar led, ar war, baradwys ohono,
gwrthryfel styfnig yn y gwynt.

Amdanaf innau, pengrwn own,
ym myddin y pensythwyr,

but I loved my hair's energy. Golden moss
like maidenhair stroked my skin, longing to escape
and sometimes, obediently, regally, I would tease
a kiss-curl like honeysuckle over one cheek.

Why that fate for it? To this day, youth loves
the life-force of hair, the way it kinks a little.
Was it the secret forest in it which fuddled the ones above?
They called it a dark thicket.

And yet, O Holy Spirit, didn't you give us the gift
of praising it, this headful of hair. This full crown, these tresses,
to be prettily dressed? What harm could there be
in this crinkly, kissable harvest? They imagined it

tumbling over naked backs, charging desire. But cropping –
a full stop to lust's sentence? Locks tied back from breasts.
To leash passion, there was a hair-wreck.
I washed up on a deserted and sensuous strand.

[Translated by Elin ap Hywel]

Crowning Glory
(for Maura Dooley)

A headful of hair was a girl's crowning glory.
It made her hair stand on end
to see the paradise of it fan over her nape,
a stubborn standard waving on the wind.

As for me, I was a roundhead,
one of the new model army of hair-striaghteners,

y rhai a ymlafnent, yn hwyr y nos
a'i gosi gyda chlipiau, cris croesau,
nes tonni. Iro saim i'w lonni,
arteithio ambell hirnos,
ar obennydd o sglefrolion,
er mwyn deffro, i'r un cribad –
a'r ambell ewyn o gyrl
yn llipa lonydd grogi dros glust.

Mewn man arall, fy nghyfaill crinwalltog
yn smwddio ei thonnau drycinog,
yn taenu rhediadau dros wanegau llyfn,
a'r gwylltion, yn sownd dan bapur brown,
sawr rhuddo ei mwng yn cyrraedd ffroen,
a'r tonnau'n gerrynt, yn crimpio yn erbyn y lli,
gyda'r penflingad blin.

Dianwes yw hanesion gwallt:
ei hoen. A'i ddirboen. Nes y daw
ei berchennog i'w dderbyn,
talog dros ei heddwch
yn erbyn chwiorydd:
a'u hunig uchelgais tynnu gwynt o'u gwalltiau.

those who laboured, late at night
titivating it with criss-crossed clips
until it waved. Anointing it with mousse to perk it up,
torturing myself by night
on a pillow of rollers,
then waking to the combing-out
and a faint foam of curl
hanging limply over one ear.

Meanwhile, my curly-headed friend
was ironing her stormy tresses,
running steel over smooth sheets,
her wild tendrils safely trussed up in brown paper,
the scorch of her mane scenting her nostrils.
Her waves a strong current, she crimped on against
                                          the tide,
a cruel scalping.

The little histories of hair are untold:
its bounciness. The pain it brings,
until its owner comes to accept it,
this fringe between sisters.
Their only ambition is to trim our sails.

[Translated by Elin ap Hywel]

Enwi Duw

'God is just a name for my desire.' – R. Alves

Tacsi.

Codi llaw am dacsi. A bydd yno. Withiau'n segura,
yn byseddu'r oriau. Edrych yn ei ddrych ôl
am yr hyn a fu. Ac o'i flaen y sgrin wynt
sydd rhyngom. A'r nos dinboeth.

Fe ddaeth unwaith. Gweld crwybr ei fetel
yn felgawod. Nid ymwthia nac arafu
na choegio siarad gwag. Rhwng gwter a phalmant
cerddais nes ymlâdd. Ochrgamu'r dorf.

Alltud unwaith eto. Ar drugaredd amser,
yn ofni'r anghynnes ddynesiad. Osgoi trem
ysgogi. Yna, Aros. Atal fy niffyg hyder.
Cerbyd i'r sawl sy'n swil neu'n swagro yw.

Nid yw'n holi cwestiynau. Cymer fy nghais
O ddifri. Hwn oedd y tacsi perffaith
yn troi'r sedd wag ochr draw imi yn seintwar
yn deml syml. Tenemos. Yn Seiat diarweiniad.

Chwiliaf am yr un tacsi o hyd. Ond cerbydau eraill
a'i oddiwedda. Cynnig siwrne a hanner
am lai. Mae pris ei dacsi'n rhy ddrud imi ei ddal
a'r enaid yn cintachu talu'r cildwrn.

Amlach na pheidio, aros nes disgwyl a wna
ar ddiwedd y ciw. Gŵyr wewyr pob aros:
sefyllian wrtho'i hun; disgwyl i'r llaw nesa
godi. Esgyn. Estyn am y drws agored.

The Many Names of God
'God is just a name for my desire.' – R. Alves

Taxi.

I hail a taxi. And he's there. Sometimes he idles,
fumbling through the hours. Looking in his rear mirror
for what's been and gone. And before him, the windscreen's
between us. That and the panting night.

He came once. I saw the reflection of his honeycombed
metal,
He isn't forward, didn't slow down,
didn't make empty conversation. Walk? Until I nearly
dropped
between the gutter and the pavement. I sidestepped the
crowd.
An exile again. At the mercy of time,
fearing a cold come-on. Avoiding a gaze,
evading contact. Then I stop. Take hold of myself.
This motor's for everyone, be she bold or shy.

He asks no questions. He takes my request
seriously. This was the perfect taxi
the empty seat opposite me, a sanctuary
a simple temple. Tenemos. Confessional with no priest.

I'm always looking for that same taxi. But other cabs
speed by. Offering a longer journey, cut price.
His taxi's too dear for me. My soul
begrudges the tip.

More often than not, his wait turns to expectation
at the end of the queue. He knows the agony
of standing around. He waits for the next upturned hand
to rise, reaching for the open door.

Os dewiswn afaelfach ei fynd a'i ddyfod
bydd yn gosod ei gloc, yn ras â'r oriog –
aros neu ddisgwyl; disgwyl nes aros – a'i rin
fydd man cychwyn y siwrne ar ein rhiniog.

Dim ond Camedd[18]
(wrth ddarllen am y diwydiant dillad isaf)

1

Mor ardderchog yw gwisg ordderch
ein dychymyg. Tryloywa'n llaes, sideru
gwrthbanau trwm ar bostyn y gwely.

Ac ar ôl dïor yr atgof digri
am staes mam-gu yn gwrido nôl
arnaf, asennau crog fel lladd-dy dynol,

daw genethod sidanaidd i'r meddwl:
sleifio ar gynfas, dyfrliwio'r co'
heb na ffrâm na bach a llygad i'w pwyo

na chrysbais cras i'w bling-wasgu;
dim weiren fagl i'w dyrchafu
ar fryniau sydd o hyd i'w gorseddu.

A'r fron sydd goron euraid a ddena
organsa yn un ffluwch o gamed,
camisôl gwanolew ei serenedd.

---

18. Darllenais yn y papur newydd am ddiwydiant y diwyg ysgafn. Dechreuodd fel cerdd ddychanol a datblygu'n fwy amwys a dwys. Darllener hi fel y mynner.

Menna Elfyn (b. 1951)

If we grasp the handle of his coming and going
he'll set his clock; the stopping and the waiting
race by; we're still expecting something when we stop –
in the journey's beginning on our new threshold.

[Translated by Elin ap Hywel]

Nothing but Curves[18]
(having read about the underwear industry)

1

How wonderful the courtesan clothes
of our imagination. Diaphanous, flowing, they droop
over heavy counterpanes at the foot of the bed.

Having unlaced the memory
of grandmother's corsets blushing at me
– hanging ribs, like a human abbatoir –

silky girls come to mind:
sliding in on memory's watercoloured canvas
– frameless, without hook or eye to hold them,

or a flannel hairshirt to flay and squeeze them,
no underwire to uplift them
to yet-unfettered heights.

The breast is the golden globe, whispering suggestions
to ruffled organza drifts,
serenely lanolined liberty bodices.

---

18. Poet's note: In the US they take their lingerie seriously, calling them 'engineering projects.' In Welsh, the word *bronglwm* (bra) years ago would send people into fits of laughter as the vocabulary of sexual politics had not yet become part of the acceptable poetic vocabulary. This tries to redress that . . .

Gwisgoedd sy'n llawn tawelwch
yw y rhain, a'u rhubanau simsan
yn rhyddhau 'bur hoff bau'r' hunan

gan droi gwlad yn gyfannedd anial.
A'r ferch yn rhydd o'i gwasgedd
yn ddalen lân rhwng dwylo'i delwedd.

2

Ond yn y golau noeth, peirianneg yw.
Purfa'r gwŷr fforensig sy'n cynllunio
o'r newydd y ffordd o gael bron gryno

i'w gwely. 'Rhyw weithio pwll yw,' medd un –
'a thri deg nodau sydd i'w deall'
er creu y llonyddwch sad arall.

Sbïwch a gwelwch nad heb gynllwyn
y mae sêr y sgrîn fawr yn brolio'u cwrel –
wrth lanio bronnau at eu genau del

a'r hen gorff yn hwb i bobl y glannau
wrth ddathlu llanw a bŵiau ar fae.
Na, nid oes lle yn yr oes hon i soddi'n strae.

3

'Nothing but curves,' medd llef hys-bys.
Ond yn droednoeth, cerddaf i'r oesoedd tywyll
lle roedd gwragedd swil mewn twyll-

olau, yn agor bach a chlasbyn;
cyn plannu'r anwel mewn drôr fel had –
matryd eu cnu tyner dan lygad

Menna Elfyn (b. 1951)

These things are full of calm,
their frail ribbons liberate
the motherland of the self,

making country a homeland all to herself:
where a woman is free of her pressure;
her self a blank sheet between her own hands.

2

– but by fluorescent light – this is hydraulics,
refined by forensic scientists, cantilevering
their brand-new way of getting

the rounded breast into bed. This is a lode to be mined:
thirty sections origami together
to create the other, the perfect orb.

Look. And you'll see that the stars of the screen
lie when they say they have hidden secrets:
their breasts push their facelifts up to their chins

and the body politic spurs on the scuba divers
as they bounce the buoys down in the bay.
There's no future these days in swimming alone.

3

'Nothing but curves,' crows the ad –
but I return, barefoot, to the dark ages
to peer at a woman who stands in half-darkness

opening a hook and eye,
placing them in a drawer where they won't be disturbed
before slipping out of her soft fleece

cannwyll. Yna, dringo matras – corlan
a'r bwlch yn cau. Uwch pwll heb waelod –
cyn cysgu ar ei bronnau ac estyn adnod.

Rhoi'r gair a'r cnawd mewn cadw-mi-gei:
sarcoffagus yw'r nos heb iddo yr un gwall
– dim hyd yn oed eillio bras – cusan dyn dall.

Glanhau'r Capel
(i Eifion Powell)

Rhai glân oedd y Celtiaid:
tra oedd darpar saint mewn ambell le
yn troi at sachlain a lludw,
roedd y Cymry'n llawer mwy cymen,
yn matryd eu hunain at y croen
wrth folchi, canu ac ymdrochi
mewn baddondai a'u galw'n gapeli.

Fe welson nhw'r Ysbryd fel un Lân –
glanhawraig â'i lliain mewn llaw,
pibau'r organ yn sugno'n drygioni;
pob smic a fflwcsyn ar ffo –
heb na thrawst mewn llygad
nac yn agos i'r to.

by the candle's eye. Climbing the mattress
she slips into her fold, closing
with a 'good night' the gap
between herself and the bottomless pit
by sleeping on her front with scripture in mind,

putting tongue and flesh safe by for a while.

The night is a sinless sarcophagus –
rasping, hard like a blind man's kiss.

[Translated by Elin ap Hywel]

Cleaning the Chapel
(for Eifion Powell)

The Celts were clean people –
in those days, some would-be saints
turned to sackcloth and ashes
but the Welsh were a tidy race:
stripping down to the skin
to wash, bathe and sing
in baths they called chapels.

To them, the Spirit was a spirit of cleanliness –
a charwoman armed with a duster,
every mote of dust hounded and banished,
the organ pipes sucking up our evil
not a single beam in anyone's eye
nor up on the roof.

Nid moli a wnâi'r Cymry
ond moeli'r adeiladu
nes teimlo yng nghanol y weddi –
rhyw gawod, gwlithen fechan
yn chwistrellu chwaon cynnes
cyn sychu i ffwrdd y gair 'pech'.

Ac yn y sedd gefn, a alwem y bad
jacuzzi oedd e i'n bywiocáu.

Wrth i ni fynd tua thre, yn ddi-frycheuyn –
braidd na chlywem y ffenestri'n chwerthin
a farnais y seddau'n chwysu dan sang eu sglein.

Menna Elfyn (b. 1951)

My people did not so much praise
as prise all ornament from their chapels,
and might have felt, in the middle of prayer
a squirt of something, a draught of warm air
polishing away their sins.

And the back seat, which we called 'the boat'
was a Jacuzzi which gave us a new lease of life.

As we turned for home, spotlessly clean
we might have heard the windows laughing,
the pews sweating in their shiny varnish.

[Translated by Elin ap Hywel]

Cusan Hances

Mae cerdd mewn cyfieithiad fel cusan drwy hances.
R. S. Thomas

Anwes yn y gwyll?
Rhyw bobl lywaeth oeddem

yn cwato'r gusan ddoe.
Ond heddiw, ffordd yw i gyfarch

ac ar y sgrin fach, gwelwn
arweinwyr y byd yn trafod,

hulio hedd ac anwes las;
ambell un bwbach. A'r delyneg

o'i throsi nid yw ond cusan
drwy gadach poced, medd y prifardd.

Minnau, sy'n ymaflyd cerdd ar ddalen
gan ddwyn i gôl gariadon-geiriau.

A mynnaf hyn. A fo cerdd bid hances
ac ar fy ngwefus

sws dan len.

Handkerchief Kiss[19]

A poem in translation is like kissing through a handkerchief.
R. S. Thomas

A kiss in the dark.
What a tame lot we were,
with our secretive yesterday's kisses.
Today, it's a common greeting,

and we watch on the small screen
world leaders deal peace

with a cold embrace,
or an adder's kiss. The lyric

translated is like kissing
through a hanky, said the bard.

As for me, I hug those poems between pages
that bring back the word-lovers.

Let the poem carry a handkershief
and leave on my lip

its veiled kiss.

[Translated by Gillian Clarke]

---

19. Poet's note: A poem in tribute to R. S. Thomas.

Hilary Llewellyn-Williams (b. 1951)

The Woman Poet

stumbles up from a disjointed sleep
to children's voices. The room is dark,
rain dulls the hidden window.
A dream, vibrant
hangs round her:
she eases it like a shawl
away and it fades
as she gropes for slippers.

Behind the breakfast clatter she finds tears
rising and falling, and anger
comes and goes. Outside
there are trees vivid with moss in the wet wind
and leaves falling, and rubbery bright
fungi sparking the gloom.
Perhaps tomorrow
there will be time. The trees blow words at her
as she gathers plates
and her mind lifts and clears.

Poems spill out of the tips
of her fingers and slide around
in the dishwater suds;
are slipped down the sink
where they spiral
and eddy for just

a moment. Then down
that black hole with a rude suck
and a derisive gurgle
they go. She smiles:
her lips are sealed.

Bagful

In your dream, you reach into my bag
to find it stuffed with hair.
Coils, hanks, skeins of black hair

nudge at your hand, a soft shock
like touching a furred animal in there –
but worse, this is loose, this is chaos

tangling your fingers, the damp filaments
that cling like algae. As you draw
your hand back, there is more, more:

nets, webs of hair, accumulation
of years, the brush-cloggings,
strands you find by the sink, the plug-pickings,

the hoover-spindle windings, the moult
on a towel, the broom-knots
twined into bristles, the pillow threads:

bunched-up, gathered, stored.
To think that so much has fallen from my head!
I could weave rugs from it, stuff mattresses,

mix it with clay and daub a whole house;
knit sweaters from it till my fingers bled,
hoard wigs of it against baldness.

You scoop some out, and shake it to the floor,
hoping someone will clear it up.
I will not; this is hardly my fault.

I have saved all my combings,
plucked them from the carpet, from the air.
If you must open my bag, that's your affair.

Breadmaking

Forgive the flour under my fingernails
the dabs of dough clinging to my skin:
I have been busy, breadmaking.
So easy, the flakes falling feathery
into the warm bowl, as I dip and measure
and pour the foaming treasured brown
yeast down to the ground wheat grain.
O as the barm breaks and scatters
under my working fingers like a scum
of tides on shifting sands, the secret cells
swell, you can smell their life
feeding and beating like blood
in my bunched palms
while I lift the lump and slap it back again.

It moves, like a morning mushroom,
a breathing side, stirring, uncurling
animal nudged from sleep; so I pummel

and thump and knuckle it into shape
to see it unwind like a spring
soft as a boneless baby on the table.
I have covered it now: let it grow
quietly, save for the least rustle
of multiplication in the damp bundle
telling of motion in the fattening seeds.
Its body's an uproar as I open the burning door –
it gives one final heave, and it blossoms out
to the brown loaf I have spread for you.
Taste the butter touching its heart like snow.

Catherine Fisher (b. 1957)

Great-grandmother

You are the furthest back.
Your name tops the family tree,
marks the end of mythology.
On the dusty trail of documents
only two snapped twigs show where you passed.
Two thin lines crossing, a crooked X
that promises, and denies,
and underneath the slightly disapproving
"Hannah O'Connor – her mark."
Your fingers, work-worn, awkward,
unused to the pen's slim fluency;
my eyes, tired after searches,
swooping on the long-sought prey –
our blood's intersection, our crossroads,
our moment of meeting.
You are the begetter of history.
Behind you, like a shadow
Ireland rises
– famine, kings, Tara, Newgrange –
– all my Dark Ages.

Immrama

First there was the island of the darkness.
When we rowed from there
the light was desolation for us.

And I remember a house with a golden chessboard
where we played too long.
What we lost I cannot remember.

As you go on it gets harder. Each landfall
an awakening of sorrows,
guile or treachery, the enticement of pleasures.

I lost my brother at the house of the feathers,
good men at the harper's table.
There are always those who would hold us back.

You get used to the voices, the clinging fingers;
in every port the warning
'Beyond here is nothing but the sea.'

Islands of glass, islands of music and berries,
the isle of the locked door,
citadels and beaches where we dared not land,

these are behind us. Daily, the delirium rises;
it may be that smudge
on the horizon is a trick of my eyes.

And would we know that land if we should find it?
They say the scent of apples
wafts on the water; there is honey, hum of bees,

salmon leap into the boat. They say the others,
the lost ones, laugh on the sand.
But behind them, who are those strangers crowding
                                      the cliffs?

In a Chained Library

Here they are, chained as if dangerous,
creatures from a bestiary left open,
foxed and gilded, a tangle of tails,
mouths, claws, spilling from the shelves.

Silent as unicorns their sweet unspoken music.
Finger them, the dry crackle of their skins
Dragons burn in margins, sea-cats uncoil;
monsters, eating letters, being letters,

as if word and flesh and beast were one
and might burst out, huge and scaly,
slithering from the nave into the crowded streets,
scorching the night with a babel of lost songs.

St Tewdric's Well

Toad on the soft black tarmac knows it's there;
screened by deadnettle, tumbled with ivy.
He enters the water like a devotee,
anointed with bubbles.

If you lean over, your shadow shrouds him;
dimly your eyes find watersnails
down on the deep green masonry, and coins,
discarded haloes.

Tewdric's miracle, not even beautiful,
slowly effacing itself in exuberant nettles,
its only movement the slow clouds,
the sun's glinting ascension.

Lost in the swish of grasses, the hot road,
blown ladybirds, soft notes from a piano;
and over the houses the estuary grey as a mirror,
its islands stepping-stones for Brân or Arthur.

Blodeuwedd

When oak, I was unbending;
would never have stooped to this.
A thousand years' slow circles
rang from my heart's wood.
Through acorn and gall I saw you
stumble into the world.

When I was broom I was golden;
my spines the haunt of birds.
I hid nothing, had no guile;
wind and rain speared through me.
In tapestries I blossomed
between unicorn and lady.

When meadowsweet, I was innocent;
white froth of fields are gone.
Spume of hedge uprooted,
of scent and butterflies.
Children and lovers watched Spitfires
through the creamy skies.

What have you made of me, wizards?
Out of me what have you formed?
Treacherous, a taloned hunter,
mutated into your fall.
The conditions that will cause death;
how is it I know them all?

Delyth George

Gwylnos
(Yn Aberystwyth, Rhyfel y Culfor, gaeaf 1991)

Cannwyll yn llosgi: ofnau'n ymgasglu.
Gwêr yn goferu: gwaed yn rhaeadru.
Dwylo'n dolennu: enaid yn trengi.
Fflam yn rhyw bylu: calon yn fferu.
Cadwyn ar dorri: byd yn ymrannu.
Diwedd y weddi   a'r cread yn nadu
    yn hwyr un nos
    ddi-glasnost.

Treiffl a Threfn

Mae i dreiffl drefn,
haenau o ystyr
ynghudd yn ei bentwr blasus.
Ond roedd un chwaer ddwl
yn ddall i hyn oll,
a gofynnodd i'r llall
sut oedd mynd ati
i hulio'r blasusfwyd
ar gyfer te parti.

'Wel,' meddai honno
yn fawr ei ffrwst:
'darn o gacen sych

Vigil
(In Aberystwyth, during the Gulf War, Winter 1991)

A candle burning: fears congregating.
Wax dripping: blood cascading.
Hands wringing: a soul dying.
A flame waning: a heart freezing.
A chain breaking: a world splitting.
End of the prayer   and the creation wailing
        late one
    glasnost-less night.

Trifle and order

A trifle has order,
Layers of meaning
Hidden in its tasty mound.
But there was one crazy sister
Who was blind to all this,
And she asked the other
How to go about making
This delectable morsel
For a tea party.

'Well,' said she
bustling importantly:
'take a piece of dry cake

a'i rhoddi yn wlych
mewn dropyn o sieri
cyn tywallt y jeli:
yna daw'r hufen
a chlamp o geiriosen.
Ac wele dreiffl,
wele drefn!'

'Ond na,' medd y llall
gan annerch y gall:
'beth pe baen ni,
am ennyd, yn oedi
ac yn newid y drefn:
yn gynta'r geiriosen
ac yna yr hufen;
wedyn y jeli
a dropyn o sieri,
ac ar y top
gacen o'r siop!'

Gwaredodd y gall.
Beth oedd ar y llall
yn creu trafferth o hyd
mewn treiffl o fyd?

soaked in a drop of sherry
before you pour the jelly:
then comes the cream
and a great big cherry on top.
And there's your trifle,
There's your perfect order!'

'But no,' said the other
addressing the sensible one:
'what if we pause a moment
and change the order:
the cherry first
and then the cream;
followed by the jelly
and the drop of sherry,
and on the top
a cake from the shop!'

The sensible one got rid of her.
What was wrong with that one,
Making trouble all the time
In a perfectly ordered, trifling world?

Gwyneth Lewis (b. 1959)

The Booming Bittern

Listen to that bittern boom.
You'll never see him. Tall reeds sway
and so does he,
courting invisibility.
Boom, bittern, boom.

See, he points up to the sky
in sympathy with wind-stirred sedge.
He has a body
but his camouflage
has made this bird all alibi.

This discretion's saved his life
so far. He sways in silence but he'll die
alone. The boom's
his only hope – his cry
might bring a brood of chicks, a wife.

To boom or not? A car alarm
risks nothing when it calls its mate.
But in a bog
you must be found, or not copulate.
So risk it, bittern. Boom, bittern, boom!

Two Rivers

Lord of the Running Rivers,
I was given two languages
to speak or, rather, they have spoken me
through different landscapes from a common spring.
The mountain's muddy; hard to see
where bog becomes trickle, the rivulet a brook
and that a cascade with identity,
a common direction and, shortly, a name.
I had my choice but never could resist
the excitable fall from scarp to estuary
in whichever language. How do rivers dream
their valleys which, like lives, they wander through
in wonder? They are silver trees
rooted in the soil of the sea,
the source their latest blossoms.
Lord of the Running Rivers, teach us how
to speak the glistening fruits of water's tree.

Lord of Dividing Rivers,
I have lived two,
which fell to my death like sentences.
The first was gifted, chose the richest loam
through fertile country, where its ox-bow bends
and indirections gave the valley fields
for grazing cows like upturned boats.
Above great oaks exploded green,
slow in the sinuous course of river time,
while elvers shot the water through like stars.
The other was jagged, fell like broken glass,
chose steeper gradients, which means poverty
(except in sky). The hungry can't live on beauty,
so this river gave itself to fords

that were coloured by dust and iron ore
which sent it through bridges further down,
full as a printing press with news of men,
of work and maculate industry.
Strange birds were seen where the sump-oil tide
rose to hide the mudbank's shame.
Lord of Dividing Rivers,
teach us to love this petrol river's flame.

O Lord of the Murmuring Rivers,
give us this day the suppleness of streams,
the virtue of water. How smoothly it translates
(not proud) into a thousand forms –
it gives itself to gardens of moss,
bog asphodel, conurbations, farms,
industrial complexes and still it flows,
always accepting, for the water knows
that nakedness means constant change.
So when, polluted, it falls through the weir,
its eddies taste of stalactites, of heath,
of heavy metals, stagnant pools – of everywhere
the experienced water flowed and loved.
Discreet, but never discredited,
it flows in filth yet its integrity
remembers always essential clarity
or, at least, the idea of purity.
Lord of the Murmuring Rivers,
grant us clean water's humility.

Lord of the Meeting Rivers,
be there when our stories run into the sea,
the multilingual estuary
which speaks sky and Sahara, watered silk and neap,
sweet water and salty. This Babel tide
will not be translated. In it we hear

more than the tale of one river's words.
Here is the source of wanting to speak
not in praise of one place, but of passing through
cool pools of beauty and then letting them go,
of becoming, of saying more than we know,
of forgetting all syntax, all local names,
in the beat of the metre sighed out by the tides.
the waters rise again to fall in rain
on other mountains, to start the brilliant train
from rock to rivulet.
Lord of the Meeting Rivers, grant us now
the language of water, its transparency,
so we may hear the tributaries speak
the silence of singing and unknowable seas.

Wholeness (extract)
II Llanbadarn Baptism
1843

The day they baptised
Margaret Ann
the Jordan
flowed through Llanbadarn.

As the river closed
above her head,
Margaret Ann heard the roar
of salmon breathing
and the water's weight,
its turbulent history,
a bond between her
and the minister.
He stood like a giant,

two pillars his legs
and the currents were black
as her sins, which spread
below and around her,
a deluge to drown her.

Her sister waved a parasol;
the saint stood like flowers
along the banks
of the crystal Rheidol
while along it, the lions
of Providence
roared out their blessings
to Aberystwyth
while she and the minister,
they both wore
the river like stockings
in hosanna[20] style
while watching two worlds –
one rural, parochial,
the other divine –
both flowing together
while the Sunday hats
were ready for Judgement
and she, the bride,
our Margaret Ann,
was dazzling,
lovely, fully at one
with the brilliant sun
which blessed and protected
the sighing palms
that had sprung up
in fertile Llanbadarn.

---

20. *hosan* = stocking, in Welsh.

Welsh Espionage (extract)
V

Welsh was the mother tongue, English was his.
He taught her the body by fetishist quiz,
father and daughter on the bottom stair:
'Dy benelin yw *elbow*, dy wallt di yw *hair*,

chin yw dy ên di, *head* yw dy ben.'
She promptly forgot, made him do it again.
Then he folded her *dwrn* and, calling it fist,
held it to show her knuckles and wrist.

'Let's keep it from Mam, as a special surprise.
Lips are *gwefusau*, *llygaid* are eyes.'
Each part he touched in their secret game
thrilled as she whispered its English name.

The mother was livid when she was told.
'We agreed, no English till four years old!'
She listened upstairs, her head in a whirl.
Was it such a bad thing to be Daddy's girl?

Parables and Faxes (extract)
V Dark Ages

Saxons are vertical,
circles we,
hence the mutual hostility
They climb, we spiral;
who shall be
the better in their eternity?

Curls tend to churls
while ladders rise;
they are legs and we the eyes
that watch the progress of the earls
across the skies
over the clods they patronise.

We are return
but progress they,
roundabout versus motorway.
We borrow but they always own
the deeds of day,
certificates for rights of way.

A thane is bright,
no plodder he,
an apex of geometry
that draws the Angles to their heights;
though fantasy
must know the fear of gravity.

The humble are fly
and know the crown
for an O in which a man can drown
or drink his death – such irony
is for the prone
who must praise the good they'll never own.

Gwyneth Lewis (b. 1959)

The Mind Museum (extract)

II History Lesson

Time was they walked on water dry
so full of ships were the teeming docks.
We dream in video what they lived by day.

Masts bobbed like crosses at a crowded quay,
sank from sight inside the gurgling lock.
Time was they walked on water dry.

Men had to travel for a fireman's pay
they sweated bullets but enjoyed the crack.
We dream in video what they lived by day.

Murmansk, Osaka, Paraguay:
the girls they met there call them back . . .
Time was they walked on water dry,

met Welshmen everywhere, and lay
by stanchions up some Godforsaken creeks.
We dream in video what they lived by day.

Back home in Cardiff, hear the halyards play
sweet music when the winds fall slack.
Time was they walked on water dry.
We dream in video what they lived by day.

Merryn Williams

Michael

Fourteen years since I held you, glimpsed darkly
your future, new parents and a new name;
wished you luck in that unforeseeable journey,
against all odds, your mother sent you on.

May, pale blue birds' eggs fracturing. Not quite naked,
you'd go out with one plain set of hospital clothes.
All else, they'd give. She'd go home empty-handed,
see your small face long years behind her eyes.

I gave you – of all things – a toy panda –
for what? You'd take no memories where you went.
Each May, I hear the cuckoo call, remember
tiled corridors and the lilacs' scent.

Black Mountain Cairns
(In memory of E. P. Thompson and Raphael Samuel)

Walking the silent tops of the Black Mountains
you find, every so often, a heap of stones,
anonymous, nothing scratched there. Not the broken
tablets which marked the boundaries of old sheep runs,
initialled by some farmer dead for a hundred years.
Nor the standing stones, isolated lower
in the valley, which track the path of the winter sun.

No, these were raised to assure the lonely traveller
someone had come here before, perhaps thinking his
thoughts.
You can walk for miles till you see one, rest, and start on
the dry, exhausting trak to the next cairn.

They're kicked over often enough, the stones scattered
on to shale. The mist clears and the peaks return,
occasionally.
Each time I pass I add another stone,
unnoticed, to the gaunt bulk of the cairn.

Elin ap Hywel

Cyn oeri'r gwaed

Marciau pensil
ar gyfrol o gywyddau.

Graffiti un meddwl
yn nodi cyffro'r cymundeb
â gwefr yr heli a'r golau'n llathru'n wyn
ar bluf gwylan Dafydd ap Gwilym,
ar wal ddi-sigl amser
ugain mlynedd a mwy yn ôl –
"Hoen ac ieuenctid rŵl ocê?"

Mae yma ysbryd bardd
sy'n awchus am lusgo paent llachar ei brofiadau
dros friciau byw,
a pheintio'r byd
yn wyrdd,
a choch,
a melyn,
ac oren,
a glas, –
wedi'i goffáu am byth
yn sgribliadau syn y graffit llwyd;
bardd a ymbarchusodd
ac sydd heddiw'n gwthio
torlif y trydan sy'n melltennu'n enfys o gerdd
drwy wifrau tyn ei hiraeth.

Before the blood cools

Pencil marks
on a volume of cywyddau.

The graffiti of one mind
noting the excitement of communion
with the thrill of the seaspray and the light falling white
on the feathers of Dafydd ap Gwilym's seagull,
on the unshakeable wall of time
twenty years or more ago –
"Youth and passion rule OK?"

There is here the spirit of a poet
eager to daub the bright paint of his experiences
on living bricks,
and to paint the world
green,
and red,
and yellow,
and orange,
and blue, –
memorialised forever
in the grey graphite's scribbles;
a poet who became respectable
and who today thrusts
the lightning bolt of electricity which ignites the poem's
                                                rainbow
through the tight wires of his regret.

O doed i mi'r doethineb
i fyw angerdd fy nghân
yn y funud fer
cyn i sbectrwm bywyd
droi yn ddu a gwyn,
a chyn troi fy mhoen
yn gyfres o sylwadau
sy'n araf golli'u lliw
ar ymylon tudalen frau fy nghof.

Cennin Pedr

Mae cyffwrdd â nhw yn weithred gnawdol bron,
gan ddwyn i'r cof
fflach min llafn yr heulwen
yn taro'r gwair, ac eco
cŵn yn udo rhwng muriau ysguborau'r ymennydd.

Mae melynder llaith a llyfn petalau'n gorwedd
fel croen rhwng y bysedd,
a'i sug yn curo'n wyrdd
yn y gwythiennau,
yn gymysg gyda'r gwaed
a welwyd yn rhwd ar gleddyf fel grug ar glogwyn.

Trwy lygad y stamen, mae chwyddwydr y gorffennol
yn dod a'n holl funudau angerdd yn ôl
yn rhithiau
sy'n agos yng nghryndod tarth y bore,
ac eto'n bell,
mor bell yn ôl a'r foment
y lladdwyd Llywelyn,
y llithrodd ei enaid i'r llwydwyll
fel defnyn yn disgyn oddi ar ddeilen.

Oh give me the wisdom
to live the passion of my song
in the brief minute
before the spectrum of life
turns to black and white,
and before my pain turns
to a series of marginal notes
slowly fading
on the brittle page of my memory.

Daffodils

Touching them is almost a carnal act,
reminding you of
the knife-edge flash of the sun
striking the hay, and the echo
of dogs howling between the walls of the mind's barns.

The damp, smooth yellow of the petals feels
like skin between the fingers,
and its sap beats green
in the veins,
mixed with the blood
rusty on the weapon like heather on a clifftop.

Through the eye of the stamen, the telescope of the past
brings back all our minutes of passion
like ghosts
which seem close in the shimmering morning mist,
and yet far off,
as far off as the moment
Llywelyn was killed,
when his soul slipped into the twilight
like a waterdrop falling from a leaf.

Mae'r cyfan yno – estyn dy law a'i gyffwrdd,
y bywyd byrhoedlog
sy'n hercio am ennyd
ac yna'n crino i'r pridd. Gwasg e
rhwng tudalennau llaith dy ddyletswydd trwm,
yn emblem o wanwyn di-dymor
yn nannedd niwloedd yr hydref. Mae'r blodau'n dal
i ddawnsio'n gibddall, yn bwpedau'r gwynt.

Gwynt y Dwyrain

Gwynt y dwyrain – yn llefain heno
a'i sisial yn sacrament
rhwng sgerbydau'r coed.

Gwynt y dwyrain – yn ei awen heno
a'i felodi'n farwnad
uwch beddrod y dail ir.

Gwynt y dwyrain – yn poeri heno
a'i lach yn ddirmyg
ar gefnau y dail du.

Gwynt y dwyrain – yn wylo heno
a'i ddagrau'n rhagrith meddal
yn angladd y pethau byw.

Gwynt y dwyrain – daw gosteg fory
a'r storm yn suddo
yn waed yn y gorllewin.

It's all there – reach out your hand and touch it,
the shortlived life
which limps along awhile
and then withers into the soil. Press it
between the damp pages of your heavy conscience,
as an emblem of eternal spring
in the teeth of Autumn's mists. The flowers are still
dancing blindly, puppets of the wind.

The East Wind

The east wind – weeping tonight
its whisper a sacrament
among the skeletons of trees.

The east wind – with its muse tonight
its melody an elegy
above the grave of the fresh leaves.

The east wind – spitting tonight
its lash of contempt
on the backs of the black leaves.

The east wind – crying tonight
its tears a soft hypocrisy
at the funeral of the living things.

The east wind – calm will come tomorrow
when the storm sinks down
bloodily in the west.

Gauloise yw'r gerdd

Gauloise yw'r gerdd –
stwmp inni sugno nicotin y dychymyg,
yn mudlosgi
rhwng bysedd yr ymennydd,
gan ryddhau emosiynau
fel rhuban o fwg glas
i droi yn ehangder 'stafell y cof,
cyn darfod
a'i daflu
i flwch
yr isymwybod llychlyd.

Llithro heibio
(Munich, Mawrth 1991)

Mae hoglau glân ar yr Almaenwr ifanc
sy'n pwyso dros y ford, hoglau fforestydd
ac eira sy'n disgleirio yn yr haul
fel darnau mân o wydr wedi'i dorri

ac mae'r ddinas
yn llathru heibio inni ar yr U-bahn
ar olwynion llyfn mae rhywun wedi'u oelio
a dan ni'n gwbod
fod popeth yn mynd i ddigwydd fel y dyle fo

The poem's a Gauloise

The poem's a Gauloise –
a stump for us to suck at
the nicotine of the imagination,
smouldering
between the mind's fingers,
releasing emotions
like a ribbon of blue smoke
to turn in the spacious hall of memory,
before being extinguished
and thrown
into the bin
of the dusty subconscious.

Slipping by
(Munich, March 1991)

There's a clean smell from the young German
leaning across the table, the smell of forests
and snow that glitters in the sun
like little pieces of broken glass

and the city
skids by us on the underground
on smooth wheels that someone has oiled
and we know
that everything's going to happen as it should

ac wrth olau cannwyll dan ni'n sôn am ryfel
ac yn edrych i'n pelen hud
i weld pobl sy'n byw y tu draw i'r eira –
tynnu lluniau o'r Gwlff ar y lliain ford
a defnyddio'r napcynnau
i ddynwared safle'r tanciau
ac wrth olau'r cannwyll mae'r nos yn llithro heibio
yn chwim, fel plentyn sy' newydd ffeindio
ei fod o'n medru sglefrio

Yn y dre heddiw
mi welais i ddyn
yn tynnu gwydr o bib
roedd o'n sugno dim ond awyr
a'i droi o'n freuddwyd i gyd

ac ar y brigau noeth mae ei gylchoedd gwydr yn crogi
a'u lliwiau yn borffor ac aur
mae rhyw gyfrinach yn eu gwneud
sy'n rhy ddrud i mi ei phrynu
sy'n rhy frau i'w chludo adre i Gymru

a dan ni'n llithro heibio wrth olau cannwyll
ac mae'r cledrau yn hynod o syth
yn llithro heibio ar olwynion wedi'u oelio
yn llithro heibio am byth am byth am byth

and by candlelight we talk of war
and look into our crystal ball
to see people who live beyond the snow –
drawing pictures of the Gulf on the tablecloth
and using napkins
to stand for the tank positions
and by candlelight the night slips by
quickly, like a child who's just discovered
that he knows how to skate

In the town today
I saw a man
pulling a glass from a pipe
he was sucking air alone
and turning it into a dream

and on the bare branches his glass spheres hang
their colours are purple and gold
there's a secret in their making
too dear for me to buy
too brittle for me to carry home to Wales

and we're slipping by in the candlelight
and the rails are amazingly straight
slipping by on oiled wheels
slipping by forever forever forever

Elin Llwyd Morgan

Rapwnsel

Mae poen yn burach na phornograffi,
yn fwy brwnt na gêm rygbi,
achos dim ond poen sy'n hollol bur,
yn tafellu'r galon fel twca
a'i gadael yn gignoeth,
yn binc a brasterog
fel salami.

Rwyf wedi ceisio codi caerau
o gwmpas fy nghalon,
ond mae 'na wastad rhyw fastad
sy'n catapwltio fel Robin Hood
i mewn i'r canol caled
a throi fy mywyd o ben i waered.

Dyw pornograffi ddim yn bur,
ddim hyd yn oed mewn *strip joints*
neu tra'n strapio putain i byst y gwely,
a phetasen ni'n 'gwneud cariad'
mi fasai 'na wastad
rhyw saib digyfaddawd
ar ôl i ni ddŵad.

Rwyt ti'n loetran
y tu allan i'r tŵr,
a gwn fy mod
yn ormod o bendonciwr,
yn ormod o boengarwr,
i beidio â lluchio
fy ngwallt i lawr.

Rapunzel

Pain is purer than pornography,
Fouler than a game of rugby,
For only pain is wholly pure,
Slicing the heart like a tuck-knife
And leaving it raw,
Pink and fatty
Like salami.

I have tried to raise forts
Around my heart,
But there is always some clown
Who catapults like Robin Hood
Into the hard centre
And turns my life upside down.

Pornography is never pure,
Not even in strip joints
Or while whipping a whore
With a bamboo cane,
And if we made love
There would always be
An awkward pause
After we came.

I see you loitering
Outside the tower,
And know that I am
Too much of a nutcase,
Too much of a masochist
Not to let my long plait down.

[Translation by the poet]

Madfall symudliw

Dwi wedi cael digon
o ddilyn fy nghynffon
fel madfall symudliw
gwyllt gwallgo gwirion
yn chwildroelli a llithro
mewn lloergylchoedd gwydlon
tra'n disgwyl i'r haul
hidlreibio'r haen osôn.

Drych amlonglog yw ofn:
edrychaf ar fy adlewyrchiad
a gweld fy wyneb
wedi'i lurgunio
yn ei ddyfroedd crisialog
a'm cudynnau'n chwifio
fel anemoni pluog.

Dwi wedi cael llond bol
o fod yn berson meidrol:
dwi isio bod yn gameleon
go-iawn, yn amliwiog,
efo amrannau fel Garbo
a chynffon gyrliog;
neu'n flodyn y mor
odiaeth a gludiog
efo bysedd petalog
yn agor a chydio
a goglais a gwingo.

Iridescent lizard

I've had enough
of chasing my tail
like an iridescent lizard:
frantic, frenzied, foolish,
reeling and slipping
in lunatic vicious circles
while I wait for the sun
to push through the ozone layer.

Fear is a many-planed mirror:
I look at my reflection
and see my face
mutilated
in its crystal waters
and my locks of stray hair waving
like a feathery anemone.

I've had it up to here with
being a person of limitations:
I want to be a chameleon,
a real one, multi-coloured,
with eyelashes like Garbo's
and a curly tail;
or a sea flower
exquisite and sticky
with petally fingers
opening and twining
and wriggling and writhing.

Machlud asid

haul yr hwyr yn aur dros aberystwyth
cwrw'n ffrwd felynfrown ysgytlaeth
ysgawen ffrwchnedd hufen ffromhyfryd
swigod trwchlaethog lli brandi bricyll
lliw shandi fflach saffirlas cen brithyll
arian byw enfysog triog tewlud
saig gliw oreneuraidd mango efydd
hylifgwenwynllyd y gwirod cnau cyll
cymun crefydd newydd sawl sylwebydd
tywydd perlddaneddog rhyfeddysgwydd
yn llowcio llamhidydd seimllyd pob sill
a ffroenluwchio fflwchbelydrau'r machlud

Acid sunset

gold evening sun over aberystwyth
beer a yellow-brown milk-shake stream
elder-scum cream livid-lovely
thick milky bubbles a pebbly brandy sea
the colour of shandy a sapphire-blue flash trout scales
molten silver prismatic thick fudgy toffee
a dish of glue orange-gold brazen mango
poison-liquid of the hazelnut liqueur
sacrament of several spokesmen's new religion
pearl-toothed weather strange-shouldered
gobbling a greasy acrobat every syllable
and drift-sniffing the bright rays of the sunset

Sarah Corbett

The Red Wardrobe

The red wardrobe where you shut in my sister,
the iron key sliding into your pocket.

The red wardrobe that fell on my sister,
its colour old blood and rusty oil
on the soft blue insides of her elbows, her wrists,

like the Chinese burns she gave me
as I cried and hated her, until I remembered
how she made herself small in corners,
how I thought she was a kitten crying until I shook her.

The red wardrobe, its doors opening and closing in my
                                                                           dream,
the warm nuts in its dust becoming mice eyes,
their long tails, scratching,

that my father splintered and burnt
the day all the women left and we had fireworks.

Ghost Mother

You are the fear
before sleep comes, the claw
in the corner of the dark
that scratches at the boards.

You are the empty moon
full of the night, a question
with only questions
for answers.

You are a turned vowel,
the inside of a hole
that sings like the rubbed rim
of a glass.

You are a smudge of hair
in the bath, the ghost
of a mouth on a fold
of paper.

You are always present
in your absence –
a fragrant skin shed
in the hallway

into which I fall.

Elin Wyn Williams

Moliannwn oll yn llon!

Canwch gân
I'r wraig o flân y tân
Sy'n smwddio'r cryse glân
Yn ddeddfol.

Taflwch winc
At gefn y fenyw
Yn y sinc
Sydd – yn ôl 'i harfer –
Yn câl pleser
Wrth addoli
Hollalluog dduw y llestri.

Lluniwch gerdd
I gloriannu angerdd
Merch y misglwyf
Wrth i'r felan
Ddripian drosti.

Cynnwch fflam
I oleuo Bedlam
Y fam
Sy'n wargam wthio'r pram
Heb gymar.

Let us all give joyful praise!

Sing a song
To the wife who all day long
Irons clean shirts by firelight
According to established rite.

Drop a wink
To the woman
At the sink
Who, never at leisure,
Gets all her pleasure
When she worships and cherishes
The almighty deity of dishes.

Write a verse
For the girl with the curse
To measure her passion
As depression
Drips
Over her.

Light a flame
To illuminate the Bedlam
Of the single mother
Whose back is bent, pushing the pram.

A bloeddiwch gri
I wroli
Gwragedd Greenham
Ar Gomin 'u
Hegwyddorion
Gwenfflam.

Dewch
Moliannwn oll yn llon
Yr uchod yr awron
A dichon daw dynion
Yn wŷr ac yn feibion
I ddeall
Ryw ddiwrnod
Nad mwlsyn mo merch!

And let out a great cry
To celebrate and glorify
The women of Greenham
On their Common, all disciples
Of their white-hot principles.

Come, at this hour,
Let us all give joyful praise
And look forward to the days
When men old and young
Will come to see, no fuss,
That a girl is no-one's wuss!

Rose Flint

In Waking

In waking my skin held a different life,
it wanted: flickering
it slid out of sleep   the cells of it
sharp as diamond   pin-points of light.
It muscled: arousal   rippled to corners
of little stiff finger, toe, slanting eyelid
filling and swelling the peony of mouth line
glossy knee hollow.   Snake-skin
shuked over me, perfume of Indies risky as spice
scenting the stinging flames   stroking
    this splendid tissue holding me
pouring its blazing senses into the leaky spaces
        of eyes   mouth   sex
you inside me   I inside out.

How we exchange, know each other more
        in this metamorphosis:
you with your day-sails
driven inward to the flood of black oceans
and   cave of furled colours
dancing outside   as if
I was light   poured over the wave.

Kate Johnson

Family Grave

As my wooden casket crumbles,
my bone settles into soil.
Beneath my fleshless palms
I feel the press of someone else –
her knuckles, polished as ivory bobbins.
The petals of bone that were her face
crush beneath the lead-weight
of my skull.
My backbone folds and is caged
within those other ribs.
I am falling into the basket
of her hips.
By the movement of earthworms
I enter my mother.

Blackberries

    They ripen
through one long night
of the full moon.

My skin peppered,
black witch
I'm pricked,
         juices

thread the white wrists'
underskin.

   Volcanic pebbles
crushed on the tongue,
warm, their stains
purpling

in a jar
the bloody swimming
light.

   Month of ripeness,
these black berries
and my own blood

rolled all night under
the yellow dragon moon.

Kate Bingham

Things I learned at University

How to bike on cobblestones and where to signal right.
How to walk through doors held open by Old Etonians
and not scowl. How to make myself invisible in seminars
by staring at the table. How to tell Victorian Gothic from
:: Medieval.
How to eat a Mars bar in the Bodleian. When to agree
with everything in theory. How to cultivate a taste for sherry.

Where to bike on the pavement after dark. How to sabotage
:: a hunt.
When to sunbathe topless in the Deer Park. When to punt.
How to hitch a lift and when to walk and where to run.
When not to address my tutors formally. How to laugh at
:: Latin puns
and when to keep quiet and preserve my integrity.
How to celebrate an essay crisis. When to sleep through
:: fire alarms.

How to bike no-handed, how to slip a condom on with one.
When to smoke a joint and when to swig champagne.
When to pool a tip and how to pull a pint. A bit of history.
When to listen to friends and whether to take them seriously.
At the same time how to scorn tradition and enjoy it.
How to live like a king, quite happily, in debt.

Nits

Lobby your ministers to sign the multilateral declaration
NOW,
and help exterminate headlice in just forty-two days
by keeping your hair as greasy as you can. People, throw
away
those fine tooth combs and feel our planet relax
as the itching stops.

Shampoo sales will slump, short-term, and the
manufacturers
of Bioderm, of course, go out of business. Factories may
close,
redundancies produce despair and crime waves in our
cities,
but the net effect on the economy will be minimal.

Let animal rights campaigners demonstrate in Hyde Park
objecting to the systematic annihilation of one species by
another
and let Jeremy Paxman interview a panel of scientists
on insect contributions to the search for a cure for cancer.

Lawyers and historians will urge the public to resist
a dangerous extension of political power, arguing that
parliament has no competence to legislate on personal
hygiene,
a fundamental human right, but we will stand firm.

There is little sympathy for the parasites
and popular opinion lies with the government.

In Passing

I would like to be a woman in a poem.
Something by Milosz, perhaps, or Brodsky,
mentioned at the end of a stanza
almost casually –

the flare of a skirt, bright red,
suspended and still vanishing round the corner
of a certain derelict building
in the poet's home town.

A laugh with music in it – bells! –
that sounds like the laugh of somebody else
the poet once knew, when he was younger.
Ah, but she never came to America.

Lemon and jasmine. Menthol cigarettes.
I won't mind that the poet
only notices what he has already remembered,
that the poem only hints.

Reading it you wouldn't be able to say
exactly who he saw,
but only that it was a woman
who reminded you of me.

Esyllt Maelor

Mam a gwraig tŷ

Mae llygaid y platiau ar y ddresel wedi serio arnaf
a bathiad y ddannodd yn nhipiadau cloc y pobty.
Catrawd o filwyr yw'r pegiau llonydd
ac mae plygiad Tŷ'n y Fawnog yn y siôl ar y lein.
Mingamu wna gweflau'r handlenni pres
a phlorod yw dyrnau'r cypyrddau yn y parlwr bach.

Mae wynebau waliau'r 'stafelloedd yn erfyn amdanaf,
a'r ceffylau bach ar eu meri-go-rownd ar wal y babi
yn gwichian nôl a blaen, nôl a blaen.

Pob jig-so wedi'i sbydu, yn ysu am anwes.
Cabalfa o geir bach cegrwth yn pledio am gau ac agor eu
                                                                    drysau,
eu gyrru, parcio a'u gyrru eilwaith.
Peli yn blysio am eu cicio, pledu, taflu'n orffwyll, a'u
                                                          drybowndio ar draws yr ardd.
Mochyn plastig yn rhochian a'r fferm yn Sioe o wartheg,
                          briwsion, bisgedi, defaid a cheffylau gwêdd.

Mae gwydrau'r glaw llonydd yn llygadu trwy'r ffenestri,
gwynt yn cosi'r cyrtans a phwffian chwerthin dan y drysau,
cadachau haul yr hwyr yn herio wrth ddwyn stribedi'r
                                                        llwch
cyn ymroi i ddangos ei hun a swagro'n rhodresgar yng
                                                      nghefn y tŷ.

Diwrnod arall yn hel ei draed o funud i funud, o funud i
                                                        funud.

Mother and housewife

The eyes of the plates on the dresser are fixed upon me
and the ticking of the kitchen clock is like the bite of toothache.
The still pegs are a regiment of soldiers
and the shawl on the line's folded like Tŷ'n y Fawnog's.[21]
The lips of the brass handles grimace
and the cupboard knobs in the parlour are like pimples.

The faces on the walls of the rooms view me with expectation,
and the little horses on their merry-go-round in the baby's room
Squeak back and forth, back and forth.

Every jigsaw's exhausted, yearning for a caress.
A cavalcade of little open-mouthed cars pleading to have
their doors shut and opened,
to be driven, parked and driven again.
Balls wanting to be kicked, passed, thrown wildly, and
dribbled across the garden.
A plastic pig grunting and the farm a Show of cows, crumbs,
biscuits, sheep and shire horses.

The lenses of the still rain gaze through the windows,
the wind flurries the curtains and bursts out laughing
under the doors,
the rags of the evening sun challenge as they steal the
strips of dust
before he settles down to showing off and swaggering
proudly at the back of the house.

Another day dragging its feet from minute to minute,
minute to minute.

---

21. Reference to a famous picture by Curnow Vosper, depicting a Welsh chapel, with an old woman called Siân Tŷ'n y Fawnog, who's wearing a patterned shawl, in the foreground: it has become an iconic image of traditional Welsh identity.

Nain

Ffenest car fyglyd a'r glaw mân heb sychu arni,
ffenest sy'n eiriol am gadach i'w glanhau.
Ffenest a wêl trwy ffenest a wêl wal gefn garegog,
frawddeg y lein ddillad wag drwy'r dydd, bob dydd.

Ond pan fo'r prynhawniau'n hel eu traed
a sŵn y distawrwydd yn cloi'r drysau, egyr y ffenest.
Daw megin y gwynt i fochio'r siwmperi gwlân. A'r
                                        trowsusau bach,
y ffrogiau a'r peisiau yn fyr eu hanadl wrth weld
cynfasau'n tin-droi ar drapîs y sioe.

Fin nos wedi'r sychu, y plygu a'r cadw daw niwl y môr i
                                                                                   wnio'i lês
ac wrth i'r llenni gau llithra dagrau'r glaw yn dawel dawel.

Grandmother

A smoky car window with the drizzle not yet dry on it,
A window that's begging for a rag to wipe it.
A window seen through a window that sees a stony back
wall,
The sentence of the washing line empty all day, every day.

But when the afternoons drag their feet
And the sound of the silence locks the doors, the window
opens.
The wind's bellows comes to plump out the cheeks of the
clean jumpers. And the little trousers,
The frocks and the petticoats short of breath as they see
The sheets turning head-over-heels on the show trapeze.

At evening, after the drying, the folding and the putting
away, the sea mist comes to sew its lace
And as the curtains close the rain's tears slip down in
silence, silence.

Deryn Rees-Jones

First

Like the impossible floodings of a fleet of clouds'
regurgitative rain, I can remember
all there was to know about that morning –
how the first light cracked across the flung-back
shutters of our window, remaking all the shadows
of our crumpled skin-white bed. Sex

had nothing to do with it –
only the way I took your body as my body
in my hands – not knowing what to do with it,
myself, as each shy stroke began to form a canvas
stretching its colours to the livid natures of the night.
At least that was the way I wanted to remember it
and called it being in love. And would I be lying
if I added too, just how intrigued I was,
quietly concerned? Like the first time
as a child, cutting my finger, smelling the blood.

I know Exactly the Sort of Woman I'd Like to Fall in Love With

If I were a man.

And she would not be me, but
Older and graver and sadder.
And her eyes would be kinder;
And her breasts would be fuller;
The subtle movements
Of her plum-coloured skirts
Would be the spillings of a childhood summer.

She would speak six languages, none of them my own.

And I? I would not be a demanding lover.
My long fingers, with her permission
Would unravel her plaited hair;
And I'd ask her to dance for me, occasionally,
Half-dressed on the moon-pitted stairs.

The Ladies

One hand slammed against the faulty lock
We scan messages on doors, chiselled
In biro and succinct
As gravestone epitaphs – that *men are bastards*
And that *Sue loves Steve, Marie's a slag*
And *Ann shags anything that moves*: assess

The catalogue of rich obscenities, puzzle
The help lines with their numbers
Scribbled out; retch
At the blue detergent, pig-shit sweet amidst
Incisive twists of toilet paper, the
Niagara flush
Of the unfettered toilet chains. It is

No wonder we avoid each other's eyes
Busy with soap and regurgitative roller towels;
Strange that next
We rearrange ourselves
In mirrors, put lipstick on, and then,

With sidelong glances
Try on each other's smiles.

Frances Sackett

Vanity
After a painting by F. C. Cowper, 1877-1958

The painter wanted embellishments,
What else could I do but dream and admire?
The props had never been so interesting,
Turning my cheeks to fire, filling the hand-glass
With a multitude of flashes, that flew like
Jolted planets, across the scanty sky of cloth
Set up behind.

        Such a change from angel-white –
The sultry taffeta, brocade in chains
Like gilded snakes that swarmed my arms,
My hands so formally arranged
To show the rings and touch the pearls
That wound their way around my neck,
Then trailed and looped against
The silken chair.

        And so he calls me 'Vanity'
And makes me feel the guilt of all
His observation. I only bared my shoulders
Once before, and that was when
A boy I loved said beauty lay
In what was unadorned.

Prinsengracht 263 – Amsterdam

if I look up into the heavens . . .
– The Diary of Anne Frank, 15 July 1944

You could just make it out –
The Westerkerk tower –
Through that arched window
In Peter's attic.

Now the large annexe windows
Are thrown wide,
Bells ring from the tower,
Pigeons coo in the back garden,
Buds break out on the old trees,
A cat yawns on a low rooftop.

We pay our toll –
Move in a long snake
Through the rooms,
English rubbing shoulders with Dutch,
German, Japanese, American.
The air, a slow mingling of garlic,
Spices and perfumes.
We read in our optional languages.

A mirror reflects the loft –
Exactly as I imagined it.

I would like to tell you, Anne,
That the house still stands tall –
Looks down at itself in the canal
And shivers a little at its memories;
As though by reflecting its good side
It could always trust in humanity
Having perfect manners
Like the people now
Passing through.

Ann Griffiths

Bechgyn Aberystwyth
(gydag ymddiheuriad i Dafydd ap Gwilym!)

Plygu rhag llid yr ydwyf,
Pla ar holl lanciau y plwyf!
Am na chefais, drais drawsoed,
Yr un ohonynt erioed.
Na llencyn, na phensiynwr,
Na gwrywgydiwr, na gŵr.

Pa rusiant, pa ddireidi,
Pa fethiant, na fynnant fi?
Pa ddrwg i ddyn dymunol
Fy nenu yn gu i'w gôl?
Nid oedd gywilydd iddo
Fy ngadael ei fwytho, dro.

Ni bu amser na charwn,
Ni bu chwant mor drech â hwn.
Ni bu nos yn y dafarn
Na bûm, ac eraill a'i barn,
Â'm wyneb at y bechgyn
A'm gobaith ar fachu un.
Ac wedi'r hir cilwenu
Dros ysgwydd at y llanciau lu,
Dywedodd un gŵr cadarn
Wrth y llall, i roi ei farn:

'Y ferch dew, draw, a'i chrechwen
A gwallt 'Boy George' ar ei phen,
Rwy'n meddwl, o'r arwyddion,
Mai tipyn o hwren yw hon.'

The Boys of Aberystwyth[22]
(with apologies to Dafydd ap Gwilym!)

I'm seething with rage, I'm just so mad,
A plague on every parish lad!
Since I never had, oh sad oppression,
A single one show me any attention.
I'm not choosy – young, or on a pension,
Straight or gay – I can't stand the tension.

What hindrance, what failure, what scorn,
Haven't I put up with? I'm just forlorn!
What harm would it do to a handsome chap
To seduce and embrace me on his lap?
And it would hardly spell the end of his good name
To let me caress him, in that there's no shame.

There never was a time when I didn't want a bit,
I've longed so much for someone strong and fit.
Not a night passed by in some pub or other
When I didn't look around for a would-be lover,
I'd stare intently at all the male population,
Hoping to pull, pretending adulation.
But after simpering at them again and again
Over shoulders and backs of the sea of men,
One stolid type piped up to his chum,
Giving this as his considered opinion:

'That fat girl over there, with her horrid smile
And her ghastly 'Boy George' hairstyle,
All the signs seem to be from the start,
Believe me, that she's a bit of a tart.'

'Pa bwrpas cwrso honno?'
Medd y llall wrtho fo,
'Gwell gen i beint, a chwmni
Criw o fois, nag un ferch hy.'

Siom yn wir, i wylaidd ferch,
Glywed y geiriau diserch.
Mewn dig, fe ymwrthodaf
Â bechgyn atgas, ac af
Heb oedi mwy, gam wrth gam
Ar ferched Comin Greenham.
Rhwystredig serch a'm cynnail
Mewn cymuned pridd a thail.

Ffieiddio dynion rhagom –
Rhoi'n hegni i rwystro bom!

'What's the point of chasing her? – she's bad,'
Said the other likely lad,
'I'd rather have a pint, and the company
of mates, than one bold girl who's zany.'

A setback indeed, to a timid girl like me,
To hear the insults flow so free.
Indignant, I therefore renounce the lads
They're mean and nasty, a bunch of cads,
So without more ado, I'm dusted and done,
Off to join the girls of Greenham Common.
Frustrated love will keep me going all the time
In a female community of earth and grime.

We'll keep men well away from us, many miles –
Give all our energy to ban the nuclear missiles!

---

22. This is a parody of — and tribute to ? — Dafydd ap Gwilym's well-known cywydd, 'The Girls of Llanbadarn'.

Kathy Miles

Wash Day

I wash your clothes weekly
as a sign of my love.
This was always the way.
I remember my mother
beating the clothes to submission,
slapping them onto marble, or
thin-stretched on the mangle's rack.
Fighting hot iron, the hiss
of burning water. Scalds still
shine white on her reddened arms.
I remember the dark smell of tweed,
hanging in front of the fire,
steam rising into the damp air,
a rainforest of garments.

You shed your clothes nightly,
a snake's habit. I pick up
these leavings, make them new again,
for you to dirty
as a token of your love.

Polishing

In her dreams, a bare room
swept clean as limbs,
dust brushed and floating
bright motes in the sun's eye.
Agitated, descending,
coating dark wood, making
a thin layer on mahogany
mocking her cloth-and-polish.

Lemon spray smelling of pale groves
cuts through the grease
with its sharp edge. Here,
the only orchards found in
the blooming of felled shaped trees,
table and dresser carved
for women to shine.

Wrought keyholes rubbed to gold
by her Midas touch, reflect
a blank space, furniture dead
as ghosts from solid roots.
Sap has long since shrunk
in their veins, embalmed in velvet,
cushions for a headstone.

She serves this dryad
of oak and pine, weekly labour
of her love. Wind sounds
its melancholy note outside,
cries like a banshee,
and dust settles, a fine cloud,
her throat constricts
from its grey hand.

Ophelia

Some nights we are all a little mad;
when the moon pulls us this way
and that, riding a sorcery of sky,
we are half-beast, half-woman, snarl
like wolves or witches at our changing.

Such evenings we are submerged,
float on strange rivers, remembrance
in our hands, or barren with grief
keen with hair streaming, strands
fanned out like weeds on stagnant water.

This vampire moon drains skin
already cold with drowning. Below
the surface it is dark and still,
a place of tiny apparitions, where
only native fish have their gestation.

Fighting up, flowers beckon their
soft gifts. Prince's feather blooms,
red-tipped as bloodied sword. Earth opens
like a ripe egg. We are sane tonight,
bright as the lunatic moon.

Samantha Wynne Rhydderch

The X-Ray Room

I am dismantled in monochrome
on the screen opposite the student doctors,
their gaze moving from me here to

me translated into porcelain
there. I am Exhibit A, my symmetry
unmasked by this cut and paste version

of my guts hermeneutically sealed
in negative. I stand by my parallel
text as if to elucidate

evisceration. My bones
in triplicate have nowhere to hide.
Their fragility becomes heraldic

when these exegetes invoke them
in Latin. You see, my other
has been deceiving me all along.

Part of the Furniture

Since I had him stuffed
and mounted in a glass case,
my husband has truly become
what he always was:
part of the furniture.
Addicted to sitting still and staring
out of the window, now I've made sure
he can do that permanently.
I know he'd thank me for it.
Always wanted to be on display,
in his best waistcoat, the centre
of attention. Suits him: far better
disembowelled than drivelling on.

Mererid Hopwood

Dadeni (detholiad)

Mae fy stori'n hen, ddarllenydd, a gwir
Ei geiriau'n dragywydd,
'di bod o hyd – ond bob dydd
yn fy neall wyf newydd . . .

*

Diniwed fel lleuad newydd oeddem,
Yn addo'n ddig'wilydd
Y gwelem gyda'n gilydd
Belydrau pob dechrau dydd.

 'mhen ar hen obennydd
Rwyf ar blufyn derfyn dydd
Yn dynn o dan d'adennydd.

Ni'n dau rhwng plygiadau plu
Ein neithiwr, dau yn nythu
Ac esgus mynd i gysgu,

Nes daw'r wawr a'i stori hud
I'n chwalu, cyn dychwelyd
I'n gwely glân, i'n gwâl glyd.

*

Rebirth (extract)

Reader, it's old, this story I sing,
The truth of its words undying,
It's always been – yet through the days
In myself I'm renewed always . . .

*

We were innocent as a crescent moon,
Making shameless vows together till noon,
And every day we shared in awe
The dawn's new rays, we woke, we saw . . .

With my head on an old pillow
I'm on the feathers of twilight now
Neatly tucked beneath your wings.

Just the two of us nestling
Amid the feathery folds of night
Pretending that we'd sleep so tight,

Till the dawn comes with its magic yarn
To break us up, before returning again
To our clean bed, our cosy den . . .

*

Tybed?! Ni fentraf gredu
Er bod lleisiau'r greddfau'n gry,
Amau yr hyn roed imi
A'r wyrth hardd drodd fy nghroth i
Yn amlen; eto, teimlaf
Chwarae rhwydd iâr fach yr haf,
Glöyn ewn tu mewn i mi
Rywsut yn troi a throsi'n
Friw afrwydd, yn wefr hyfryd
Yn fy neffro'n gyffro i gyd –
Ac o wrando ei gryndod
Ynof fi, mi wn ei fod.

Adnabod y dyfodol
Yw dy law'n gadael ei hôl,
Neu annel dy benelin
Ar ras i ffoi 'mhell dros ffin
Denau fy ngwast elastig.
I'r oriau mân, chwarae mig
A wnei di, a ni ein dau
Yn gymun yn ein gêmau.

Ar y sgrîn, gweld fy llinach
Mewn ynni un babi bach,
A hanner gweld fy hunan
Yn y sgwâr, yn llwydni'r sgan.
Yn y darn rhwng gwyn a du
Mae egin pob dychmygu,
A'r smotyn mewn deigryn dall
Yw'r fory, yw'r fi arall –
Hwn yr un a fydd ar ol,
Yr un, ac un gwahanol.

Could it be?! I can't trust myself to believe
Though the voices of instinct are firm,
Doubting what has been retrieved
And the lovely miracle that turned my womb
Into an envelope; yet now I sense
The light touch of a butterfly
Fluttering playfully inside, intense,
Turning and turning strangely,
Becoming a pulsing bruise that gives
A pleasant twinge which leaves me stirring,
Wide awake, and from feeling its trembling
Inside me, I know it lives . . .

A recognition of tomorrow,
That's your hand leaving its sign,
Or the poke of your elbow
Rearing to escape across that thin
Frontier which is my elastic waist.
Till the small hours you're there, ever gay,
Playing hide and seek with no haste,
You and me as one in our play.

On the screen, seeing my heritage
In the energy of one little infant,
And half-seeing myself on the page
Of the machine, the grey fuzz of the scan.
It's in the bit between black and white
The seed of all imagining,
The spot in the tear that blinds your sight
It's the future, it's the other being –
This is the one who will be left,
Both the other and the self.

Fy hanes yw dy hanes di, un cylch
Yn cau a'i ddolenni'n
Ddi-dor, un yw ein stori,
A hon sy'n ein huno ni.

*

Mae seren ein hamserau heno 'nghynn,
Ac yng nghân fy rhwymau
Clywaf gwyn dy gadwynau;
Heddiw yw awr dy ryddhau.

Yn dy lef mae fy nefoedd, un waedd wen
Yn ddyheu'r blynyddoedd,
A mi'n flin, mae hyn o floedd
Yn fiwsig naw o fisoedd.

Heno, 'rôl nawmis uniawn, yn fy nghol
Fy nghalon sy'n orlawn,
Cariad naw lleuad sy'n llawn –
Yn ei goflaid rwy'n gyflawn.

Yn y cariad gweladwy
Deall mai arall wyf mwy.
D'eni heno yw nadeni innau
I stori gariad ac ystyr geiriau
Fel 'mam' a 'dad' tu hwnt i 'mhrofiadau,
A bywyd eilwaith mewn byd o olau.
Yn yr heddiw llawn lliwiau, ar unwaith
Af ar daith i'th yfory dithau.

*

My story is yours, one circle
Closing, and its linking
Is forever, our story is one,
And this lulls us together.

*

The star of our times is tonight aflame,
And in the song of my chains
I hear the moan of your manacles;
Today is the day of your release.

Your cry is my heaven, one white cry
Yearning for the years ahead,
With me shirty, your enormous shout
Is the music of nine long months.

Tonight, after those months, in my lap
My heart is replete,
The love of nine moons is at the cusp –
In his embrace I am complete.

I perceive that from now on I am Other.
Giving birth to you tonight is my rebirth
It's the start of the story of father and mother,
The words have meaning, like the tale on the hearth,
And life again is a world full of light.
In today's rainbow, suddenly what might
Be your future appears and I take my path . . .

*

Ond heno'n dy wely tan dawelwch
Na all ein twyllo, yn y tywyllwch
Un haenen oer o ofn yw 'nhynerwch,
Gwewyr a'i ystyr tu hwnt i dristwch –
Oer ddwylo ar eiddilwch fy mabi,
A minnau'n sylwi ar dwymyn salwch.

Heddiw yw diwrnod 'nabod anobaith
Wrth weld y cariad liw'r gwêr yn dadlaith
Hyd y gannwyll – rwy'n ei wadu ganwaith,
Rwy'n fud, heb allu lleisio'r anfadwaith.
Un ifanc, un a'i afiaith yn diffodd,
A'i wen anodd lle bu chwerthin unwaith.

*

Dere 'run bach, mae'r machlud
Yn bwrw'i aur, ac mae'n bryd
Cloi corlan dy deganau
A hi'r nos oer yn nesáu.
Dere i wrando'r stori
Am y wawr, a gad i mi
Mewn nyth twt, am unwaith 'to,
Dy ddal. Estyn dy ddwylo
Bach gwyn yn dynn amdanaf
Cyn llithro heno i'th haf.
Dere, fe ddaw'r bore bach
A'i Frenin a'i gyfrinach.
Cwsg, cwsg fy nhywysog gwyn,
Darfod mae'r dydd diderfyn.

*

But tonight in your bed, in the stillness
Which cannot deceive us, in the darkness,
One cold layer of fear is my tenderness,
A spasm with its meaning beyond sadness,
Cold hands on my baby's softness
And me standing vigil over your illness.

Today is the day of absolute hopelessness
Seeing love the colour of wax melt down
Along the candle – I deny it a hundred times,
But now am mute, my power of speech has flown.
A young one, the quick of his being slowly quenched,
His hard-won smile faltering as his face blenched.

*

Come little one, the sun
Is shedding its gold, and it's time
To close up the pen of your toys,
As the cold night approaches.
Come and listen to the tale
Of the dawn, and let me
Hold you just once more in
A cosy nest. Stretch out your little
White hands around me
Before sliding tonight into your summer.
Come, the morning will arrive
With its king as its secret.
Sleep, sleep my little white prince
The limitless day comes to its end . . .

*

Amynedd ni ddaw â munud yn ôl,
Nac eiliad o'i fywyd
Mwy mi wn, ond am ennyd
A'r un bach, mi rown y byd.

*

I'r heddiw rhoddaf wreiddyn
Wedi'i godi o'r doe gwyn,
I flaguro ryw 'fory
Nes troi'n ardd y ddaear ddu.

Ac wrth y bedd mae 'ngweddi'n
Un fud, Dad – sef dy fod Ti . . .

Patience won't bring a moment back,
Not one moment of his life so brief,
No more, I know, but to have that moment back
I'd give the whole world, and lose my grief . . .

*

Today I plant a tiny flower,
Plucked from the white of yesterday
To blossom at some future hour,
When the black earth brings forth a nosegay.

And at the grave my silent appeal
Is simply, Father – that you are real . . .

Biographies of Poets

Gwenllïan ferch Rhirid Flaidd (*fl.* 1460)
Only one of her poems (the englyn included in this anthology) has survived. Thought to have been the daughter of the poet, Tudur Penllyn, and Gwerful ferch Ieuan Fychan, who was a descendant of Rhirid Flaidd.

Gwerful Mechain (c.1462-1500)
Born sometime between 1460 and 1463. Evidence from her own poetry and that of her contemporaries indicates that Gwerful was a member of the Fychan family from Llanfechain in Powys. Her surname, therefore, is based on the name of her birthplace, rather than on the name of her father. Her work is full of specific references to places around her home. Her father was Hywel Fychan ap Hywel and her mother was Gwenhwyfar ferch Dafydd Llwyd. She had at least three brothers, Dafydd, Madog, and Thomas, and a sister, called Mawd. Gwerful married John ap Llywelyn Fychan ap Llywelyn ap Deio and manuscript evidence suggests that she was the mother of at least one daughter, called Mawd or Mallt. Gwerful has posed a problem for critics and biographers by representing herself in one of her best known poems, *"Cywydd i ofyn telyn rawn"* (A cywydd to ask for a harp) as the landlady of a pub called the Ferry. The unlikelihood of a woman belonging to the aristocratic Vaughan family 'lowering herself' to keep a tavern led some critics to believe that there must have been two different poets called Gwerful, one presumably responsible for the erotic verse and the other for the devotional. The reader would not be hard pressed to guess which of the

two Gwerfuls would be held responsible for which kind of poem! Actually, critics now agree that the notion of the 'two Gwerfuls' was a false one, and that the poet's self-representation in the poem in question is tongue-in-cheek. As Ceridwen Lloyd-Morgan judiciously points out, *"peryglus iawn . . . fyddai derbyn fod yr hyn a ddywed beirdd amdanynt eu hunain yn eu cerddi yn adlewyrchu'n gywir bob amser y ffeithiau am eu bywyd."*[1] (it would be very dangerous . . . to accept that what poets say about themselves in their poems is always an accurate reflection of the facts about their lives). There is evidence from the poems, however, to support the view that she and the poet Dafydd Llwyd of Mathafarn, with whom she exchanges a number of provocative poems, were lovers. Some forty poems by her are preserved in manuscript, mainly in the form of cywyddau or englynion, and ranging in tone and subject matter from the pious and didactic to the outrageously humorous and erotic. Nevertheless, as Ceridwen Lloyd-Morgan has observed, she apparently does not write praise poems nor elegies of the conventional kind, as practised by her male peers. She does enter wholeheartedly into the poetic practice of the *ymryson* (poetic battle or debate), however, and this relish for discussion and dialogue is also evident in the poetry of the female poets who followed her. Gwerful's poetry is female-centred, vigorous, and imaginative; moreover, the relatively large number of manuscript copies of her work testifies to her popularity over the centuries. In 2001, *Gwaith Gwerful Mechain ac eraill*, an edition of her work by Nerys Ann Howells, was published by the Centre for Welsh and Celtic Studies in Aberystwyth. The fact that it has taken so long for the work of such an important figure to be acknowledged

---

1. Ceridwen Lloyd-Morgan, "'Gwerful Ferch Ragorol Fain': Golwg Newydd ar Gwerful Mechain" *Ysgrifau Beirniadol* XVI (1990) p. 89.

by the Welsh academic establishment may be regarded as a symptom of its erstwhile prudery and misogyny. Let us hope that time is past.

Alis ferch Gruffydd ab Ieuan (ap Llywelyn Fychan) (C16)
lwydwen . . .) From the Vale of Clwyd. Her sister, Catrin, was also a poet, as was their father. Her englyn to her father on his wanting to marry a much younger woman shows the influence of Gwerful Mechain's englyn on the same theme (*Gwelais eich lodes lwydwen*)

Catrin ferch Gruffydd ap Hywel o Landdeiniolen (*fl.* 1555)
From Anglesey. A few of her englynion and the included poem on the cold summer of 1555 have survived in manuscript.

Katherine Philips, née Fowler [The Matchless Orinda] (1631-64)
Poet, born in London but married into the Welsh family of James Philips in 1647, at the age of 16. From then on she lived mainly in Cardigan. A precocious and fairly prolific poet, she earned considerable fame in her own lifetime (hence the admiring epithet). She maintained a coterie of like-minded friends and wrote extensively of the joys of platonic love. Some recent criticism interprets her passionate works addressed to female friends as lesbian love poems, though this reading is strongly contested by others. Publications: *Poems by the incomparable Mrs Katherine Philips* (1664); modern edition: *The Collected Works of Katherine Philips* ed. Patrick Thomas, in 3 volumes (1990-3).

Angharad James (1677-1749)
Poet, daughter of James Davies and Angharad Humphreys, Gelli Ffrydau, Llandwrog. She and her sister, Margaret,

received a good education at home, including the study of Latin and music. When she was twenty she married William Pritchard, who was sixty; the poem in dialogue with her sister about the relative advantages of choosing an old or a young man as a husband would appear to be related, therefore, to the circumstances of her own life. In adult life her home was at Y Parlwr, Penanmaen, Dolwyddelan.

Jane Brereton [Melissa] (1685-1740)
Jane Brereton was born in 1685 to Thomas Hughes and his wife, Ann Jones, near Mold, Flintshire. Encouraged by her father to develop her intellectual capacities, Brereton began writing poetry as a child for her own amusement. Brereton was married in 1711 to Thomas Brereton, the wastrel son of William Brereton, distinguished soldier of the ancient Brereton family of Chester. Thomas Brereton managed to squander the considerable fortune inherited on his father's death, and his wife was reluctantly persuaded to separate from him shortly before he drowned whilst crossing a river when the tide was coming in. Jane Brereton lived in London for a while during her marriage, but returned to Wales on her separation from her husband and died in Wrexham in 1740.

Margaret Davies (c.1700-1785?)
Several of Margaret Davies's notebooks containing her transcriptions of poems are preserved in the National Library of Wales and have been the source of a number of hitherto unpublished poems in this collection. She was an avid collector of poems and a poet in her own right, having been taught the strict metres by Michael Pritchard. She was the daughter of Dafydd Evan of Coetgae-du, Trawsfynydd and was a prominent figure in Meirionethshire and Caernarfonshire literary circles.

Anna Williams (1706-83)

Anna Williams was born and raised in Rhosmarket near Haverfordwest, the daughter of Zachariah Williams, an inventor; she moved to London with her father in the late 1720s. In 1727, Zachariah Williams entered the Charterhouse, an establishment which functioned both as a school and as an almshouse for gentlemen fallen on hard times; it is unclear in which capacity Mr Williams was involved. Williams was herself well-educated and spoke fluent French and Italian. Furthermore, during her father's time at the Charterhouse she is known to have assisted Stephen Gray, the eminent scientist, with his experiments in electricity and the human body.

Williams became friends with Samuel Johnson in the 1740s, by which time she had already begun to lose her sight. In 1752 Johnson convinced Williams to undergo an operation to save her sight, which unfortunately resulted in her total blindness. After that time Williams lived intermittently in Johnson's household until her death in 1783. Williams' *Miscellanies in Prose and Verse* was published by subscription in 1766. She went on to produce one more volume of poetry, namely: *Romance of A Dull Life* (1771).

Anne Penny, née Hughes (*fl.* 1729-80)

Anne Penny was born in Bangor, where her father was a clergyman. In later life she lived in London and, like her compatriot Anna Williams, had connections with Samuel Johnson. Her publications are: *Anningait and Ajutt* (inscribed to 'Mr Samuel Johnson', 1761), *Select Poems from Mr. Gesner's Pastorals* (1762), *Poems with a Dramatic Entertainment* (1771) and *A Pastoral Elegy* (1773).

Mary Robinson, née Darby [Perdita] (1758-1800)

Born in Bristol, Mary Robinson's maternal ancestry was Welsh, stemming from the Seys family of Boverton Castle, Llantwit Major. She was the third of five children; her father abandoned the family when Mary was seven. They moved to London, where her mother made ends meet by running a school for girls, where Mary herself was educated. She was an exceptionally beautiful girl and had many suitors from an early age. She married Thomas Robinson, also of Welsh extraction, when she was fifteen; they led a precarious life thereafter, often fleeing to Wales from their creditors, since Thomas was a feckless drunk. At the instigation of David Garrick, Mary went on the stage, to great acclaim. Her most famous role was as Perdita in *A Winter's Tale*. The Prince of Wales (later George IV) saw her on stage and took her as his mistress. Her reputation was irretrievably lost. She wrote a polemic condemning the institution of marriage, as well as numerous novels, including *Walsingham, or The Pupil of Nature* (1797) and several volumes of poetry, including *Poems* (1775) and *Poetical Works*, 3 vols. (1805). She died at the age of forty-two.

Jane Cave (*fl.* 1770-96; d. 1813)

Jane Cave was born and raised in South Wales. Her English father was an exciseman who was stationed for his daughter's formative years in Talgarth, Breconshire. John Cave came into contact with Howel Harris and his religious community at Trefecca, and became a fervent Calvinist Methodist. Jane Cave herself was married to another exciseman in 1783 and left Wales with her husband soon after. She bore two sons and is known to have lived in Bristol and Winchester before returning to Wales where she died in Newport, Gwent in 1813. Between 1783 and 1794, four editions of her volume of verse, *Poems on Various Subjects, Entertaining, Elegiac and Religious* were published. Many of Cave's poems are witty explorations of issues still pertinent to women's experience, such as marriage, motherhood, female friendship and women's health.

Ann Julia Hatton, née Kemble [Ann of Swansea] (1764-1838)
Born into the theatrical Kemble family in Worcester; her sister was the famous actress Sarah Siddons. Julia herself was lame, which seemed to have prevented her from following a theatrical career herself. While she was still a teenager she married and was abandoned by a man named Curtis; it is tempting to interpret the cynical and disillusioned view of men expressed in many of her works as a reflection of personal experiences such as this. In 1792 she married William Hatton and travelled with him to America; on their return they became the lease-holders of the Swansea Bathing House. In 1806 William Hatton died and, after a sojourn in Kidwelly, where she ran a dancing school, she returned to Swansea, where she devoted herself to writing. Her family apparently paid her to stay in Swansea, in order to be as far away from them as possible. She published nine three- and five-decker romantic novels, including *Cambrian Pictures* (1810) and *Deeds of the Olden Times* (1826) and two volumes of elegiac and somewhat dolorous lyric verse, *Poems on Miscellaneous Subjects* (1783) and *Poetic Trifles* (1811). Her poem 'Swansea Bay' has been much anthologised.

Ann Griffiths (1776-1805)
Born at Dolwar-fach in Llanfihangel-yng-Ngwynfa, Montgomeryshire. The family were well-off country people, her father being a *bardd gwlad*. Ann's mother died when she was seventeen, after which she became mistress of the household. The whole family gradually came under the influence of Methodism, Ann herself undergoing an intense experience

of conversion in 1796. The family home became a centre of Methodist worship in the district; the rest of Ann's all too brief life was dedicated to her religion, for which she composed the hymns for which she is today remembered and revered. Ann married in 1804 but died in the following year, after giving birth to a baby daughter, who also died. Eight of Ann's letters survive, one in her own hand; these letters are highly regarded both as masterpieces of Welsh prose and as a vivid rendition of the life of the early Methodist congregations. Some seventy of her hymns survive, though she herself did not seek either to preserve or publish them. The fact of their survival is a result of their transcription by John Hughes, who married Ruth Evans, a maid at Dolwar-fach, and who recited the hymns from memory, since she herself was illiterate. They appeared in a posthumous collection in 1806. Ann Griffiths' hymns are really poems of intense, personal religious fervour. They are influenced by folk song and the Bible. From the point of view of the student of women's poetry, her verse is remarkable for the daring outspokenness of its central female speaker and that speaker's longing for a quasi-conjugal relationship with Jesus Christ. Publication: *Casgliad o Hymnau* (1806).

Felicia Hemans, née Browne (1793-1835)
Born in Liverpool, she moved with her family to North Wales in 1800 and lived in Wales, near Abergele and later St Asaph, for most of her life. Her mother was well-read and influential. Felicia was something of a child prodigy. She spoke six languages and published her first book of poems at the age of fourteen. She married Captain Hemans in 1812 and had five sons. He left the family in 1818, after which she supported the family through her writing, which was copious and generally admired. Select Publications: *Poems* (1808), *The*

Domestic Affections and Other Poems (1812), *Tales and Historic Scenes in Verse* (1819), *The Sceptic: A Poem* (1820), *Welsh Melodies*, 3 vols. (1822-9), *The Siege of Valencia* (1823), *The Forest Sanctuary and Other Poems* (1825), *Records of Women, with Other Poems* (1828), *Songs of the Affections, with Other Poems* (1830), *Scenes and Hymns of Life, with Other Religious Poems* (1834), *National Lyrics* (1834).

Maria James (1795–c.1845)

The dates of Maria James' birth and death are unconfirmed. What is certain is that at the age of seven she emigrated with her family from Snowdonia to the United States. James was a monoglot Welsh speaker when she left Wales and recalls learning her first words of English during the voyage to America as "'take care' and 'get out of the way' seemed reiterated from land's-end to land's-end". [Maria James, *Wales and Other Poems* (New York: John S. Taylor, 1839) p. 49]. James' family joined a community of Welsh quarry workers in New York State, and, at the age of ten, she was sent to the household of the Garretson family in nearby Rhinebeck to take up a position as housemaid and companion to the young daughter of the house, Mary. James remained with the Garretsons for the next five years, during which time she was educated along with Mary, and began to write poetry for her own satisfaction.

When James was fifteen she was sent away to a position as apprentice in the lace-making industry in New York City where she remained for the next nine years. She then returned to take up her previous role as much-loved servant of the Garretson family. On her return James is said to have been very sad and pious and writing poetry more frequently than ever. Presumably through the well-intentioned agency of her employers, her work began to appear in local newspapers and magazines. In 1838 the Garretsons showed one of James' poems to Mrs Potter, a visiting friend from New York City; in 1839 Mrs Potter's husband, A Potter, D.D., of Union College New York edited and wrote an introduction to a volume of James' work entitled *Wales and Other Poems*. After this publication nothing further is known of Maria James. Many of the poems in *Wales and Other Poems* offer rare and interesting insights into the experience of a nineteenth-century working-class woman poet.

Jane Williams [Ysgafell] (1806-85)
Born in London to a family with roots in Montgomeryshire, Jane Williams later lived in the family home, Neuadd Felen, in Talgarth. She was an erudite and forthright author who vigorously repudiated the allegations made against Wales and the Welsh in the Blue Books report of 1848. She was patronised by Lady Llanover and lived most of her life with her 'attached friend', Mary Willey. Her best known work is her edition of the autobiography of Betsy Cadwaladr, the Balaclava nurse. She also edited the writings of Thomas Price (Carnhuanawc). Her major works, including a *History of Wales* (1869) are in prose, but she also published two volumes of verse, viz. *Miscellaneous Poems* (1824) and *Celtic Fables, Fairy Tales, & Legends: Versified* (1862).

Elin Evans [Elen Egryn] (1807-76)
Born in Llanegryn, Merionethshire, daughter of the village schoolmaster, who, along with Gwilym Cawrdaf, taught her the craft of poetry. She later lived in Liverpool. Her volume of verse, *Telyn Egryn* (1850), recently republished by Honno, is generally considered to be the first book of poetry by a woman published in Welsh.

Anne Beale (1816-1900)

Born in Somerset; came to Wales in 1840 as a governess to the family of an Anglican vicar near Llandeilo. She wrote with empathy and enthusiasm of her adopted Welsh home. Primarily a novelist, Beale published one collection of verse, *Poems* (1842), which had a list of eminent subscribers, beginning with the Countess of Cawdor, of Golden Grove, Llandeilo and the Lady Dynevor of Dynevor Castle.

Emily Jane Pfeiffer, née Davis (1827-90)

Born in Milford Hall, Montgomeryshire, into a wealthy banking family. However, the family fortunes collapsed and Emily was therefore denied the education she craved. She married a German businessman and they lived in London, where her husband supported and encouraged her writing. On her death, she left a substantial sum of money to support higher education for women in Wales. Her major work is *Glân-Alarch: His Silence and Song* (1877), an epic poem tracing the history of Wales through the voice of the bard, Glân-Alarch. Other collections include *Gerard's Monument and Other Poems* (1878) and *Flowers of the Night* (1889). She also published some translations of Heine's verse. Contemporary reviewers were generally ecstatic, e.g. *The Times* said: "Mrs Pfeiffer shows that it is quite possible for a woman to write verse that shall be agreeable even to palates that scarcely care to quench their thirst with anything less than the nectar of the gods."

Sarah Williams [Sadie] (1838-1868)

Born in London, of Welsh Nonconformist parents. Delicate in health, she died at an early age; her only volume of verse, *Twilight Hours: A Legacy of Verse* (1868) was published posthumously. The attitude expressed towards Wales and the Welsh language in her works is one of longing and regret.

Sarah Jane Rees [Cranogwen] (1839-1916)

Born in Llangrannog, Ceredigion. Teacher, editor, temperance campaigner, sailor, preacher, poet. Publications: *Caniadau Cranogwen* (1870); many prose works in *Y Frythones* (which she edited for some time) and *Y Gymraes*. She was the founder of the Temperance Union of the Women of South Wales and a renowned public speaker in her day. She never married though, ironically, she won the Crown at the National Eisteddfod for a poem on the subject of 'The Wedding Ring'. Her most passionate works, though, are addressed to women.

Catherine Prichard [Buddug] (1842-1909)

Born in Llanrhuddlad, Anglesey. Temperance campaigner. Wrote for magazines such as *Y Frythones, Y Gymraes* and *Y Genhinen*. Publications: *Caniadau Buddug* (1911) posthumously compiled and edited by her husband.

Alice Gray Jones [Ceridwen Peris] (1852-1943)

Born in Llanllyfni, Caernarfonshire. Teacher and temperance campaigner. One of the founders of the North Wales Women's Temperance League. Regular contributor to *Y Frythones* and later editor of *Y Gymraes*. Publication: *Caniadau Ceridwen Peris* (1934).

Ellen Hughes (1862-1927)

Born in Llanengan, Caernarfonshire. Journalist, poet, and preacher. Publications: *Sibrwd yr Awel* (1887), *Murmur y Gragen* (1907).

Elizabeth Mary Jones [Moelona] (1878-1953)

Born Rhydlewis, Ceredigion. Novelist, teacher, and poet. A prolific prose writer, her most famous work was *Teulu Bach Nantoer* (1913). Many of her works reflect her ardent commitment both to Welsh nationalism and to women's suffrage. She was also a Francophile and translated some works by Alphonse Daudet into Welsh.

Eiluned Lewis (1900-1979)
Born in Newtown, Montgomeryshire. Educated at the University of London. Fleet Street journalist and subsequently a novelist and short story writer. Publications: *December Apples* (1935), *Morning Songs* (1944) (verse). Novels: *Dew on the Grass* (1934), *The Captain's Wife* (1943), *The Leaves of the Tree* (1953). Also published a collection of essays, *In Country Places* (1951) and *The Land of Wales* (1937). Edited the letters of Charles Morgan (1967).

Dilys Cadwaladr (1902-1979)
Born in Four Crosses, Caernarfon. She won the Crown at the National Eisteddfod in 1953, with a pryddest entitled 'Y Llen'. During the 1940s she lived on Ynys Enlli (Bardsey Island) [cf. Brenda Chamberlain and Christine Evans] Worked as a teacher. Published only one collection of short stories (1936). Married a Dutchman, Leo Scheltinga, after the war.

Jean Earle (b. 1909-2002)
Born in Bristol, brought up in the Rhondda. Publications: *A Trial of Strength* (1980) *Visiting Light* (1987), *The Sun in the West* (1995), *The Bed of Memory* (2001).

Lynette Roberts (1909-1995)
Born in Buenos Aires of Welsh parents. Married Keidrych Rhys in 1939 and lived in Llanybri, Carmarthenshire. She published two volumes of verse with Faber under the editorship of T. S. Eliot, who championed her unusual, hermetic, surrealist work. *Poems* was published in 1944, followed by *Gods with Stainless Ears*, an epic war poem, in 1951. She also published two prose works, *Village Dialect* (1944) and *The Endeavour* (1954). Llanybri itself and the surrounding landscape was an important inspiration for her work. In later years she became a Jehovah's Witness and renounced poetry altogether.

Brenda Chamberlain (1912-1971)

Born in Bangor, Chamberlain was a painter, prose writer, and poet. She trained as a painter in London and then settled with her husband, John Petts, in Llanllechid, near Bethesda. She and Petts produced the *Caseg Broadsheets*, a series of six poetry pamphlets illustrated by Chamberlain and Petts, during the war years. Lynette Roberts was one of the poets included in the series. After the breakup of her marriage in 1946, she travelled to Germany and then settled on Bardsey Island (Ynys Enlli). In 1961 she moved to the Greek island of Ydra. During these periods, she chronicled the islands' landscapes and people in visual art, prose and poetry. She returned to Bangor at the end of her life. Her publications include *The Green Heart* (1958), *Tide-Race* (1962), *The Water Castle* (1964), *A Rope of Vines* (1965), and *Poems with Drawings* (1969). Her work is distinctive and idiosyncratic, often autobiographical, and with an interesting combination of the mystical and the down-to-earth. She is one of the few artists who truly excelled in more than one art form.

Eluned Phillips (b. 1915?)

Born in Cenarth, Ceredigion. Freelance writer. Won the Crown at the National Eisteddfod twice, in 1967 and 1983. Wrote a biography of Dewi Emrys (1971). Published *Cerddi Glyn-y-mêl* in 1985.

Joyce Herbert (b. 1923)

Born in the Rhondda. Educated at Cardiff University. Began publishing verse in the 1940s, followed by a period when she was primarily involved in political activism and published little verse, until the 1970s when her work began to appear again. Publication: *Approaching Snow* (1983).

Alison Bielski (b. 1925)

Born in Newport, Gwent. A prolific and unjustly neglected poet, with a distinctive voice. Publications: *Twentieth Century Flood* (1964), *Across the Burning Sand* (1970), *Monogrampoems* (1971), *Eve* (1973), *Shapes and Colours* (1973), *Zodiacpoems* (1973), *Mermaid Poems* (1974), *The Lovetree* (1974), *Discovering islands* (1979), *Seth* (1980), *Night sequence* (1981), *Eagles* (1983), *That Crimson Flame: Selected Poems* (1996), *The Green-Eyed Pool* (1997). Has also published works on local history. Formerly the honorary joint secretary of the English-language section of the Academi Gymreig.

Christine Furnival (b. 1931)

Born in Chelsea of partly Welsh parentage. Educated at Cambridge. Lived in Carmarthenshire from 1973-1983. Publications: *A Bare-Fisted Catch* (1968), *Prince of Sapphires* (1976), *The Animals to Orpheus* (1977), *Towards Praising* (1978). Also writes plays for radio and stage and translates from the Italian.

Nest Lloyd (b. 1934)

Born in Llangeler, Ceredigion. Apart from poems in anthologies, she has recently published a fascinating memoir of her childhood in West Wales during the Second World War in the anthology *Iancs, Conchis a Spam: Atgofion Menywod o'r Ail Ryfel Byd* ed. Leigh Verrill-Rhys (Honno, 2002).

Sally Roberts Jones (b. 1935)

Born in London of partly Welsh parentage, brought up in Llanrwst, Denbighshire and Llangefni, Anglesey. Lives in Port Talbot. Educated at the University of North Wales, Bangor. Librarian, publisher, and local historian, as well as poet and novelist. Publications: *Turning Away* (1969), *Sons and Brothers* (1977), *The Forgotten Country* (1977), *Relative Values* (1985). Novel: *Pendarvis* (1992).

Gillian Clarke (b. 1937)

Born in Cardiff. Poet and teacher of creative writing. Educated at Cardiff University. Lives in Talgarreg, Ceredigion. Co-edited *The Anglo-Welsh Review* 1976-1984. Publications: *The Sundial* (1978), *Letter from a Far Country* (1982) *Letting in the Rumour* (1989) *Selected Poems* (1985), *The King of Britain's Daughter* (1993), *Collected Poems* (1997), *Five Fields* (1998). Has also written work for children and translated from the Welsh of Kate Roberts and Menna Elfyn. Her work is widely known and admired, and is frequently set in school syllabi. She has been an important influence on, and inspiration for, contemporary Welsh female poets, beginning to publish her work at a time when 'Anglo-Welsh' poetry was conceived of as being almost exclusively masculine.

Jane Edwards (b. 1938)

Born on Anglesey. Educated at Coleg y Normal, Bangor; subsequently became a teacher. Novelist and short story writer. Winner of numerous Arts Council and Eisteddfodic prizes. Publications (novels and short stories): *Dechrau Gofidiau* (1962), *Byd o Gysgodion* (1964), *Bara Seguryd* (1969), *Epil Cam* (1972), *Tyfu* (1973), *Dros Fryniau Bro Afallon*(1976), *Miriam* (1977), *Hon, debygem, ydoedd Gwlad yr Hafddydd* (1980), *Cadno Rhos-y-ffin* (1984), *Y Bwthyn Cu* (1987), *Blind Dêt* (1989), *Pant yn y Gwely* (1993).

Christine Evans (b. 1943)

Born in West Yorkshire of partly Welsh descent. Educated at the University of Exeter. Has lived on the Llŷn peninsula since 1967, spending her summers on Ynys Enlli (Bardsey Island) the subject of her most recent collection, *Island of Dark Horses*. Teaches English in Pwllheli, her father's birthplace. Publications: *Looking Inland* (1983), *Falling Back* (1985), *Cometary Phases* (1989), *Island of Dark Horses* (1995).

Nesta Wyn Jones (b. 1946)

Born in Dolgellau, Merionethshire. Educated at the University of North Wales, Bangor. Winner of numerous Welsh Arts Council prizes for her volumes of verse. Farms at Abergeirw, near Dolgellau. Publications: *Cannwyll yn Olau* (1969), *Ffenest Ddu* (1973), *Rhwng Chwerthin a Chrio* (1986) and *Dawns y Sêr* (1999). Has also published a travel journal: *Dyddiadur Israel* (1982).

Glenda Beagan (b. 1948), Rhuddlan

Born in Rhuddlan. Educated at the Open University, University of Wales Aberystwyth, and Lancaster University. Published two collections of short stories: *The Medlar Tree* (1992) and *Changes and Dreams* (1996), as well as *Vixen*, a volume of verse, in 1996.

Marged Dafydd [Meg Elis] (b. 1950)

Born in Aberystwyth. Educated at the University of North Wales, Bangor. Journalist, prose writer, poet, and translator. Won the Prose Medal in the National Eisteddfod in 1985. Prominent member of Cymdeithas yr Iaith Gymraeg (The Welsh Language Society). Publications: *Cysylltiadau* (1973) – poetry; *I'r Gad* (1975), *Cyn Daw'r Gaeaf* (1985) – novels; *Carchar* (1978) – short stories.

Einir Jones (b. 1950)

Born in Traeth Coch, Anglesey. Educated at the University of North Wales, Bangor. Twice winner of the Crown in the National Eisteddfod. A teacher by profession. Publications: *Pigo Crachan* (1972), *Gwellt Medi* (1980), *Daeth Awst, daeth nos* (1991), *Gweld y garreg ateb* (1991).

Menna Elfyn (b. 1951)

Born in Pontardawe. Educated at the University College of Wales, Swansea. Has worked as a teacher but has been a full-time writer for a number of years. A prominent member of Cymdeithas yr Iaith Gymraeg (The Welsh Language Society) and well known as a pacifist and feminist, as well as the foremost Welsh woman poet of her generation.

Her commitment to the language, social justice, peace, and the woman's movement is in evidence in her poetry, but the political nature of her verse is never allowed to become sloganeering because of the precision of her technique and the sensuous delight of her imagery. Her work is the embodiment of the feminist dictum that 'the personal is political'; for Elfyn, current events are taken personally, while the intimately personal becomes a world event. She has become well-known as a performer of her own poetry and has travelled extensively throughout the world as a kind of one-woman ambassador for Welsh poetry. Her poetry tours began in Wales where she was a participant in successful collaborations with other poets in *Fel yr Hed y Frân* (1985), *Cicio Ciwcymbyrs* (1988) and *Dal Clêr* (1993); the latter resulted in the publication of a joint volume of verse with her collaborators, Ifor ap Glyn, Cyril Jones, and Elinor Wyn Reynolds. Her last three collections of poetry have been bilingual works, in which her poems are translated by a range of prominent Welsh poets working through the medium of English, including Gillian Clarke and Elin ap Hywel.

Publications: *Mwyara* (1976), *Stafelloedd Aros* (1977), *Tro'r Haul Arno* (1982), *Mynd Lawr i'r Nefoedd* (1985) *Aderyn Bach Mewn Llaw* (1990), *Dal Clêr* (1993), *Eucalyptus* (1995), *Cell Angel* (1996), *Cusan Dyn Dall/Blind Man's Kiss* (2001). Edited the following collections of Welsh women's poetry: *Hel Dail Gwyrdd* (1985) and *O'r Iawn Ryw* (1992). For children: *Madfall ar y Mur* (1993) Plays: *Madog* (1989), *Trefen Teyrnas Wâr* (1990), *Y Forwyn Goch* (1992) and *Melltith y Mamau* (1995).

Hilary Llewellyn-Williams (b. 1951)
Born in Kent of partly Welsh descent. Educated at Southampton University. Has lived in Wales since 1982. Publications: *The Tree Calendar* (1987), *Book of Shadows* (1990), *animaculture* (1997).

Catherine Fisher (b. 1957)
Born in Newport, Gwent. Educated at the Gwent College of Further Education, she is a teacher in her home town. A poet and highly successful novelist for children. Publications: *Immrama* (1988), *The Unexplored Ocean* (1994), *Altered States* (1999). Many award-winning children's novels, such as *The Conjuror's Game* (1990).

Gwyneth Lewis (b. 1959)
Born in Cardiff. Won the Literature Medal in the Urdd Eisteddfod twice while still at school. Studied English at Cambridge, then creative writing in the USA. Did research on literary forgeries at Oxford. Publishes poetry in both Welsh and English. Publications: *Sonedau Redsa* (1990), *Cyfrif Un ac Un yn Dri* (1996), *Parables and Faxes* (1995), *Zero Gravity* (1998).

Delyth George
Brought up in Cefneithin. Educated at Aberystwyth. Wrote her PhD on *Love and Passion in the Welsh Novel 1917-85*. Publishes articles and reviews in *Barn*, *Y Traethodydd*, and *Llen Cymru*. Wrote a monograph on Islwyn Ffowc Elis (1990).

Merryn Williams
Educated at Cambridge University. Primarily a poet and a literary scholar, who has published works on Hardy, Wilfred Owen, Margaret Oliphant, and translations of the work

of Federico García Lorca. Has also published a novel for children, *Clare and Effie*, with Honno Press.

Rose Flint
Born in London but lived for many years on the Welsh-English border. Publication: *Blue Horse of Morning* (1989).

Sarah Corbett
Born in Chester; brought up in North Wales. Educated at the Universities of Leeds and East Anglia. Publications: *The Red Wardrobe* (1998); *The Witchbag* (2002).

Kate Johnson
Born in Manchester but has lived in both Anglesey and Cardiff. Publication: *Gods* (1996).

Kate Bingham
Lives in London. Educated at Oxford. Has published two novels and a volume of verse, *Cohabitation*. Received an Eric Gregory Award in 1996.

Elin ap Hywel
Educated at Queen's College, Cambridge and the University of Wales, Aberystwyth. Won the Literature Medal at the Urdd Eisteddfod in 1980 for her volume of verse, *Cyfaddawdu*. Published *Pethau Brau* in 1982. One of the founding editors of Honno, the Welsh Women's Press. Known also as as a translator, especially of the work of Menna Elfyn.

Elin Wyn Williams
Born in Pontyberem. Educated Aberystwyth. Won the prose medal at the Urdd Eisteddfod in Dyffryn Nantlle.

Elin Llwyd Morgan
Born in Cefnbrynbrain. Daughter of Jane Edwards, the novelist. Brought up in Anglesey. Educated at UCW Aberystwyth. Translator and scriptwriter. Publication: *Duwieslebog* (1993).

Deryn Rees-Jones
Born in Liverpool of Welsh parentage. Educated at Bangor and London. Currently teaches Literature and Creative Writing at Liverpool Hope University College. Publication: *The Memory Tray* (1994).

Frances Sackett
Born in Chirk, Clwyd and brought up in North Wales. Educated at the University of Manchester. Currently lives in Stockport. Publication: *The Hand Glass* (1996).

Kathy Miles
Lives in Aberaeron, Ceredigion. Founder-member of the Lampeter Writer's Workshop. Publications: *The Rocking Stone* (1988); *The Third Day* (1995).

Esyllt Maelor
Born in Meirionethshire and brought up on the Llŷn peninsula. Has worked as a teacher. Won the chair in Eisteddfod Dyffryn Ogwen in 1990.

Ann Griffiths
Born near Ammanford. Studied at Aberystwyth; wrote her PhD on Welsh poetry 1320-1600.

Mererid Hopwood
Lives in Llangynnwr, Carmarthen, though originally from Cardiff. Formerly a lecturer in German at the University of

Wales, Swansea; later worked for the Arts Council of Wales; now a freelance writer. Won the Chair at the National Eisteddfod in 2001 – the first time it had ever been won by a woman. Learned her craft in strict metre poetry by attending evening classes given by the poet Tudur Dylan.

Samantha Wynne Rhydderch (b. 1966)
Brought up in Llanelli; family originally from New Quay, Ceredigion. Studied Classics at Cambridge University. Published her first collection, *Rockclimbing in Silk* in 2001.

Acknowledgements

Thanks to Professor Dafydd Johnston for his advice and encouragement on the tricky business of translating early Welsh women's poetry. Thanks to Cathryn Charnell-White for her help.

Our great thanks to all the poets and estates for allowing their work to be published and to the following publishers for allowing us to reproduce the works. In a few cases, despite our best efforts, we have been unable to contact the owners of the copyright to the poems. The publishers would be delighted to hear from any copyright holders not here acknowledged and would be pleased to make any necessary change to future editions. All translations are by Katie Gramich unless otherwise stated.

Glenda Beagan – poems taken from *Vixen* (Honno, 1996).
Alison Bielski – poems taken from *That Crimson Flame: Selected Poems* (University of Salzburg Press/Poetry Salzberg, 1996).
Kate Bingham – poems taken from *Cohabitation* (Seren, 1998).
Brenda Chamberlain – 'I dream too much over and over' taken from *Poems with Drawings* (Enitharmon Press, 1969); 'Seal cave', 'Women on the strand', 'Talysarn', 'Shipwrecked Demeter', 'Dead ponies' – taken from *The Green Heart: Poems* (Oxford University Press, 1958).
Gillian Clarke – poems taken from *Selected Poems* (Carcenet, 1997).
Sarah Corbett – poems taken from *The Red Wardrobe* (Seren, 1998).
Marged Davies (Meg Elis) – 'Y Milwr' taken from *Hel Dail Gwyrdd*, editor Menna Elfyn (Gomer, 1985).

Jean Earle – poems taken from *Visiting Light* (Poetry Wales Press, 1987) printed with permission from Seren publishers.

Jane Edwards – 'Gwreddiau' taken from *Hel Dail Gwyrdd*, editor Menna Elfyn (Gomer, 1985).

Elen Egryn – poems taken from *Telyn Egryn*, editors Ceridwen Lloyd-Morgan and Kathryn Hughes (Honno, 1998).

Menna Elfyn – 'Cân y di-lais i British Telecom', 'Y gneuen wag', 'Eucalyptus', 'Siapau o Gymru' – taken from *Eucalyptus: Detholiad O Gerddi/Selected Poems, 1978-1994* (Gomer, 1995); 'Pomgranadau', 'Diwinyddiaeth Gwallt', 'Coron Merch', 'Enwi Duw' – taken from *Cell Angel* (Bloodaxe, 1996); 'Dim ond Camedd', 'Glanhau'r Capel', 'Cusan Hances' – taken from *Cusan Dyn Dall* – Blind Man's Kiss (Bloodaxe, 2001).

Christine Evans – poems reprinted with permission from the poet and Seren Books.

Margiad Evans – poems taken from *A Candle Ahead* (Chatto & Windus, 1956).

Catherine Fisher – poems taken from *Immrama* (Seren, 1982) and *The Unexplored Ocean* (Seren, 1994).

Rose Flint – poems taken from *Blue Horse of Morning* (Seren, 1991).

Christine Furnival – poems taken from *Prince of sapphires* (Breakish: Aquila Press, 1976) and *Towards Praising* (Swansea: Christopher Davies, 1978).

Delyth George – poems taken from *O'r Iawn Ryw*, editor Menna Elfyn (Honno, 1991).

Ann Griffiths – translations taken from *Ann Griffiths: Hymns and Letters*, editors Alan Gaunt, Alan Luff and Kathryn Jenkins (Stainer and Bell, 1990).

Ann Griffiths – 'Bechgyn Aberystwyth' taken from *O'r Iawn Ryw*, editor Menna Elfyn (Honno, 1991).

Joyce Herbert – poems taken from *Approaching Snow* (Poetry Wales Press, 1983).

Mererid Hopwood – 'Dadeni' reprinted with permission of the poet and Dinefwr Press.

Elin ap Hywel – poems taken from *Pethau Brau* (Y Lolfa, 1982).

Kate Johnson – poems taken from *Gods* (Poetry Wales Press, 1987).

Einir Jones – poems taken from *Gweld y Garreg Atab* (Gwasg Gwynedd, 1998) printed with permission from Dinefwr Press.

Nesta Wyn Jones – poems taken from *Rhwng Chwerthin a Chrio* (Gomer, 1986) and *Dawns y Sêr* (Gomer, 1999).

Sally Roberts Jones – poems taken from *The Forgotten Country: Poems* (Gomer, 1977).

Eiluned Lewis – poems taken from *December Apples* (Lovat Dickson and Thompson, 1935).

Gwyneth Lewis – poems taken from *Parables and Faxes* (Bloodaxe, 1995) and *Zero Gravity* (Bloodaxe, 1998). 'Two Rivers' and 'Wholeness' (extract) reprinted with permission from Modern Poetry in Translation, Kings College London.

Hillary Llewellyn-Williams – poems taken from *The Tree Calender* (Poetry Wales Press, 1987) printed with permission from Seren Publishers.

Nest Lloyd – 'Iâr' taken from *Hel Dail Gwyrdd*, editor Menna Elfyn (Gomer 1985); 'Merched Llanio' taken from *O'r Iawn Ryw*, editor Menna Elfyn (Honno, 1991).

Elin Llwyd Morgan – poems taken from *Duwiselebog* (Y Lolfa, 1998). 'Rapunzel' printed with permission from Modern Poetry in Translations, Kings College London.

Esyllt Maelor – poems taken from *O'r Iawn Ryw*, editor Menna Elfyn (Honno, 1991).

Gwerful Mechain – poems taken from *Gwaith Gwerful Mechain ac eraill*, edited by Nerys Ann Howells (*Cyfres Beirdd yr Uchelwyr*, 2001).

Kathy Miles – poems taken from *The Rocking Stone* (Poetry Wales Press, 1988).

Eluned Phillips – 'Y Perthi Coll' taken from *Cerddi Glyn-y-Mêl* (Gomer, 1985).

Katherine Philips – poems taken from *The Collected Works of Katherine Philips* vol. 1 ed. Patrick Thomas (Stump Cross Books, 1990).

Deryn Rees-Jones – poems taken from *Signs Round a Dead Body* (Seren, 1998).

Lynette Roberts – poems taken from *Poems* (Faber, 1944).

Samantha Wynne Rydderch – poems taken from *Rockclimbing in Silk* (Seren, 2001).

Frances Sackett – poems taken from *The Hand Glass* (Seren, 1996).

Elin Wyn Williams – 'Moliannwn oll yn llon!' taken from *O'r Iawn Ryw*, editor Menna Elfyn (Honno, 1991).

Merryn Williams – poems taken from *The Sun's Yellow Eye*, editor Johnathon Clifford, sponsored by Rosemary Arthur (National Poetry Foundation, 1997).

ABOUT HONNO

Honno Welsh Women's Press was set up in 1986 by a group of women who felt strongly that women in Wales needed wider opportunities to see their writing in print and to become involved in the publishing process. Our aim is to develop the writing talents of women in Wales, give them new and exciting opportunities to see their work published and often to give them their first 'break' as a writer.

Honno is registered as a community co-operative. Any profit that Honno makes is invested in the publishing programme. Women from Wales and around the world have expressed their support for Honno. Each supporter has a vote at the Annual General Meeting.

For more information and to buy our publications, please write to Honno at the address below, or visit our website: www.honno.co.uk

Honno
Unit 14, Creative Units
Aberystwyth Arts Centre

Honno Friends
We are very grateful for the support of the honno Friends: Gwyneth Tyson Roberts, Jenny Sabine, Beryl Thomas. For more information on how you can become a Honno Friend,
see: http://www.honno.co.uk/friends.php